Lump Sum Compensation Payments Research Project: The Circle Rechecks Itself

Prepared for

the Aboriginal Healing Foundation

By

Madeleine Dion Stout
Rick Harp

2007

Table of Contents

Figures

Foreword

In a report of this nature, where faithful reproduction of individual experiences and perceptions is of critical importance, one proceeds with due care and circumspection when attempting generalized assertions concerning Aboriginal people. The Aboriginal Healing Foundation feels however that preliminary generalizations pertaining to two subjects are required at the outset of this project.

Communication of the Indian Residential Schools Settlement Agreement

The first generalization relates to the confusion surrounding the *Indian Residential Schools Settlement Agreement* and associated matters such as the Common Experience Payment or the Independent Assessment Process. Statements of interviewees recorded in this report may suggest to the reader ignorance or misunderstanding. Confusion however derives not necessarily from these, but in many cases from: a) changes of government strategies and initiatives around all facets of the residential school issue, b) a lack of clear policies and institutional jurisdiction, and c) an absence of coordinated communications efforts among the agencies responsible for *Indian Residential Schools Settlement Agreement* initiatives. To be fair, one should acknowledge that the I*ndian Residential Schools Settlement Agreement* is an enormous bureaucratic undertaking and that some shortcomings are to be expected. However, it is also the case that communication to Survivors has often been sporadic, incomplete, contradictory, or inaccurate.

Traditional Views of Money

The second generalization relates to money. While a range of views about money may be found among Aboriginal people, as it may indeed among any group of individuals, a core set of themes in this report supports the following statements. The first is that Aboriginal cultures are informed by collectivist world views in which the traditional ethic of sharing is paramount. Sustained efforts by successive governments to assimilate Aboriginal people have weakened, but not overtaken, collectivist views. Money is therefore often viewed by Aboriginal people as a collective good, to be shared with family, friends, and community. The cultural norms of sharing will inform how money arriving into Aboriginal communities through the *Indian Residential Schools Settlement Agreement* is viewed, disbursed, and dispensed.

While traditional cultural norms may shape how money is viewed and used, money nonetheless enters Aboriginal communities attended by unease, especially when the source of this money is government. In simple terms, money is often viewed with suspicion as an instrument which government will use to manipulate and undermine Aboriginal people. Speaking of compensation, one interviewee asserted that "Those who were living traditional lives [...] abandoned this way of life for the money. The government threw this money out and caused chaos" (31). Ulterior motives and negative consequences are suspected where government money is concerned.

Furthermore, the values of cultures organized around exchanges of money at times contradict the values of traditional, non-monetized Aboriginal cultures. As one interviewee puts it, "The almighty dollar has broken down our relationships and community-mindedness"(41). Perhaps the most effective illustration of this contradiction is the differing views of land within Aboriginal and non-Aboriginal cultures, the former regarding land as a trans-generational communal resource and the latter as a divisible good fit for individual ownership and economic exploitation. Where such fundamental contradictions subsist, money is necessarily viewed by Aboriginal people with wariness as assimilation's "Trojan horse."

Although this report does not attempt a formal study of the social ideology of money, such a consideration is implicit throughout. There is much theoretical complexity and contradiction between the economic individualism of "Western" societies and the traditional cultures of Aboriginal people. At the practical level, collectivist values will be balanced against individual rights, in particular the right of former residential school attendees to receive and use their money free of judgement, paternalistic meddling, or external pressure. The Aboriginal Healing Foundation ultimately places faith in the resilience and capacity of Aboriginal people. Our communities will work out their destinies in the manner they deem most fitting. Toward this end, the report presents a strategic framework and a set of priority recommendations that come from Survivors themselves.

Aboriginal Healing Foundation

Acknowledgements

This report is subtitled "The Circle Rechecks Itself" to show how everyone and everything is related over time and across boundaries when it comes to dealing with the impact of lump sum payments on Survivors, families, and communities.

We heard this collective message from 117 individuals we interviewed, and we now take it as a reminder of just how much effort and commitment it takes to produce a document like this. We marvel at the people who not only shared stories, experiences, and lessons from past lump sum payments, but who welcomed us into their homes, communities, and lives. We cannot thank them enough for embracing each of us as one of their own and for contributing so richly and readily to this report.

We would like to extend our special thanks to the leadership who made our site visits so successful: Chief Bryan McNabb (Gordon First Nation), Chief Adrian Stimson Sr. (Siksika Nation), Chief Fred Robbins (Esketemc First Nation), Norman Yakeleya (MLA, Sahtu), and Dr. Nellie Cournoyea, (CEO Inuvialuit Regional Corporation). We would also like to applaud and thank some Champions for Survivors who helped us navigate the communities we visited: Ed Bitternose, Carla Waterchief, Douglas Dillon, Ruth Majoras, William Blackwater, Harold Cook, Violet Doolittle, Mitzi Bob, and Yvonne Rigsby-Jones. The RCMP whom we met went the extra mile to meet us and for this we are grateful. But, at the end of the day, the Survivors are the real heroes.

Last, but not least, we want to express our deepest appreciation to the Aboriginal Healing Foundation (AHF) for giving us the opportunity to work with kindred spirits both inside and outside of the organization. This report rests squarely on the patient and professional support we received from AHF employees: Jackie Brennan, Janice Horn, and Flora Kallies. Most of all, we would like to honour Dr. Gail Valaskakis, Research Director at the AHF, for her visionary, steadfast, and inspiring support throughout.

The Legacy will take on new meaning when Everyone is accounted for, Everything is done, and the circle has rechecked itself one more time. To this end, we humbly submit our small effort.

Definitions

Aboriginal people or Aboriginal – includes First Nation, Métis, and Inuit regardless of where they live in Canada and regardless of whether they are "registered" under the *Indian Act of Canada*.

AFN – Assembly of First Nations is the national organization representing First Nation citizens in Canada. The AFN represents all citizens regardless of age, gender, or place of residence.

AHF – The Aboriginal Healing Foundation is a not-for-profit organization established in 1998 with funding from the Canadian government. Its mission is to support Aboriginal people in building sustainable healing processes that address the legacy of physical and sexual abuse in the residential school system, including intergenerational impacts. AHF provides funds to healing projects and promotes knowledge about the issues and the need for healing.

Alternative Dispute Resolution (ADR) – Intended to be a less formal, less complicated, and faster alternative to the courts for the resolution of residential school-related abuse claims, this out-of-court system was designed and implemented by the Canadian government beginning in December 2002. Under the ADR process, claims are heard by a neutral, third-party adjudicator instead of a judge, and fall under one of two streams: Model A (serious physical and/or sexual abuse) and Model B (less serious physical abuse and/or claims of wrongful confinement). The ADR process also offers health services such as counselling and commemorative activities for Survivors.

Common Experience Payments (CEP) – Part of the proposed *Indian Residential Schools Settlement Agreement*, the CEP is a lump sum payment that recognizes the experience of those who attended an Indian residential school, including its impacts. Former students who had their attendance verified and who apply for the CEP would be eligible to receive $10,000 for one school year or part thereof plus an additional $3,000 for each subsequent year or part thereof. Survivors must have been alive on 30 May 2005 to be eligible for a CEP. To receive an advance payment on their CEP of $8,000, Survivors must have been 65 years and older as of 30 May 2005.

Community Well-Being Index – A measurement to determine the relative well-being of communities throughout Canada. It does so by evaluating several socio-economic factors (income, active labour force, education, and housing conditions) and combining them into a numerical score, ranging anywhere from 0 to 100.

Indian Residential Schools Agreement-in-Principle (AIP) – On 20 November 2005, the federal government announced a multi-party agreement-in-principle toward the resolution of Indian residential schools claims. Other parties to the AIP included the Assembly of First Nations, legal representatives of former residential school students, and representatives of the churches involved in running the schools. With the details to be worked out later that year (see *Indian Residential Schools Settlement Agreement*), the AIP proposed a *common experience payment* and a new *alternative dispute resolution* process for claims of serious abuse, among other elements of compensations.

Indian Residential Schools Settlement Agreement – Formally approved by Cabinet on 8 May 2006, this agreement is a politically negotiated residential school compensation package. It was reached between the parties involved in the prior agreement-in-principle of November 2005 (see *Indian Residential Schools Agreement-in-Principle*). The agreement proposes a *common experience payment* and an *independent assessment process*, along with measures to support healing, funding for commemorative activities, and the establishment of a Truth and Reconciliation Commission. Under the terms of the settlement agreement, approval must be gained from the courts of nine Canadian jurisdictions. Following court approval, former residential school students have five months to voluntarily opt out of the deal; however, should more than 5,000 opting outs occur, the deal would not come into force.

Independent Assessment Process (IAP) – Introduced in the *Indian Residential Schools Settlement Agreement*, it replaces the ADR process. Five years after the date of the agreement, the IAP will be the only option of pursuing a sexual or serious physical abuse claim, unless one has formally opted out of the agreement. Through the IAP, the government will pay 100 per cent of the compensation, after validation of the claims by an independent adjudicator.

LSP – Abbreviation for lump sum payment.

NNADAP – The National Native Alcohol and Drug Abuse Program is a Health Canada program now largely controlled by First Nation communities and organizations. Since its origins in the 1970s, the program's goal has been to help First Nation and Inuit communities set up and operate programs aimed at reducing high levels of alcohol, drug, and solvent abuse among on-reserve populations.

NAHO – The National Aboriginal Health Organization is an Aboriginal-designed and -controlled body committed to influencing and advancing the health and well-being of Aboriginal people by carrying out knowledge-based strategies. Incorporated in 2000, NAHO is a unique not-for-profit organization founded upon and committed to unity, while respecting diversity. With Aboriginal communities as its primary focus, NAHO gathers, creates, interprets, disseminates, and uses both traditional Aboriginal and contemporary Western healing and wellness approaches. At all times, the organization reflects the values and principles contained in traditional knowledge and practices.

RCAP – The Royal Commission on Aboriginal Peoples was established in 1991 to examine all issues relevant to any or all Aboriginal people including recent events such as the Oka Crisis and the Meech Lake Accord. The commission culminated in a final report published in 1996. The commission consisted of several high profile Aboriginal people including Paul Chartrand, Viola Robinson, and Mary Sillett and was co-chaired by René Dussault and Georges Erasmus. Together, they undertook the study of the historical relations between the government and Aboriginal people. The commission made numerous recommendations to address all issues affecting Aboriginal people. These recommendations related to restructuring the relationship between Aboriginal and non-Aboriginal people that is fundamental and grounded in ethical principles. Members of the commission travelled to numerous Aboriginal communities to interview Aboriginal people on their past and current conditions.

Residential schools – The residential school system in Canada, attended by First Nation, Métis, and Inuit students. It may include industrial schools, boarding schools, homes for students, hostels, billets, residential schools, residential schools with a majority of day students, or a combination of any of the above.

Survivor – an Aboriginal person who attended and survived the residential school system in Canada.

The Legacy – means the ongoing direct and indirect effects of physical and sexual abuse at residential schools. It includes the effects on Survivors, their families, descendants and communities (including communities of interest). These effects may include and are not limited to family violence, drug, alcohol, and substance

Executive Summary

The Aboriginal Healing Foundation (AHF) was established on 31 March 1998 as a result of *Gathering Strength—Canada's Aboriginal Action Plan*, a federal strategy to renew the relationship between Aboriginal people and the Government of Canada. The AHF was given a $350 million one-time healing fund with an eleven-year mandate to commit this funding towards initiatives that address the legacy of physical and sexual abuse in the Indian residential schools of Canada. Between 1831 and 1998, at least 130 industrial, boarding, and residential schools, including hostels, operated in all territories and in all but three provinces (New Brunswick, Prince Edward Island, and Newfoundland). In 1991, it was estimated that approximately 105,000 to 107,000 Aboriginal people were alive who had attended residential school. Today, that number is about 86,000. Recent extrapolated figures indicate that approximately 287,350 Aboriginal people have experienced intergenerational impacts. This means there are, at minimum, 373,350 individuals whose lives have been intimately touched by residential schools.

Four different lump sum payment (LSP) options have been offered to Survivors to compensate them for the suffering they experienced at residential school. The first option secured LSPs through civil and criminal lawsuits initiated by Survivors against the Canadian government and the churches. This process, which began in the 1990s, was criticized by some Survivors as exclusionary, time-intensive, financially and emotionally draining, and less than rewarding. The second option, the Alternative Dispute Resolution (ADR) process, was intended as a less formal, less complicated, and faster alternative to the courts. However, it only dealt with physical and sexual abuse, and imposed rigid compensation guidelines for different types of abuses. Similar to court cases, Survivors following the ADR route needed to prove their claims. The third option, the recently negotiated *Indian Residential Schools Settlement Agreement*, includes the Common Experience Payment (CEP) process that would, if passed, offer a common financial package to all Survivors. Using a "10+3" formula, each Survivor alive as of 30 May 2005 would receive $10,000 for the first year (or part of the first year) of attendance at a residential school and an additional $3,000 for each subsequent year. The final option, the Independent Assessment Process (IAP), also part of the settlement agreement, is meant to replace the ADR process, and promises to process any residential school abuse-related claim within a 9-month period.

Under the *Agreement in Principle* announced by the federal government on 20 November 2005, which was then finalized as the *Indian Residential Schools Settlement Agreement* on 8 May 2006, approximately 86,000 former residential school students stand to receive, on average, $28,000 each in compensation through CEPs, which includes an advance payment of $8,000. This wave of payments would represent a massive and sudden influx of money into Aboriginal communities across Canada.

In anticipation of imminent LSPs, the AHF initiated the *Lump Sum Compensation Payments Research Project*. This project offers an impact assessment of past compensation payments on Survivors, their families, and communities as experienced by them. The project consisted of two phases: a first-phase literature review and a second-phase key informant survey. The second phase involved 117 field interviews conducted across western and northwestern Canada. These interviews were carried out at seven sites: Gordon First Nation (Saskatchewan); Siksika Nation (Alberta); Esketemc First Nation and Tsow-Tun Le Lum Society on the Nanoose First Nation (British Columbia); and Inuvik, Yellowknife, and Fort Good Hope (Northwest Territories).

The first phase of the research project revealed that very little research has been conducted about LSP impacts on individuals nor has much work been carried out about the positive and negative uses of such large sums of money. Both the literature review and the survey analysis underscored the urgency of developing a strategy for efficient, culturally appropriate, and accessible supports for LSP recipients.

Recipients and non-recipients of LSPs were interviewed during the key informant survey of the research project. Of 117 people interviewed, 80 per cent were Survivors, 36 per cent of whom had received LSPs. Interview questions were designed to elicit the following: participants' experience with compensation payment processes; perceived positive and negative impacts of payments on individuals, families, and communities; suggested supports for LSP recipients; potential barriers to those supports; and potential Aboriginal and non-Aboriginal resources. The main LSPs discussed during the key informant survey included payments that came from court-based litigation, the ADR process, and the $8,000 advances of common experience payments.

The key informant survey provided feedback from recipients and non-recipients of LSPs, and identified a wide range of community impacts stemming from these payments. These impacts began with the application process, which was looked upon negatively by the majority of survey participants who complained of its excessive cost and duration. While a minority found the LSP process beneficial and positive, most saw it as financially inequitable and emotionally draining. However, once the monies arrived, many recipients turned their LSP into a positive financial opportunity to help out family, purchase needed items, clear up debts, and invest. On the negative side, recipients noted that LSPs often led to troublesome increases in problems such as drug and alcohol abuse, pressure from family for money, and encroachment by financial predators. Receiving LSPs also triggered negative residential school memories for Survivors. Some non-recipients linked LSP readiness and general Survivor healthiness to shed light on Survivors' responses to LSPs. While some constructive impacts were recognized, most non-recipients viewed LSPs in a critical light, citing the increased vulnerability of Survivors in general, but particularly if they are elderly, female, ill, and living on the street.

A comprehensive intervention strategic framework for LSPs is proposed in this research project, and it begins with a discussion of the following cross-cutting issues: class, age, gender, religion, geographic location, culture, historic trauma, elder abuse, resources and funding, and research. Undergirding the framework are four strategic principles: the first principle—*Survivors' rights and autonomy are central*—requires that LSP initiatives always respect the ultimate right of Survivors to make their own decisions; the second principle—*Survivors are their own best resource*—urges communities to maintain Survivor involvement in all initiatives; the third principle—*the family has a rightful place at the table*—means that interventions should be ideally tailored to, and inclusive of, an LSP recipient's immediate family members; and the fourth principle—*the community is the natural catalyst*—reinforces the fact that when responses are genuinely developed by and for the community, they nurture and reinforce a sense of local ownership and responsibility over policy and programming.

In the interests of inspiring and informing immediate-, medium-, and long-term action, this research project puts forth five strategic goals: reform healing, reframe health, reinforce safety and security, reverse crises, and realign capacity. Two strategic interventions are identified for each strategic goal.

In order to reform healing, it will be important to a) elevate communal healing, and b) to research and evaluate change over time. A public apology, "give-aways," and ceremonies that mark the country-wide distribution of LSPs will help shift healing from the legacy of residential schools beyond communities so that it becomes collectively owned by all those affected. Healing reform will require keeping a close eye on the unique and pivotal role of the voluntary/non-governmental sector in Aboriginal communities to the possibilities of private sector involvement in healing initiatives and to exploring key concepts like citizen engagement, social capital, and social cohesion, and relating these to home-grown concepts. Prioritizing impact assessments and evaluations will be key, as will training front-line workers on the early detection of risks and impacts of LSPs and collaborating with individuals who have expertise on effective interventions.

To reframe health, two strategic interventions will have to be undertaken: a) promote holistic health and interventions, and b) link health to wealth. A renewed interest in the healing effects of ceremonies and traditions place these front and center in community programs and practices, and this is no less the case where LSPs are concerned. Moreover, health disparities, mental health, addictions, and cultural competence have to be considered if health is to proceed holistically and across the spectrum of care. Elders' teachings about self-reliance, productivity, and usage of money have to be embedded into the meaning of culture for the long-term benefit of Survivors, families, and communities. Health can be viewed as an economic resource that can be pressed against the residential school legacy, which has compromised the socio-economic status of Survivors, families, and communities. Therefore, there is a need to mobilize financial and monetary support services through training, along with the provision and promotion of economic and education opportunities to leverage the Survivors' money for their own benefit.

The third strategic goal, reinforce safety and security, involves the following strategic interventions: mediate the risks for the most vulnerable and use the media to the best advantage. LSPs can escalate problems such as domestic violence, frauds and scams, and elder abuse and increase the need for RCMP involvement. Community ownership and leadership with the LSP issue are markers for success for the RCMP who strongly support inter-agency collaboration and working within existing community structures and processes. One of the important functions for communities is to safeguard the financial well-being of at-risk groups that include elders, women, youth, street people, and the infirm and to provide them with refuge from harm if necessary, along with children and those who opt out of the settlement agreement. Elder abuse will have to be addressed on a priority basis, as well as the development of disability and injury prevention and awareness initiatives. Public service advertising media campaigns can help to minimize the negative effects of LSPs, including scams and frauds, by promoting dialogue and hope through Aboriginal languages wherever possible. It will also be important to develop media messages to educate children and youth about the legacy of residential schools and LSPs.

To reverse crises, the way forward is to a) focus on crisis management, and b) understand the crushing burden of Survivors' decision-making. Communities will have to adjust to doing things in a short period of time before, during, and after the arrival of LSPs with new or renewed skills in crisis management, and they will have to apply these and other preventative and preparatory approaches against a whole range of challenges. Crisis response plans, protocols, and practices will need to be set up. The AHF's national LSP intervention strategy should be distributed to communities in order to share insights on dealing with LSPs and and the evolving position of communities on the legacy of residential schools and healing. Education sessions about the truth and reconciliation process will be needed to help Survivors, families, and communities look beyond LSPs. Supportive mechanisms like talking circles and specialized treatment programs and centres will have to be made available to Survivors. In addition, Survivors will have to learn the fundamentals of negotiation skills, problem solving, and anger management.

The final strategic goal aims to realign capacity with two strategic interventions: a) build on existing alliances, and b) work with relevant and ready community supports. Since almost every facet of community life is governed by the ideals of connection and communication, capacity building in this area becomes vital when LSPs are received. By offering Survivors the means to act on their own priorities when human resources are at a real premium, LSPs offer them a true stake in delivering their own care supplemented by inter-community networking and support. Two important ways to do this is to link communities through the Internet so that they can exchange lessons learned and best practices related to LSPs and identify a staff person who can coordinate LSP-related activities and initiatives. Families and youth are critical community supports in minimizing the negative effects of LSPs and in maximizing the benefits.

Though each community is free to rank the 26 recommendations developed out of this research project, the following are considered to be the six most important on a priority basis:

+ Develop crisis response plans, protocols, and practices immediately by setting up meetings, assessing community vulnerability, securing funds, identifying choices and avenues for action, and becoming familiar with existing federal and provincial/territorial mandates in crisis management.

+ Launch public service advertising campaigns through a variety of media outlets to promote the positive impact of lump sum payments and to decrease the negative effects while depicting an alternative future for Survivors and creating opportunities for dialogue on issues like elder abuse. Aboriginal languages should be used where desirable and feasible.

+ Adopt innovative and anticipatory measures to safeguard the well-being of at-risk groups by laying out banking and purchasing options for elders, women, youth, street people, and the infirm to avoid scams and frauds, and by providing them with temporary refuge from harm if necessary, along with children and those who opt out of the settlement agreement.

+ Support Survivors who are interested in entrepreneurship and in saving, investing, and pooling lump sum payments through timely and accessible counselling and training.

+ Identify and dedicate a community Survivor coordinator who can bring all paid and unpaid partners together on a regular and on an emergency basis to help meet the needs of Survivors, efficiently and effectively, by ensuring smooth and steady information sharing, service provision, and programming.

+ Address the call for a formal apology to recognize the legacy of residential schools and its effects on First Nations, Métis, and Inuit communities.

Introduction

The Aboriginal Healing Foundation (AHF) was established on 31 March 1998 as a result of *Gathering Strength—Canada's Aboriginal Action Plan*, a federal strategy to renew the relationship between Aboriginal people and the Government of Canada. The AHF was given a $350 million one-time healing fund with an eleven-year mandate to commit this funding towards initiatives that address the legacy of physical and sexual abuse in the Indian residential schools of Canada. Between 1831 and 1998, at least 130 industrial, boarding, and residential schools, including hostels, operated in all territories and in all but three provinces (New Brunswick, Prince Edward Island, and Newfoundland). In 1991, it was estimated that approximately 105,000 to 107,000 Aboriginal people were alive who had attended residential school. Today, that number is about 86,000. Recent extrapolated figures indicate that approximately 287,350 Aboriginal people have experienced intergenerational impacts. This means there is, at minimum, 373,350 individuals whose lives have been intimately touched by residential schools.

The AHF commissioned the *Lump Sum Compensation Payments Research Project* (see Appendix A) in pursuit of the following aims: a) to assess the impact that past lump sum payments have had on First Nation, Inuit, and Métis Survivors, and their families and communities; b) to help identify the benefits and costs of such payments; and c) to prepare recommendations on what might be helpful with respect to the imminent distribution of Lump Sum Compensation Payments (LSPs), including Common Experience Payments. According to the AHF, approximately 86,000 former residential school students stand to receive, on average, $28,000 each in compensation, with an average recipient age of 60 years old. This wave of payments represents a massive and sudden influx of money into Aboriginal communities across Canada.

A literature review (Appendix B) was conducted in the first phase of the research project, and it referred to the monetary awards every former residential school Survivor is eligible for under the *Agreement-in-Principle* announced by the federal government on 20 November 2005, which was then finalized as the *Indian Residential Schools Settlement Agreement* (Appendix C) package approved by Cabinet in May 2006. The most striking finding of this literature review was the lack of empirical research on the personal experiences of individuals (Aboriginal or otherwise) who had received either reparation-type or revenue-type monetary payments (Dion Stout and Jodoin, 2006).

Indeed, evidence revealed that very little research attention has been devoted to the impact and use of lump sum payments by individual recipients, making the key informant survey of the *Lump Sum Compensation Payments Research Project* all the more critical (Dion Stout and Jodoin, 2006).

The key informant survey that made up the project's second phase involved on-site visits and interviews with Survivors, including recipients and non-recipients of previous residential school-related lump sum payments as well as with other key community stakeholders. This report combines the scant findings of the literature review with the large volume of data produced through the key informant survey, which has weighted the report heavily toward the latter findings.

Methodology

The methodologies used in this final report include document and literature reviews along with in-depth interviews. The survey phase of this research project adopted a qualitative methodological protocol, using in-person interviews as well as a few telephone interviews. The survey participants included individuals who have had direct experience with, or knew of lump sum payments stemming from the legacy of residential schools. The survey probed key concerns and gathered consensus opinions on the LSPs that have been paid to Survivors of residential schools.

Instrument

Keeping the findings of the literature review in mind, a questionnaire with open-ended questions was developed by the project researchers, which were then vetted through the AHF (see Appendices D and E). Separate sets of questionnaires were developed for recipients (Survivors who have received LSPs) and non-recipients (key community stakeholders, including Survivors who have not received LSPs). It is important to note that while the purpose, scope, and length of both questionnaires were very much alike, this somewhat comparative approach helped to identify the similarities and differences in input provided by recipients and non-recipients, even though no attempt was made to conduct a compare and contrast analysis as such.

Both questionnaires focused on the following areas: involvement with residential schools and lump sum payments; perceptions of the payment process; negative and positive impacts on individuals, families, and communities; implications for healing; workable supports and suggestions; perceived barriers to these supports; and the role various organizations and people can play when compensation payments are made to Survivors of residential schools.

Survey participants

The AHF provided the project consultants with an initial list of four communities where individuals had received substantial settlements for wrongs committed against them in residential schools. After community profiles were written on all four communities (see Appendix F), site visits were made to Gordon First Nation (Saskatchewan), Siksika Nation (Alberta), Esketemc First Nation (British Columbia), and Inuvik (Northwest Territories). Key community contacts also recommended the site visits that were added in the Northwest Territories (Yellowknife and Fort Good Hope) and in British Columbia (Tsow-Tun Le Lum Society on the Nanoose First Nation).

The AHF sent letters to the political leadership in the first set of communities it identified as potential sources of information for the research project. At the same time, it also notified officers at adjacent detachments of the Royal Canadian Mounted Police (RCMP) and other key community informants to determine their interest in participating in the survey. The lead project researcher sent similar correspondence to the communities that were eventually added to the original list of potential survey participants. The survey package that was sent out included introductory letters, survey questionnaires, and a description of the project.

The survey package specified the purpose of the survey, explained that the information collected would be treated in a confidential manner, and introduced the project researchers, a Survivor and an immediate descendent of a Survivor. Involving a male and female researcher provided survey participants the option of talking to one or the other if they so wished. The survey protocol tried to maximize the participation of recipients and non-recipients by allowing for proper preparation and response time for the interviews. To this end, the lead project researcher maintained ongoing contact with each community leader or representative and with other potential survey participants through phone calls, emails, or letters.

Administration of the Survey Questionnaire

Letters from the AHF to community leaders and the RCMP were sent out in late September and early October (2006). With the exception of the site visit that was added in January (2007), all the site visits took place from early November to the first week in December (2006). Both project researchers visited the first four communities with the lead project researcher attending to the rest. For the most part, community leaders and representatives identified and recruited potential survey participants, but the participants themselves often suggested other individuals and parties who could contribute to the project.

The number of survey participants involved exceeded earlier expectations, perhaps because residential school-related compensation payments were receiving wide media coverage, and various community consultations had been held on the topic and related activities and initiatives were ongoing. As well, the communities who took part in this survey were involved in healing projects funded by the AHF.

While a few telephone interviews were held, all other interviews were in-person and mostly one-on-one, and generally lasted sixty minutes. On average, three days were dedicated to each site visit. Since the majority of those interviewed were Survivors, the project researchers took the extra step of identifying local community counsellors that could be called upon if necessary. Along the same vein, each participant was told that the project was not intended to re-examine the atrocities of residential schools, nor was it meant to find fault, or tell people what to do with their lump sum payments.

The project researchers took detailed notes during the interviews, which they later transcribed. Interviews tended to be semi-formal and conversational, though every effort was made to cover the interview questions fully and meaningfully with participants. Home visits with the elderly and others, and flexible interview times, helped to maintain consistent community participation in the survey.

Data analysis

The interview notes were systematically and thematically analyzed by how frequently subject areas were mentioned and by their relevance to the project objectives. All feedback was summarized and synthesized for the purpose of putting forward an integrated analysis and comprehensive final report, which is qualitative in nature.

Limitations of Key Informant Survey

The following limitations of the key informant survey deserve consideration:

+ For a research project with national significance, the sample size of the key informant interviews was small and concentrated in select communities in the western and northwestern regions of the country;

+ The level of analysis rests on the input from recipients and non-recipients and no effort is made to disaggregate the findings any finer than that;

+ Ideally, both researchers should have been present at all the site visits to lend even more consistency to the interview process and the information gathered;

+ Some participants were not entirely clear on the jobs, roles, and organizational affiliation of the researchers;

+ The perspectives of highly motivated and involved participants were targeted by the survey, leaving out other important voices including the Métis and non-Aboriginal people who also have a stake in the LSP payment process and its outcome. Furthermore, Inuit were poorly integrated into the survey;

+ A few key participants who could have made valuable contributions to this research project could not be contacted because they had relocated or were unavailable when the interviews were conducted;

+ Considering the significance of this study, no empirical research exists to draw on to substantiate the findings.

Background

Throughout the key informant survey, participants referred to a variety of LSP compensation processes. This section offers a brief overview of these processes including their perceived strengths and weaknesses.

Litigation

The first set of lump sum payments came directly or indirectly through civil and criminal litigation by Survivors against the Canadian government and churches. These lawsuits began in earnest in the 1990s (Llewellyn, 2002). Such legal actions took the familiar form of a trial, where claimants often faced intense cross-examination by opposing lawyers over their allegations of abuse. Typically, trials are "open to the public, and their proceedings and decisions are part of the public record" (Llewellyn, 2002:267), and such accessibility is seen as one of litigation's chief virtues. Based on the legal evidence and arguments put forth, a trial judge rules for or against a claimant, and awards compensation accordingly. In some cases, however, settlements are reached out of court between Survivors and other parties.

Common criticisms of the court-based process include the burdensome costs involved. Although some legal firms claim to have overcome this barrier through contingency fees (i.e., a post-trial percentage of any Survivor compensation awarded), some of those very same firms have been accused of gouging their clients (Llewellyn, 2002). Llewellyn details other perceived shortcomings of the litigation route for Survivors:

> [V]ictims often find the process of testifying and facing cross-examination painful, as it brings back memories and opens old wounds … Even among those who do not find the process painful, many express dissatisfaction with their experience. Victims often enter a trial with the expectation that they will have an opportunity to tell their story freely. However, the purpose of a civil trial is to prove liability, and everything is done for this express purpose … As a result, victims often do not have a chance to tell of their experiences fully or to express their feelings in a way they find satisfying or healing (2002:269–270).

Llewellyn also discusses the inherently "adversarial," winner-take-all nature of litigation, which, in her opinion,

> focuses the parties' attention on winning rather than on ascertaining what happened and what ought to be done about it. It locks parties into their positions as plaintiffs or defendants and into the behaviour expected of each. It thus fails to explore the ways in which the plaintiffs and defendants might share common goals or share common interests in how the dispute is resolved (2002:272).

A final criticism of litigation stems from the fact that any court ruling faces a potential appeal to a higher court, creating a high degree of uncertainty as to the length of the process. Indeed, it was the lengthiness and costliness of litigation that prompted the push for an alternative process by members of all parties involved (Llewellyn, 2002).

Alternative Dispute Resolution

Inherent in its name, the ADR (alternative dispute resolution) process is intended to be a less formal, less complicated, and faster alternative to the courts for the resolution of disputes stemming from specific residential school-related abuse claims. As it is used here, 'ADR' signifies those out-of-court structures and rules specifically designed and put into place by the Canadian government for the purpose of hearing and resolving residential school-related claims.

The federal government first announced the ADR process in December 2002. According to Indian Residential Schools Resolution Canada (IRSRC), the ADR is:

> a voluntary process that offers a timely and alternative method to resolve claims of physical abuse, sexual abuse and wrongful confinement suffered at Indian residential schools (Indian Residential Schools Resolution Canada [IRSRC], n.d.b:para. 1).

Instead of a judge, the ADR process utilizes an adjudicator—a neutral, third party "decision-maker." According to the Indian Residential Schools Adjudication Secretariat:

> All adjudicators are chosen with the participation and agreement of the Chief Adjudicator, representatives of Aboriginal people, lawyers who act for residential school claimants, church organizations and the Government of Canada (Indian Residential Schools Adjudication Secreatariat, n.d.:para. 13).

But critics of the ADR process claim it is flawed precisely because it is a creation of government. Advocates of this view would seem to have support in the Ontario Court of Appeal, whose December 2004 decision in the *Cloud vs. Canada* class action case stated the following:

> [ADR] is a system unilaterally created by one of the participants in this action and could be unilaterally dismantled without the consent of the appellants. It deals only with physical and sexual abuse. It caps the amount of possible recovery … It does not compare favourably with a common trial (Ontario Court of Appeal, 2004:para. 92).

In any event, similar to a court case, "claimants have to prove their claim" to an adjudicator's satisfaction "in order to be compensated" on the basis of pre-determined guidelines. As with court-based litigation, lawyers tend to be part of most ADR applications and hearings. Although the choice is ultimately up to the Survivors, the complicated legal issues involved virtually require the support of counsel. That said, the government will help defray these legal costs to a maximum of 15 per cent of any successful claimant's total compensation payment (IRSRC, 2003:12, 19).

Claims are resolved through one of two ADR streams: 'Model A' and 'Model B.' The former accepts claims of the most serious cases of physical abuse and/or sexual abuse, while the latter hears the 'less serious' claims of physical abuse and/or claims of wrongful confinement (IRSRC, 2003). Unlike the public nature of a trial, ADR conducts private hearings, although certain points in the process may allow for group participation where applicable. Adjudicators have 30 days from the conclusion of a hearing to render a decision, at which point claimants have an additional 30 days to accept or reject the decision. Although no similar timeline exists concerning the number of days it takes to convene a hearing once an ADR application is initially filed, proponents of the process certainly feel the 30-day decision deadline is an improvement over the lengthy uncertainty of litigation.

"Compensation amounts are similar to those paid in court in each province or territory" (National Aboriginal Health Organization [NAHO], 2004:5). Again, under ADR, Survivors reserve the right to reject any adjudicator's decision and are free to go on to pursue redress elsewhere. A limited form of appeal is available, however, in that Survivors are permitted a one-time request for review of the first adjudicator's decision by a second adjudicator. This option is also open to the government, which has additional recourse to the Chief Adjudicator in asking for a review. To accept compensation, Survivors must sign a release form surrendering their future right "to sue the government for claims relating to their residential school experience" (IRSRC, 2003:32). However, claims for loss of language and culture are not included in this release. Moreover, Survivors must "meet with a lawyer to receive legal advice on the release" (IRSRC, 2003:12). The government picks up this cost.

Unlike the courts, the "Resolution Framework," as the ADR is also known, offers a toll-free, all-day crisis line, and officially promises "independent counseling and personal supports, including payment of travel for a family member or friend" (NAHO, 2004:5) to attend hearings. The Framework also funds and facilitates "various commemorative activities … meaningful to" (NAHO, 2004:6) Survivors.

The most recent statistics for the ADR break down as follows (IRSRC, n.d.c):

> Number of applications received to date: 7,614
>
> Number of applications sent to the IRS Adjudication Secretariat: 3,382
>
> Number of decisions to date: 2,416
>
> Total value of decisions to date: $126.5 million
>
> Number of 'Model A' decisions: 1,770
> Range of decisions: $6,000 - $260,000
>
> Number of 'Model B' decisions: 646
> Range of decisions: $250 - $3,500

The above statistics provided by IRSRC do not include an explanation as to why 4,259 of the original 7,607 applications failed to proceed on to the Indian Residential Schools Adjudication Secretariat, or the status of those 966 applications that have yet to culminate in a decision.

Common Experience Payment

Unlike individualized compensation obtained through litigation or the ADR process, the proposed Common Experience Payment (CEP) is a more 'global' LSP that would be extended to every former student, not just those able to prove specific incidents of physical/sexual abuse. In other words, compensation would be universally forthcoming to any and all students able to prove they shared the 'common experience' of attending Indian residential school, irrespective of whether they were ever abused. Negotiated by the Assembly of First Nations and a variety of governmental, religious, and legal players the CEP is part of the comprehensive political *Indian Residential Schools Settlement Agreement* formally approved by Cabinet in May 2006. The so-called "10+3" CEP compensation formula provides $10,000 for the first year of residence at a school, with an additional $3,000 for each subsequent year of residence. One estimate pegs the average LSP at $24,000, based on 5 to 6 years of attendance (Mahoney, 2006).

To be eligible for the CEP, Survivors must have been alive on 31 May 2005 (the day negotiations were initiated). Survivors aged 65 years and older as of 30 May 2005 were eligible to receive an advance of their $8,000 common experience payment. Once it passes the required series of court approvals, followed by a mandatory five-month waiting period, the CEP will not be subject to legal fees, income tax, or (subject to negotiation with the provinces) 'claw-backs' through social assistance cut-offs.

The following are IRSRC (n.d.a) data available as of 2 April 2007 concerning the $8,000 CEP advance payments:

Total number of applications received: **13,547**

Number of applications verified and processed for payment: **10,326**

Number of applications in process: **272**

Number of incomplete applications (awaiting further information from applicant): **0**

Number of applications unable to process

Notified - unable to confirm residential school residency: **1,328**

Notified - did not meet the payment criteria (age/deceased): **1,621**

Total value of all applications processed for payment: **$82.6 million**

Independent Assessment Process

The *Indian Residential Schools Settlement Agreement* introduced another LSP procedure known as the Independent Assessment Process (IAP). Intended to replace the ADR, the IAP would deal with sexual abuse, severe physical abuse, plus severe psychological effects of abuse through what proponents are calling a "greatly improved, more generous and far speedier" mechanism (Mahoney, 2006:slide 19). As with the ADR, legal fees would be covered to a maximum of 15 per cent of any final IAP-related LSP. In terms of mandatory timelines, the IAP pledges to process any given file over a time period of no longer than nine months in total (IRSRC, 2006). Similar to the ADR process, IAP adjudicators would utilize a point system to award compensation, and any decision may be subject to review by participants.

Participant Profiles

A total of 117 individuals took part in the key informant survey, the majority of whom came from seven communities across the western and northwestern parts of the country. Most of the participants were former residential school students of First Nation ancestry. The following is a more detailed demographic picture of the survey participants.

Figure 1) Participants by Geographic Location

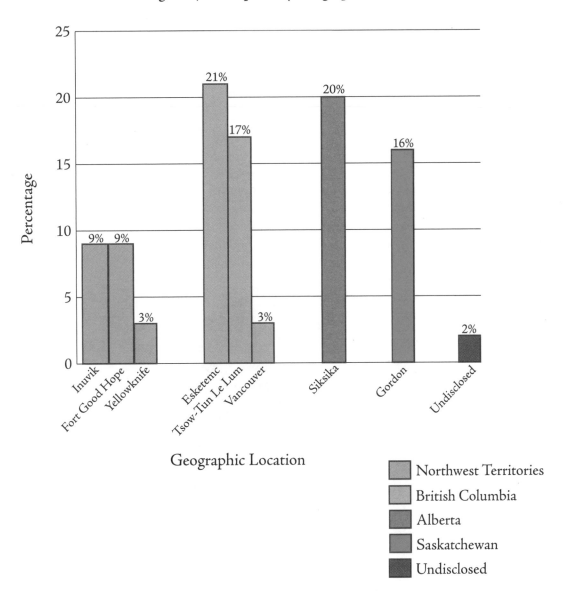

The province with the most survey participants was British Columbia at 49 individuals, and included site visits to two communities: Esketemc First Nation and Nanoose First Nation. The number of interviews in the Northwest Territories and Alberta were 25 and 24, respectively. In Saskatchewan, 19 individuals took part in the survey.

Site visits were made to communities who had previous experience with lump sum payments and had worked closely with the AHF on healing initiatives. Among those communities, two had the greatest number of participants, Siksika Nation in Alberta and Esketemc First Nation in British Columbia, at 24 individuals each. Together, they contributed over 40 per cent of all participants. Meanwhile, the Tsow-Tun Le Lum Society on the Nanoose First Nation had 20 participants and Gordon First Nation had 19. Three individuals were interviewed one-on-one in the Vancouver area while two participants did not want their locations disclosed.

The breakdown between interviews that were conducted in urban and rural settings is 20 per cent and 80 per cent, respectively. The clear majority of interviews—94 to 23—were held on-reserve rather than in large cities or towns.

The main method for conducting interviews was to carry them out in-person as opposed to over the phone or on-line. A male and female researcher both attended each interview as often as was feasible. Most interviews were conducted in First Nation administration buildings while a few were held in public buildings such as offices, schools, hotels, and restaurants. Several were held in private homes, especially in the Northwest Territories. Due to personal requests by participants, bad weather conditions, or the sheer distance between researchers and participants telephone interviews were conducted in lieu of in-person meetings. In total, 65 interviews were conducted in-person with individuals or groups, while seven were carried out by means of telephone. Three RCMP officers numbered among the one-on-one interviews. In terms of individual versus group interviews, 8 focus group interviews were held with 52 participants.

Figure 2) Participants by Gender

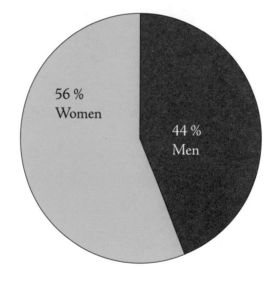

The gender breakdown among participants showed more women participants than men (56 % versus 44 %) at 65 females and 52 males. More men have had past experiences with LSPs, but under the settlement agreement both men and women will be receiving compensation payments.

Figure 3) Participants: Survivors versus Non-Survivors

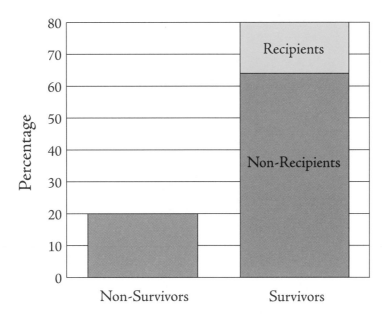

As this figure shows, most of the survey participants—8 out of every 10—were Survivors of residential schools. However, among participating Survivors, most of them (64%) had yet to receive any residential school compensation. In some cases, Survivors chose not to disclose whether or not they had received compensation. That said, the overwhelming majority had voluntarily disclosed this information.

Virtually all of the interviews were held in November 2006, beginning with 19 interviews in the early part of the month (Saskatchewan), 25 interviews mid-month (Northwest Territories), and 23 interviews at the end of the month (Alberta). A group interview was held in January 2007 (British Columbia).

While participants were not asked to self-identify as First Nation, Inuit, or Métis it can be said that the majority of participants were First Nation, with the remainder being Inuvialuit. No one clearly identified as Métis.

Summary of the Key Informant Survey

Overview of Participants

Care has been taken to ensure that the perspectives and voices of both recipients and non-recipients of lump sum payments (LSPs) are represented in this report including the level of its analysis. Therefore, where possible, the following findings are attributed to recipients and non-recipients so as to maximize the integrity of their respective contributions.

Recipients

All the participants who are Survivors and who received a residential school LSP had received this payment either through a court case settlement, the federal ADR process, or last year's CEP advance payment. A few have received two LSPs. The eldest participating recipients were in their early eighties, and included First Nation and Inuvialuit Survivors. The duration of their attendance at the schools ranged from one to nine years, extending as far back as the mid-1930s, or occurring as recently as the early 1980s. The schools they attended were located across the prairies and the Northwest Territories, and were operated by Catholic and Anglican churches.

Recipient participants included prominent members of residential school Survivor groups who have helped dozens of fellow claimants obtain LSPs, totalling anywhere from $1,000 to $100,000. These groups have provided information and guidance to Survivors, as well as helped them fill out residential school compensation forms. They rely entirely on volunteer help and are well acquainted with, and deeply passionate about, criminal court processes. In the process, others have spawned a movement for justice for Survivors. Some were involved in trials that were heard in the 1990s and featuring plaintiff groups as large as 26 people, while others settled out of court.

Many recipients described having quite vivid, "quite present" memories of residential school to this day, which, in some cases, were the product of incapacitating abuse at the hands of priests. A few were the third generation in their family to attend the schools. While most recipients were critical of the residential school experience, at least one voice did not appreciate the focus on negative residential school impacts, countering that, in some cases, the schools saved people from desperate situations. A few managed to hang onto their language; most did not.

Some recipients had lived in their community for decades; others travelled a fair bit. A good number had work experience in such fields as corrections, victim advocacy, childcare, carpentry, and maintenance. Some had engaged in long-term employment and had post-secondary education. Some were past and present politicians with First Nation governments and included experienced office-holders.

In addition, some recipients shared their familiarity with addictions and illness: their own or that of their inner circle. Common experiences that were brought to the table included child removal by Child and Family Services authorities, suicide, family violence, cancer, alcoholism, and other addictions. Meanwhile, many continue to pursue their own paths to healing, as they draw on sobriety and men's groups for support.

Most LSPs discussed by recipients concerned court cases and settlements, with a few from ADR or the $8,000 CEP advance payment of 2006. Court-ordered LSPs arrived in the mid- to late-1990s, and voluntarily disclosed amounts received by participants ranging from a low of $2,000 to a high of $105,000, not necessarily accounting for legal fees.

Non-Recipients

The involvement of non-recipients with residential school Survivors ranged from the personal to the professional. This group of participants was made up of former students who, at the time of their interview, had not received a lump sum payment. This group also included key stakeholders in the community, many of whom were close to Survivors. One non-recipient was the fourth generation of her family to attend residential school. Another recalled that her community's residents "started going to residential school back in the 1800s. Three or four of my mother's sisters died [there], probably from broken hearts and trauma." Participants in the non-recipient group attended or made reference to schools that were run by Anglican and Roman Catholic churches in Alberta, Saskatchewan, British Columbia, and the Northwest Territories. Many of these former students went for much of their childhood—8 to 11 years in some cases—and were taken from their families as early as age five. Some non-recipients attended up to 8 years without ever going home. At the other end of the extreme was a non-recipient who ran away after less than a week, and never went back. A few noted staying in dorms while at high school. Attendance at residential school extended as far back as the early 1950s. Some went to day school for early grades, then to residential school afterward. Taken as a whole, the experience of students from virtually every grade is represented by the non-recipient participants, from early childhood to teenage years. Some attended more than one residential school. Many still live near their former school or the site where it once stood.

The trauma of residential school came up regularly among non-recipients. Along with general and specific references to "physical, mental, spiritual abuse," some non-recipient participants reported being victims of sexual abuse while inside these institutions:

> Most of my best friends from [residential school] have committed suicide and when I tried to do the same, I heard their voices encouraging me to live. I've carried toxic shame from carrying four sexual assaults from older students. Only in the last year have I tried to stand up for myself. Once I went through healing, I became good to myself.

One Survivor who has worked with many Survivors, and children and grandchildren of Survivors, offered this description of the persistent and pervasive legacy of the schools:

> Whether indirectly or directly, I saw the impact of residential school. The violence, anger, and denials. Having lived in residential school, I know the perpetrators, and I know some of the male victims here [and where most] of their victims were from … This community has suffered immensely from the impact of abuse in residential schools. From there I've seen alcoholism and violence.

But at least one non-recipient did "not remember any physical abuse in residential school." Another had a parent who spoke only of happy residential school stories, which sometimes became sad later on. This ambivalence reflected in the recollections of many former students.

Non-recipients who were members of well-established or recently formed Survivor groups and societies contributed a critical portion of the survey findings. Some have become local experts on the various LSP processes and the changes that will come once the settlement agreement is implemented. A few non-recipient participants were among the more active in their Survivor groups, working as coordinators or executive members at the regional and national levels. Some non-recipients had not received LSPs despite knowing recipients who lived in the same community.

The health services sector was well represented among participating non-recipients. From nurses' aides to social workers to counsellors and therapists, the length and diversity of participants' experience were extensive. They included many addictions counsellors among other kinds of counsellors. From youth to adults, in groups or one-on-one, they would work with their clients to "get through the day [and] help them cope." Client referrals to medical supports and services for physical and sexual issues, depression, and suicide put these professionals in constant touch with their community. This made them well aware of what and where treatment resources were currently available. Some, but not all, were locally based; some have worked in more than one community. A few worked at the regional level and beyond. Moreover, the reality of limited access to such services meant that some counsellors would take in clients from other communities. Indeed, the demand among former residential school students for counselling often exceeded the supply. One provider has "seen up to 100 Survivors," with most of them being men. Another counsellor spoke of driving "at eleven thirty at night to the drunk tank [at the nearby town] to talk to Survivors." Another referred to how it has taken 13 years to finally make inroads on the residential school fallout where they live. Among the dozens of participants such understanding, dedication, and concern for former residential school students were not uncommon. Those who work as volunteer caregivers and helpers for Survivors are very much included in this assessment. Some counsellors were schooled and employed by Aboriginal-specific organizations like Nechi, NNADAP, and the National Native Addictions Partnership Foundation. Providers who took part in the survey used a wide range of methods in their work with clients such as workshops on stress, inner child therapy, and male rage. They are well-placed to offer solutions grounded in fresh thinking and action. For example, one provider said that Survivors exhibit all the classic characteristics of post-traumatic stress disorder, but to acknowledge this would make government "antsy." A common thread is the health professionals' commitment to building and supporting the personal capacity of Survivors. As one practitioner put it, "We are not problem solvers. We facilitate processes. We help them to accept responsibility for their behaviour."

Some non-recipient participants had a more personal experience with serious addiction, be it their own or that of someone close to them. Some can count as far back as 31 years ago since their last drink. They are acutely aware of the "difference between staying dry and living sober," and how being in recovery is an ongoing, lifelong process. Similarly, people were involved in a variety of voluntary associations like men's groups and Alcoholics Anonymous, both as participants and organizers.

In the realm of justice, some non-recipient participants had previously been caught up in the justice system as offenders, while others were professionally and/or personally connected to them, including those involved in law enforcement and legal representation.

Non-recipient participation also came from a variety of community and regional educators, serving young and mature students in high school and college through courses in nursing, counselling, and life skills. One partnered with local Aboriginal organizations and industry and other educational institutions.

The non-recipient group also included a number of First Nation chiefs and councillors, past and present, and those who live and work closely with them. The staff and management at Aboriginal government services also contributed; most were well-established bodies, but one agency was just one year old. A fair number of senior and junior band-level administrators in social services, health, social development, elders' services, operations, and management were also interviewed.

Some non-recipients interacted with Survivors as part of criminal lawsuits against abusers. The range of experience extends from formal support of an investigation that led to charges and/or convictions (in one case, abuse stemmed back to the late 1970s) to being the spouse of an abuse sufferer, which carried "net effects" (overall effects) of its own. One "did lots of advance payment research for elders in response to questions from Survivors," and facilitated the "necessary research into documentation." Survivor assistance came from relatives, but more likely by means of more formal advocates, paid or unpaid.

Non-recipients' connection to Survivors also included volunteers who helped elders with the ADR process: "Today, we assist anyone who went to residential school and help to fill out forms, mail them out for them, help them find evidence that they were in residential school." In fact, one person's hearing was imminent at the time of the interview. Such involvement is perhaps among the most time-consuming and difficult, as evidenced in this comment:

> Personally, I help fill out ADR forms [but won't anymore after this month]. It's too upsetting and draining for me to hear the horror stories. I saw it from the beginning to the present. The first amounts awarded weren't all that high, considering the abuse involved.

Advocates and practitioners of Aboriginal culture and language who grew up on the land also numbered among the non-recipient participants. A few were formally active in spiritual matters, from traditions rooted in Aboriginal beliefs to Christian faiths, or a melding of both. A growing number of people are employing traditional methods and medicines to help Survivors, and this participant group includes individuals on both sides of that development.

One person used to be a co-worker of a former residential school supervisor, while a few worked at some of the last schools to close. One participant reported no involvement with Survivors. Some non-recipients were connected indirectly to the residential school experience through relatives and other loved ones, through parents and grandparents especially, but also as spouses, parents, in-laws, and/or siblings. Many viewed the schools' effects in completely negative terms. "Residential school damaged my husband," said one participant, but not all saw the schools that way. "My dad worked all his life. Residential school taught him how to work. Survivors have to get over it," as another participant put it. Citing the abuse that went on at many schools, some non-recipients told of Survivors they knew who died prematurely or developed addictions in response to negative memories of what went on in residential school: "My cousins drank themselves to death as adults." Many have been told the stories of abuse experienced or witnessed by their elders, although some have never been told anything.

The payments discussed by non-recipients were received as far back as the mid-1990s and went as high as $125,000. The recipients they mentioned had pursued their cases individually or as part of a larger group. Some non-recipient participants knew people whose LSP came in the form of the $8,000 advance payment under the *Indian Residential Schools Settlement Agreement*. Some non-recipients knew of recipients through media reports on residential school legal cases and the compensation that was awarded. Again, all of the aforementioned connections were described by both Survivors and non-Survivors. Then there were those non-recipient Survivors who had made a conscious decision not to pursue any compensation at all:

> I'm a problem solver, and I was once a Survivor, and now feel I'm a healed, healthy woman. I was eligible but chose not to apply. I didn't feel money would do anything for me; I felt like I was taking something I didn't need. Money could've been better used for programs.

That said, there were also those who did not think it right "to criticize people who receive advance payments."

A fair number of non-recipients reported no contact of any kind with LSP recipients or their families, even though they were aware that such payments had reached people in the community. Others were simply "not directly aware of any elder who got a 'first round' lump sum payment through litigation." Some chose to highlight the fact of relatives they felt should have received compensation but did not. In a slightly different vein, one female participant was adamant that many women like her were not compensated because "the LSP was for men and run by men" only.

Experiences and Perceptions of Compensation Payment Processes

Among participants who had successfully obtained LSPs, three areas came up the most when asked about the path they had walked in order to win their payments: the participation of lawyers, the emotional toll of presenting their stories, and the duration of the process. A general comment from one recipient suggested that, overall, the process was not very 'Survivor-sensitive,' as it too often relied on people who, being either too young or too unfamiliar with residential school, had no empathy for the Survivor experience.

According to the picture painted by non-recipients, the pursuit of residential school compensation turned out to be its own ordeal for Survivors. Next to no one in this group of former students and others had anything positive to say about any aspect of the residential school compensation claim process itself. Participants offered feedback on the legal process for both the first round of lawsuits in the 1980s and 1990s as well as the more recent ADR process. Based on the feedback of non-recipient participants, it would seem that for most Survivors there has yet to be a process for determining and allocating residential school compensation that has either been based on, or sensitive to, their needs. One non-recipient view on the LSP process could be taken as emblematic for the majority of participants: "Government should have met with the community first to make arrangements on how to pay it out. There should have been prior consultation." Another non-recipient added that "Survivors should be involved in the ADR form development process. My main question is: Were Survivors involved in the process?" Despite the fact that it was their suffering and their persistence that led to the process in the first place, many former students felt shut out.

It should be mentioned that a few non-recipients either had no knowledge or awareness of LSPs, or of Survivors' particular experience with them: "I know LSPs happened but when and how this took place, I don't know." "I don't know if Survivors were satisfied." "All I know is that some of them did not get very much." "The people who received payment did not talk about the LSP."

Legal costs seen as excessive

Lawyers came under frequent fire by LSP recipients and non-recipients, and were often portrayed as profiteers who only cared about their 'cut' of the payments. Both groups offered more than one account of people who owed thousands of dollars to legal counsel after the LSP arrived. Examples include a $96,000 settlement that became $50,000 after legal fees, and a lawyer that reportedly took in a million dollars from LSPs awarded to a group of Survivors. Questioning the fairness of such "disproportionate" arrangements, recipients protested that they were the ones who were severely abused and beaten in residential school, and not the lawyers. Another Survivor said a lawyer put a claim on his money, but the local government fought to get his money back. Some non-recipients found that the various LSP processes did not take the often-limited resources of elders into account. As one volunteer helper recalled:

> Some elders had no phones or vehicles, so I had to travel out to their homes, which were hard to reach on the other side of reserve. Another elder felt bad that they weren't home when I visited, so she later visited me, even though she wasn't very mobile. (She uses a walker, and has no car.) She'd found a way to come in, saying, "I remember a name." She came all that way just to say that! I was touched.

The more skeptical non-recipients went so far as to suggest that money was there to be made through the compensation process by everyone but the Survivors. One individual likened ADR to "an inverted pyramid," with Survivors at the bottom, when it came to

> who made the most off IRS [Indian residential school] Survivors. Lots of therapists get $800 a day for sitting in on hearings just to listen. My sister threw the therapist out. She didn't know who the person was. Only the adjudication board approves therapists. Survivors didn't get to pick.

In light of these concerns, it can come across to some Survivors as somewhat contradictory to worry about their potential spending choices when, as one Survivor put it, "everyone else is getting wealthy off the IRS process." Given that "the lawyers get the cheque first" before any amount is disbursed to Survivors, it left many Survivors more than a little wary of them. Some made the argument that Survivors who win LSPs should not have to pay any legal fees whatsoever—the government and church should. Some Survivors have responded by taking greater ownership over the LSP process by negotiating their own percentages, for example. One recommended that people fill out their own forms.

Stories about lawyer misconduct were common among recipient and non-recipient participants. Described by one recipient as "invaders" who descended upon communities to sign up Survivors en masse for class-action suits, law firms were accused of not telling people what it was they were signing or that it "automatically" made them their client. One such firm reportedly came onto a reserve and "herded Survivors like cattle, [filing] tons of names in the Court of Queen's Bench without even telling them." Once names are gathered on such lists, participants reported, nothing would happen until, tired of the inaction, they got a new lawyer, whereupon a "threatening" letter would arrive saying firms will "sue for a percentage of residential school compensation." Another person said a lawyer was "harassing her for $20,000 even though he did nothing at the ADR." The comment, "My husband's lawyer was very good," would be the lone note of praise for lawyers.

Process highly emotional, even traumatizing

Many recipients commented on the sometime intense emotions that arose during the pre-payment process as they relived negative residential school experiences and revisited old hurts. Part of their "heartbreaking and bitter" pain came from having their credibility automatically questioned under the process, but simply revisiting their past so thoroughly proved difficult too. As one non-recipient noted, "It triggered a lot of emotions and pain for the recipients. There was not enough preparation for them. One went through a very tough time [because] he ended up going back three times." Non-recipients spoke of how the process "brought out a lot of shame" for Survivors, creating "emotional turmoil" and "opening a can of worms." For some Survivors, memories of their school days were always close to the surface: the scrutiny of the various LSP hearings exposed it for all to see, and not without consequences. In the words of one non-recipient:

> My brother got a large sum, $80,000 to $100,000. It took seven to eight years. By the time he got the money, he shot himself the day after. He was found by his daughter. He went deep. That's why I'm scared. It triggered a lot.

This would not be the only case of a suicide attributed to a Survivor's having testified, according to recipients and non-recipients. "One guy killed himself after disclosure because of what came up. He had no support. He couldn't handle it." Others, meanwhile, had "turned to alcohol and drugs" to cope with the fallout of telling their story. One non-recipient's account illustrated the wider impact that disclosing abuse can have on family members:

> When I spoke to my son who had a hard time in his application, [I saw that] the applicants who went to see lawyers were made to feel small. I found out as a mother who had no daughters that my sons had been sexually abused. I cried and cried.

Similarly in another case, it would not be until the court hearings that "wives found out for the first time that their partners had been sexually abused. This was traumatic."

Although one person did mention that their lawyer referred them to a psychologist, others noted a general lack of counselling on-hand, both during and after sessions. Some recipients spoke of unexpectedly breaking down as they shared their stories, while others were just as surprised when they became verbally aggressive. Relentless questioning by lawyers in court unnerved some recipients. Some almost did not apply at all out of fear. For one recipient, "this is Indian residential school all over again." Another felt that requiring Survivors to not only prove their stories, but to tell them over and over again, was to be re-victimized. This led some to question whether they were in a sufficiently healthy frame of mind coming out of the process to determine whether their level of compensation was fair. Some recipients claimed that they "would not recommend the courts to anyone." Still others resisted the restrictive protocol of these proceedings, from aggressively asserting their equality with those who ran the hearings to always referring to what happened to 'all of us' instead of just 'me' at residential school.

While recognizing that a certain amount of pain is unavoidable, some non-recipients argued that the process made things worse. They accused the government of insensitivity for not taking these emotional aspects into consideration when setting up and operating these LSP processes: "Someone has to prepare Survivors for when this happens. We can never get that through to bureaucrats." And so, with "no aftercare after your

ADR process" and a "help-line that you can't get through to," many Survivors were left to feel "re-victimized" by the process.

Forced by that process to prove they were abused, Survivors who enter the government-run LSP system have had to contend with its major default assumption: that Survivors are not telling the truth, and must bear total responsibility for showing otherwise. In other words, they are presumed guilty until proven innocent. This apparent bias might explain why not enough care was taken to have more resources and a more sensitive process in place for Survivors at such hearings.

Regarding the ADR process, however, some non-recipients reported "paid stress leave" for adjudicators who found the stories of abuse too much to take, "but there's nothing for front-line workers. It's a double standard," suggesting that the needs of adjudicators may have received more attention than those of Survivors or the people who helped them.

Payment processes seen as too long, too complicated and restrictive

Beyond their design, one of the major concerns expressed by recipients and non-recipients about the various compensation payment processes was their duration, taking anywhere from three to 12 years to complete. Many had complaints about the length of time it took to begin a process, the length of that process once it got underway, and the often onerous logistics it took to be involved. Indeed, 'slow' or 'slowness' and 'long' or 'very long' were descriptions that came up frequently. These criticisms cover the various court cases, ADR, and even the $8,000 advance payment associated with the *Indian Residential Schools Settlement Agreement*.

The amount of travel to a large city far away from home, coupled with the agitation and anxiety of an unfamiliar process, were such aggravating factors that by the end claimants were evidently ready to "settle for whatever they could get." Other recipients felt no choice but to hold out for larger LSPs after initial low offers from the government led to an extended back-and-forth process.

The length of LSP processes had consequences. Cases cited by recipients included a class action suit filed in the late 1980s of which, by the time it was all over a decade later, two of the group's members had taken their own lives. In another case, thirteen elders within one Survivors' group alone had passed on before the final outcome was reached. A non-recipient spoke of a "long and painful" trial from the early nineties where the victims "got frustrated with waiting [as] court dates were postponed over and over again."

More specifically, concerns were shared by non-recipients about how Survivors grew "very angry and upset with the long forms they had to fill out," which bogged down the process in bureaucracy. On top of that, said one non-recipient, one accused perpetrator

> had so many cases against him, the Survivors had to sometimes wait a year before their cases went ahead. What if one supervisor abused 15 boys? When they finally found these supervisors, they were very old. In order to receive money for compensation, they waited. It was not a healthy process because it brought back bad memories.

Such lengthy court processes were made worse due to their perceived secrecy, as a non-recipient said, "Compensation was a very 'hush-hush' process. The new payments under CEP are more open." Then there was the travel time required to bring victims to trials and hearings, which only extended the process. Labelled by one non-recipient as "a white bureaucracy put in by government that keeps people down," the ADR process was seen as inaccessible and it was "hard to get hearings." This view was shared by both recipients and non-recipients. Moreover, the hearings that did occur were followed by frustrating waits of three months before a decision was made, prompting this critic to state, "Government can't seem to process hearings while people die." Another non-recipient urged authorities to speed things up and to "rush the payments so no more people die before they get the benefits."

A non-recipient alleged ADR adjudicators were scheduled to a maximum of "two sessions a day over two weeks, at four hours a day." This allegation was echoed elsewhere: "I don't know who put in the quota for hearings. They only hear so many cases at a time." According to some non-recipients, this situation clearly frustrated Survivors who, after enduring the long wait it took to merely get a hearing, felt that their cases were utterly rushed through the system with their story barely heard.

Another non-recipient Survivor spoke of the apparent restrictions around ADR application forms: "When we started the group, we only had two form-fillers for everyone. There are 168 names in our [Survivors] group, but only twenty ADR application forms have been filled." The group was assisted by lawyers with training, and the federal IRSRC office contracted a counselling group to help out. The participant went on to say the group was informed that "there are only two recognized form-fillers in all of [the province], and [the IRSRC said], 'If you use a non-IRSRC-sanctioned form-filler, it's not in your best interests.' We want that training."

Once the compensation was finally approved, some non-recipients noted that "it took a long time for the payments to be paid." Recipients spoke of routinely broken promises about when an LSP would arrive, and the need to be persistent with lawyers in order to locate information about the status of an LSP. A non-recipient mentioned how some elderly Survivors apparently received advance payments, but others "died waiting" for them. This sparked a recipient's push for expedited hearings for the sick and elderly.

By comparison, some Survivors found their ADR process less cumbersome than the courts, though this process was also not without its detractors. A few recipients were assisted in their ADR proceedings in that the abusers' guilt had already been established. As for the *Indian Residential Schools Settlement Agreement*, the vagueness about when the CEP will arrive annoyed some Survivors. "We hear we'll get money 'mid-summer.' We don't know what that means."

Meanwhile, one non-recipient complained of the apparent government disregard toward someone who "interviewed and filed claims for over 200 people," a total of "2,000 hours work over 18 months." The individual was under the impression that financial support for this work would be forthcoming at twenty cases. Meanwhile, Survivors "constantly called" the individual asking when their hearing would happen. Another non-recipient mentioned how

> friends who've applied for advance payments wait and wait for payments, [and] have placed calls to trace their cheques. It is residential school all over again for them. I'll give you a candy tomorrow if you behave, but tomorrow never comes.

With all of these options (lawsuits, ADR, CEP, and IAP) put forth at one time or another, the apparent result is "much confusion regarding any kind of settlement" among Survivors, leading a non-recipient to remark that "they keep changing the process." "The ADR is frustrating, [and now it's] about to close. We're asking for information on what IAP is all about."

Another repeated source of concern among non-recipients over LSP processes was the matter of who or what was eligible for compensation. Many felt the criteria and timelines were restrictive and unfair. This Survivor's experience of "the third time around" was not unusual:

> When the Indian residential school claims first started, I was told I didn't qualify, and only a few got it. The second time I applied, I was told what happened to me 'wasn't serious enough.' That's why I was hesitant to do it this time.

Compensation levels inadequate and/or inequitable

By virtually every measure, Survivors took issue with the quantity and quality of compensation awarded to them under the LSP process. Some recipients were very upset and frustrated at the gap between what they had expected to receive and what was actually awarded. One individual reported being originally offered $700,000 but somehow received just $50,000 by the end. Others got a quarter of what they had anticipated. A non-recipient's story of one parent's experience is telling in this regard:

> My mom got $2,000 for nine years—not much! She wasn't satisfied, but my mom took the money and just wanted to continue with life. She gave [her children] $100 each. I think she was angry because my dad committed suicide at 71, before the payments came. He was angry too at [the school]. They were violent perverts. Dad wouldn't talk about it to us, not even to the RCMP. Mom has nightmares about residential school, although the more she talks, the less she has them.

Other recipients complained they did not receive the minimum amount promoted in the ADR literature, but did not want to push it for fear of receiving no payment at all. Yet, in some cases, non-recipients saw a fatigue factor set in and Survivors would resign themselves to the outcome: "The money for compensation is just not enough. I think some have concern, but they're tired of this process."

Some recipients felt they went through "the same things as everybody else," but got less money from the courts than others did. They decried the legal system's inequity: "the courts do not look at us equally and the same." Many non-recipients observed that it was only natural for recipients to compare their respective LSP with others', and they frequently perceived an inequity and imbalance in what different people received: "One elder wanted to fix up his cabin but he got less than students who were there a shorter period of time." Some non-recipients could not understand why one person would get as little as a $1,000 LSP, but others got $60,000. The discrepancies in the awarded amounts were not always immediately apparent. As well, many recipients believe the approach used under ADR, a.k.a. the 'Model A' and 'Model B' framework, seemed to vary greatly in its application from Survivor to Survivor despite cases appearing reasonably similar. It seemed to some recipients that those who were least abused would all too often receive a greater LSP than those who were constantly abused. One couple was upset that one of them got a greater LSP than the other. A suggestion was to have the government pay out the highest amounts available for each compensation scale to Survivors right across the board. Some non-recipients questioned the timing of LSPs as well: "One [elder] was very frustrated because he was older than his friend who got [money] before him. Then he told his story, went on the radio, and got his money."

There were also recipients who complained of the LSP inequity between jurisdictions. Citing different compensation schedules for different parts of the country, elders questioned why some regions were assigned a higher payment ceiling than others. Other recipients questioned the timing of LSPs: two Survivors who had won compensation more or less at the same time might receive their cheques weeks apart from each other.

Some recipients believed that Survivor awards are more generous now than those given out in previous years, possibly because of lawyers' inexperience with such cases at the time. Some non-recipients echoed this perception:

> I read that [previous] lump sum payments for Aboriginal people have compensated them for far less than for now - $150,000 versus $400,000. There is no fairness in this. Maybe the recipients just accepted the money [back then] because it was such a large sum.

There were recipients who felt compensation was greater in places like the United States. These differences led a recipient to suggest that Survivors not always be quick to "jump at the first offer." Another recipient said the "10+3" compensation formula put forth under the *Indian Residential Schools Settlement Agreement* should be multiplied by ten times that amount.

A strongly delivered criticism of the payment process from non-recipients centered upon a perceived bias against female residential school students. Some argued that "only men benefited" as far as receiving compensation or treatment, and "there was no sensitivity to women" or their issues:

> Women are the family keepers and caretakers, yet we were not compensated. They wasted all the money on men. I want to be compensated for all the embroidery I did for the nuns, making pillows and sheets, Monday to Sunday. I was 9 to 11 years of age when I was doing this. Today I'm claustrophobic. This is the frustration of the women who were basically left out.

While many questioned the quantity of compensation, others took issue with its quality. According to one recipient, "Our suffering is priceless. Money can't make it disappear," suggesting financial compensation was inadequate in more ways than one. There are those recipients who felt tens of thousands of dollars amounted to little compared to what is actually needed to make up for or ease the pain caused at residential school. Others said money and an apology are but the least that could have been done, and do not constitute genuine contrition or compassion. One recipient alleged that workers' compensation boards pay more for a broken leg than what the Canadian government has offered for years of mental and spiritual anguish suffered by Survivors.

Processes unjustly preclude culture and language claims

Some recipients were fundamentally unhappy that the loss of culture and the loss of language have never been on the table under any LSP process. One particularly passionate recipient vowed to bring future action on these fronts: "You make the government aware there will be future lawsuits. It's not going to end here." There was also concern that the documents Survivors must sign in order to take hold of their LSPs are a government attempt to trick people into "surrendering" their rights to such future culture and language lawsuits.

ADR better than court, but still confrontational and legalistic

Many participating non-recipients found the Alternative Dispute Resolution compensation payment process to be excessively confrontational and adversarial in nature, with its near-total onus on Survivors to prove they even went to the schools. In that sense, ADR was as legalistic as any court proceeding, disappointing those Survivors who may have assumed it would employ a less combative method of settling IRS claims. Accordingly, non-recipients found ADR's "legal jargon alienating," a process "full of terminology associated with court and judges." "Authority being a dirty word for Survivors," as one non-recipient put it, they are much less likely to embrace a process that reminds them of this. Indeed, the recipients who found ADR to be relatively simpler and often quicker than the courts nonetheless saw it as far from perfect: "Some [of those involved] did not respect what you went through. They wanted to make you feel guilty. I had to remind myself that it was not my fault. I'm still dealing with residential school."

During one ADR process, a recipient was reportedly told that, as a 19-year-old, she/he could have stopped an incident of sexual abuse, even though earlier testimony indicated that the incident was just the latest in an eight-year series of ill-treatment. With the church and government "trying to prove [they] are liars," some recipients found the process to be "very depressing." Those who considered speaking against officials worried that it could hurt their settlement.

A non-recipient expressed the belief that "since the Tory government came in, it's become stricter, more aggressive. At one ADR hearing, they reportedly "grilled [a relative] all day, and kept asking the same questions in different ways, for over eight hours in total." Non-recipients questioned how ADR placed the burden of proof of residential school attendance entirely on the shoulders of Survivors despite the fact that "church and school records are not always reliable," or that many Survivors "cannot even access their information, so there are delays." With people "lacking documentation, tracing documents has been a problem." Moreover, said a non-recipient, for many applicants "it can feel like a slap in the face to be told their application was incomplete [after what] they'd been subjected to." As another non-recipient complained, there are "so many hoops we have to go through. To get different information from different sources is frustrating." In one case, a "95-year-old got a quick process because of her age but no money" in the end because of a lack of records. Elsewhere, a non-recipient disclosed how "an 80-year-old, sickly [Survivor] applied but got denied because they can't find his records [even though] prior to 1960, this residential school did not keep records." Then there were those people who "could not access records because the residential school burned down, as so many have."

A non-recipient who had helped 50 elders receive advance payments recalled how their applications got stalled because Aboriginal names had been spelled differently by various non-Aboriginal residential school personnel. In another situation, "some of the applicants had changed their names after residential school … [T]hese kind of technicalities complicated their application process." Time and time again, it seemed that even though the mistake or issue was not that of the Survivors to begin with, but they were the ones left to deal with it.

Alternative methods of proving attendance were not necessarily accepted under the ADR, as some non-recipients reported. "My mother was told 'we can't find records,' that none before 1940 [exist, but] we have photos, witnesses, and declarations—they demand more." In another community, they found what we needed to do now is to have sworn affidavits to prove people attended residential school. Some elders here did not have a birth certificate, for instance. Documents required for an elder's application include a passport, treaty number, and a health care number.

It is a different situation and a similar outcome for this former student and non-recipient: "I was sexually abused … [but had] to produce evidence I was sexually abused because my abuser died years ago. They're asking me to produce evidence I can't deliver on." Notwithstanding these testimonies, there may be some inconsistency between adjudicators. A non-recipient claimed some adjudicators accepted a signed affidavit on its own while others did not.

On top of the burdensome requirement for documentation, there was a non-recipient's report of elders who found it hard to recall names of people involved in claims or dates. More than just a matter of memory, it was also painful and often something that could not be done all at once. The ADR hearing itself was also criticized by non-recipients for moving too quickly, that only two to three hours maximum were allocated. Information would come back to Survivors' memories after the fact, thereby removing their chance to tell their full story. One Survivor spoke of the difficulty she had testifying: "I had blanked out because it was too much to keep uppermost in my head. I repressed it. I won't even tell my husband this stuff. It's too emotional to bring this up, to recall everything."

One non-recipient spoke of a lawyer who helped revive the memory of an older person about repeated strappings at residential school, but with no idea as to why they took place. The lawyer then apparently sat down with an adjudicator and discussed the best way to approach the Survivor to elicit those details. Yet other non-recipients claimed that "no preparation is allowed for the ADR process" whatsoever, in that anyone accompanying Survivors to an ADR hearing could not meet with them beforehand, which suggests adjudicators across the country may not be applying the rules consistently.

If working cooperatively with elders to bring out their emotion-laden stories is seen as tantamount to 'coaching' a witness, some non-recipients pointed out that "elders don't talk about abuse" openly, often using "coded language" to discuss what can obviously be disturbing and troubling incidents from their childhood. As a result, they can be easily misunderstood by adjudicators unfamiliar with these codes. In addition, English may be a second language for a Survivor, which is why some non-recipients pushed for "someone who can interpret, someone who's fluent in the language" at hearings. A related point stems from the fact that none of the paperwork used by any compensation process are in an Aboriginal language, which increases the likelihood that "forms are not filled out properly as a result." And, as one non-recipient was quick to point out, few of the adjudicators themselves are of Aboriginal descent, and those that are may or may not speak an indigenous language. There were also claims among non-recipients that four "Indian adjudicators were fired," but no one was told why.

"In discovery sessions, elders are isolated," recalled one non-recipient. The sad irony is that such a dynamic replicates the worst features and methods of abuse suffered by children at the hands of residential school staff. Although not a conventional court procedure, one participant suggested it would feel much safer for Survivors if the process allowed for bringing whole families together, or at least former students as a group, to make it easier to cope with having to recall traumatic incidents. But that emotional and psychological intensity can also get caught up in an unintended set of financial incentives within the compensation process that prompt Survivors to stay in a dark and wounded place. Thus, some "Survivors played a waiting game, so that they could not get better until final examination for discovery. Men in particular put off healing and stay victimized [because] if you're sick, the more credible you'll appear, the more money you'll get." Such systemic incentives to prolong one's pain have not served Survivors well.

On the other hand, some recipients complained of people misrepresenting what had happened to them at school. One allegation claimed that someone who had never even gone to school had received compensation. Some recipients accused lawyers of complicity in this. One Survivor told of being asked by ADR staff to vouch for other elders' attendance at school.

Another issue raised among recipients was the apparent awarding of an additional $10,000 to Survivors who used the services of a government-approved psychologist. A recipient questioned why their own preferred healer was not eligible for this money, adding that psychologists cared more about money than Survivors.

Indian Residential Schools Settlement Agreement criticized

The negotiated *Indian Residential Schools Settlement Agreement* contains many confusing and restrictive provisions, according to LSP recipients. For example, perceiving that the same type of abuse happened at day schools as residential schools, and both under the same regime, recipients were bothered by the exclusion of day students under the agreement. Non-recipients echoed this sentiment about the differential treatment accorded to former day school students who were "treated [in] the same, really harsh" ways as residential school students.

One recipient expressed worry that the $10,000 offered for the first year of residential school attendance would serve as a cap on compensation for any single-year student, even if they had faced horrific experiences in that time. Other recipients took issue with the "abuse claim rating system," and questioned whether Aboriginal participation was involved in setting the award amounts for the various abuse categories. Finally, some recipients, as with non-recipients, labelled the eligibility 'cut-off' date of 30 May 2005 as "arbitrary" and unfair. It was not clear to them why the children of abused Survivors were unable to pursue compensation on their parents' behalf simply because they had passed away prior to this date. Similarly grating for others were the anticipated delays in applying for LSPs due to the lack of good school records.

Process positive for some

As arduous as it was for many Survivors to tell of their residential school past, there were those recipients who actually found the process to be beneficial in the end. "It helped me get out my story. I was well-treated," said one participant. Exhausting and distressing as it was, disclosing the abuse proved to be a positive part of the LSP process in that it "revalidated" some Survivors' sense of who they were, as they gained an understanding of what led to their behaviour as adults. Other recipients lost their sense of shame as they realized others went through similar experiences. In this way, the LSP process may have indirectly helped Survivors find closure by offering, however imperfectly, the opportunity to deal with the problem head on and put it behind them.

Meanwhile, in terms of the overall LSP process, one recipient felt that it went smoothly, while another recipient's case moved through the system in what was felt to be a relatively short 12 months. There was another report of an LSP arriving two months after it was awarded. Some recipients spoke of the helpful support they were permitted to draw on from other members of their claimant group and family members during their hearings. One non-recipient indicated satisfaction with what they experienced of the LSP process: "My husband did not seem frustrated with the process. He's well educated, so had no problem filling in forms. [There was] frustration directed at the church."

Positive Impacts of Payments on Individuals, Families, and Communities

Broadly comparing the two participant groups, recipients were relatively more forthcoming with examples of positive effects of lump sum payments than non-recipients. That said, members of both groups were quick to emphasize a shared belief that money only goes so far toward compensating victims. As one recipient put it: "It's not about money: it's getting people accountable and telling our story."

One non-recipient declared that "no amount of settlement is going to justify" what many Survivors experienced. For them, it is ultimately about far more than financial considerations. Indeed, some non-recipients fundamentally rejected strictly cash-based forms of compensation as either inadequate or inappropriate. One such Survivor had this to say of LSPs: "The payment did not take away our pain. It took away momentary stress, and helped us refocus our financial situation." Another non-recipient added: "The money alone is not a way for government to say we've paid our dues and be off the hook. Lump sum payments may just feed the damage done." One non-recipient had even harsher words for monetary compensation, judging it a "complete failure, unethical, and destructive [with] no redeeming factors." In this view, "financial compensation [is just] one way" of addressing residential school abuses.

Indeed, some recipients questioned whether the compensation had much connection to wellness at all: "Healing is a top priority for me, not the money, which is limited." That sense of limitations of the money was shared by a number of recipients, who seemed less concerned with the amount of their LSP and more focused on letting go and acceptance: "I am quite contented with my payment. I don't love money that much. I forgave my abusers who are long gone, so I don't hold a grudge." And yet, some non-recipients spoke of Survivors who looked past the monetary aspects to see the symbolic value of LSPs as the source of their most positive impact:

> I think a lot of recipients feel partially healed, that they are being recognized for what happened in the past. They feel someone out there cares. They are being given money because they are something, not nothing. The money brings peace of mind, and so they can heal.

In these cases, LSPs serve as a form of recognition and affirmation that can allow people to feel that "their past is redeemed," said one non-recipient.

The effects of money can be as varied as the people who receive it. As one recipient remarked: "Money is just a way for government to 'make amends,' I guess. It's up to me to accept it. You can't go on and on." In such cases, money almost seems to function as a mirror, 'reflecting' a person's situation and outlook when their LSP arrives. How much an LSP potentially helps or hurts a given recipient is thus, to some extent, particular to them. For example, one recipient attributed the mostly positive outcome of LSPs for recipients in their community to its 80 to 90 per cent sobriety rate. Others felt that "to deal with money properly, you need to have had it first," a testament to one's prior experience with handling money. Perhaps one positive impact of LSPs may be the way they offer some recipients the chance to demonstrate their capacity to put the payment in proper perspective.

Some non-recipients spoke of how positive outcomes of LSPs seemed to correlate with the healthiness and stability of the Survivor: "If a person does not have his life in order, more drinking and gambling will take place. If a person has their life in order, they'll probably pay off their debts, like I will." As one non-recipient put it: "The impact will depend on how mature people are, and how ready they are for the lump sum payment." Another noted that "those who've been stable enough have done well," and estimated that this applied to about "one-third of recipients." Having a job also seems to help, according to some non-recipients: "Those who work can utilize money as a means."

Even amidst the most difficult circumstances there are hopeful signs. One non-recipient had an abused, alcoholic sibling who chose to help the family with their $8,000 CEP. And as one health provider said, "We know some people are going to die from this money. It's a given, we've seen it, but we can help the majority."

There were a few recipients who had no idea of the social impacts of LSPs on others. This was either because they found it too "hard to gauge," too political, or they simply did not care to know what their neighbours did with their money.

LSPs offered chance to help out with family

The most common positive LSP outcome reported by recipients was the chance to spend some or all of their money on family and friends. A number opened modest to large banking or investment accounts for children or grandchildren; others simply handed over money directly. In one case, someone gave out virtually all their money, keeping just a fraction for themselves. Such selflessness was echoed elsewhere.

Education assistance was a common choice among recipients, including funds for computers. One of the more elaborate family-oriented uses of an LSP was a parent's offer to provide $50,000 in "educational incentives" to their children to encourage them to go to school.

From clothes and food to a trailer and van, many recipients said they bought items for their children and grandchildren. Travel with family was also a popular choice. One recipient went even further, buying a skidoo and tents to ensure they could regularly spend time outdoors together with loved ones. Another recipient consulted with their spouse and opted to help an expectant daughter prepare for the baby's arrival by covering the costs of building a new addition to their home. For many recipients, it seems helping others was its own reward and one that was newly afforded through LSPs.

Some non-recipients felt the impact of an LSP was somewhat 'diluted' in certain situations. "Some families are large, so $8,000 does not go very far in the end" to have "spent it wisely on family," although this was generally seen as positive. Some non-recipients described this behaviour as very consistent with a traditional ethic of sharing:

> When I get my money, I can't keep it in the bank, I share it. When my dad got his compensation, he shared it with the eleven of us … My dad [just] turned 91 years old.

> I told my husband, 'When the money comes in, I'll buy you a nice truck.' I'd put a down payment on a house for the older boys. If the money comes in time, we'll most likely spend it on our oldest daughter.

Other non-recipients indicated they would revisit their wills or "plan to invest in [the] children's university education." A grandparent intends to "save it for my grandchildren. I'll just keep $2,000 for myself." But not everyone knew of recipients who were necessarily so generous: "My brother who got the ADR did not give a cent to my sisters who are single. He's the angry, drinking brother."

LSPs invested

In quite a few cases, recipients directed a portion of their LSP straight into the bank, be it into long-term investments or other accounts. These financial arrangements include term deposits as well as other locked-in options that would only periodically pay out returns: "I want to put some away, to not take the thing all in one shot." Non-recipients also noted cases where recipients made investments, both private and public. "I know someone who invested $8,000 in an account," said one. Elsewhere, a group of three families asked a bank for help with their money, from which they now earn annual dividends. Another family's investment pays for an annual holiday. One Survivor advises others to "put money away for retirement as I'm planning to do." A non-recipient recalled recipients who opted to use their LSPs to support their community, which gave Survivors the option to allocate five per cent of their ADR payments toward local healing and education programs.

LSPs used to clear up debt

Another popular use for LSPs among recipients was to clear up indebted accounts and relieve the stress and pressure of living in poverty, at least temporarily. Depending on the amount of the LSP and debt involved, recipients could take care of some fairly large bills; for example, putting a down payment on a home or even paying it off outright. Others cleared outstanding loans or credit cards. One person set up a business with their LSP.

Non-recipients also knew of Survivors who had used either a portion or all of their LSP to eliminate outstanding debt: "A minority of elders paid their bills."

LSPs spent "in a good way"

Many recipients were glad to have the chance to acquire previously unaffordable goods such as vehicles, new furniture, children's clothes and bikes, tools for work or hunting, and a boat. Home and vehicle repairs also came up. These sorts of purchases seemed to meet with the approval of most participating recipients, and appeared "uplifting" for those recipients who did not enjoy regular access to such financial means. Non-recipients echoed these positive outcomes of LSPs: "My father-in-law bought a truck and furniture and still has these things." They also noted how LSPs were also put to some very practical uses:

> Not everyone had a negative experience. My brother-in-law built himself a cabin where workshops are held. He hunts and traps there. He has everything he wants on the land. From his experience at residential school, he turned his life around and set up his camp where healing workshops are held. He teaches how to live off the land.

Other items of this sort mentioned included a phone, a canoe and motor, a skidoo, or even just "wood and other necessities." Meanwhile, some non-recipients expecting an LSP for the first time under the CEP planned to indulge their passions and hobbies. "I love music and will get a beautiful guitar with my LSP," said one participant. "I'll go on a nice holiday," said another.

LSPs put toward care

For some recipients, an LSP permitted them to pay the costs associated with travelling to and/or participating in treatment centres, healer-run ceremonies including sweat lodges, or counselling sessions. Non-recipients occasionally saw LSPs playing a positive role in terms of health: "It added to healing for some, a minority. A majority blew it, with help from family and friends." A reference was made to "one couple using money for help from counsellors," a case similar to that of another family:

> We gave our daughter $10,000 when my husband got his payment. She was able to put a down payment on a cottage. My family went for counselling after the court case but we went on our own, though there were rumours counselling would be made mandatory with [residential school] cases. This never happened.

As mentioned earlier, non-recipients looked to a Survivor's starting point as the critical variable in determining the impact of LSPs. "Those individuals who were on a healing journey, who were few and far between, they did okay. As for the others, it accelerated and exacerbated the problems of individuals." In other words, to the extent healing is already underway when a payment arrives, LSPs can play a role in enabling or deepening opportunities to build upon it. Meanwhile, other non-recipients believed healing occurred as an indirect, almost accidental, result of LSPs:

> Even though the lump sum payment was humiliating, it forced recipients to name their experience and to deal with it. People got past their denial. They revealed their secrets.

> If people did not know they needed healing before [the money], you felt so crappy afterwards, you went for healing. Community pressure and sanction forced some into seeking help.

The potential for connecting healing and the receipt of LSPs was discussed by non-recipients, who referenced the efforts of legal advocates to incorporate counselling into the compensation process for some former students: "The lawyers said go for counselling for going through court. Lawyers encouraged them for instrumental purposes, and they ended up having counselling that helped them in the end."

Survivors were also offered optional "financial and mental health counselling [which] some people took." Another non-recipient noted that "some lawyers were ethical, [with] more integrity, and recommended therapy sessions before disclosures were made." A link between LSPs and healing can be made with the extent that this option was utilized and positive effects generated. However, it must be noted that mechanisms for making this happen were rarely mentioned by non-recipients.

Negative Impacts of Payments on Individuals, Families, and Communities

According to one lump sum payment recipient, "If you don't start healing, the money will kill you." There were many negative impacts linked to LSPs among the recipients. One Survivor estimated that only one-third of fellow recipients managed their payments well, and the remaining two-thirds struggled. Among non-recipients, negative impacts of LSPs came up a lot more frequently than positive ones. A few non-recipients were unable to comment, citing insufficient first-hand knowledge, little opportunity to discuss it with elders, or just feeling that "it is none of my business."

LSPs led to greater substance abuse and dysfunction

Increased drug and alcohol abuse was among the more commonly cited consequences of LSPs by recipients. This impact on people's lives seemed to be felt almost immediately: "When I got the payment, I was sober for 12 years overall. After I got the money, I drank for four days in a row." Many recipients offered accounts of Survivors reeling from the abuse brought on by LSPs. For some non-recipients, the toll of LSPs extended well beyond the Survivors themselves:

> In some ways, the payments took away from healing because money makes people 'go crazy.' Everybody in small communities will be affected by heavy drinking. Everyone is affected. When a group is drinking, this multiplies the burdens for individual families. Those who were living traditional lives—hunting and trapping—abandoned this way of life for the money. The government threw this money out and caused chaos.

A few recipients who took trips to larger population centres ended up on the street after two solid weeks of substance abuse. Some drinking sprees lasted longer, up to three or four months, said recipients, and these binges occasionally resulted in death. In some cases, the drinking only revealed itself afterward once it was too hard to keep it a secret any longer.

Families were broken apart by the drugging: "I lost my wife and kids for a while. That money brought me a lot of problems." A recipient recalled one set of siblings who each had received LSPs, and used them to join with friends in hosting one continuous party, which only ended when their funds ran out: "Everybody wants to be your friend when you have money. All of a sudden you're left alone and broke and you're shunned because you have nothing left to give."

"Where money comes in, abuse follows," said one non-recipient health provider. In fact, a great many non-recipients felt that LSPs inevitably led to greater community dysfunction: "As soon as I hear we're getting money, my stomach churns because I can see the outcome already." In places where rates of suicide and substance abuse are already high, giving money to people with addictions "just adds fuel to the fire." Some non-recipients are convinced that the relationship does not get any more direct: every time money comes in, the crime rate and the child welfare rate go up. For one counsellor, the sad truth is that more lump sum payments equal more clients. Based on previous outcomes, many non-recipients expressed their fear that Survivors will not survive their experience with LSPs. A health provider recalls "getting calls non-stop from people who were suicidal and angry the first few months" after the money arrived.

Participating non-recipients shared multiple accounts of alcoholism seemingly reactivated—even after 30 years of sobriety—by the sudden introduction of LSPs:

> One elder who got the $8,000 just went crazy with it. He's an alcoholic, and when you have a couple of shots you want to drink more. He spent his [money] in 2 or 3 weeks. He got $1,000 out of the bank each day and he was getting rolled. People gravitated to him, drank with him, partied with him, and they were shopping [with his money] after he passed out.

My husband's nephew got $70,000. Before he got the money, he was more grounded. He used to make his own regalia. He loved dancing. He's no longer near powwows today. As soon as he got his money he was gone. His parents were alcoholics. My mother-in-law picked him out of an abusive lifestyle, which he reverted back to once he got his money. [Someone] saw him buy a bottle of hair spray lately, but not for beauty.

Outcomes like these led some non-recipients to conclude that it made no sense for people desperately struggling with addictive tendencies to be given LSPs. Seeing increased drug abuse after LSPs came, social service providers say that payments not only amplified existing negative behaviours and problems in their communities, but they opened up doors to experiment with substances recipients could not afford before, like cocaine. For other non-recipients, the same risks were there for potentially deepening and worsening compulsive gambling and shopping.

Overall, while not every participating recipient worried that LSPs would inevitably usher in widespread alcohol and drug abuse ("some will drink it up, but not all"), others could scarcely recall more than a handful of Survivors who did not indulge in such abuse when the payments came. One recipient offered this reason as to why some recipients tended to spend their money unconstructively: "To me, $30,000 is nothing, not in terms of what people went through, but in terms of what you can buy. A truck costs $40,000, but for an alcoholic, it's a lot of bingeing."

A counsellor shared this anecdote about working with Survivors: "I asked them the question, 'When do you do better?' They answered, 'When I don't have money.'" Indeed, some counselling staff maintained that to get a sense of what LSPs will unleash, all one has to do is to look at what already happens in Aboriginal communities now on the days cheques for welfare or the child tax credit come in: "Everybody gets drunk in their home, children are neglected, and we have to remove children."

Alcohol abuse and sexual abuse problems tend to escalate at those times of increased money flow, said non-recipients. With LSPs, they feared such behaviour "will be rampant. There's a drug dealer for every mile on this reserve." However, one community-based law enforcement officer said they "could not determine any direct statistical policing impact where we had an increase in calls" when previous LSPs arrived.

Children of recipients faced special risk

Non-recipients say that the youngest members of families receiving residential school compensation will likely face their own particular risks when LSPs arrive: "Things are going to get worse with new payments. Eighty per cent of my files are on kids who have had fallout [from LSPs]." Another counsellor describes a family that had received money:

> [W]e took away a 14-year-old into care. The dad had bought a 1964 Thunderbird and furniture. His car burnt in his yard, and all his new material things were gone in a year. The [child] is now seventeen, and asking for money for bread and toilet paper.

There were also references by non-recipients to "addicted babies of recipient families" and "stoned" children of Survivors who get LSPs. Fears of subjecting children to increased risks of violence, sexual abuse, and incest were also expressed by non-recipients.

LSPs triggered emotions and anxiety

Once the money arrived, many recipients found their residential school memories came flooding back soon thereafter, triggering an intense emotional reaction in the process. Hopes of achieving closure through an LSP were quickly dashed when recipients realized that their issues had not gone away. In fact, it was the payments themselves that brought it all back. Potent enough for some recipients that they contemplated suicide, others were led by their feelings to question why they even received the money. Indeed, one non-recipient pinpointed how payments can trigger guilt and shame for Survivors:

> People did not value the compensation money because it was dirty money. That's why they mismanaged it. They lost all their pride. They gave it all away. Who wants this money when it reminds them of something negative?

Another non-recipient recalled a recipient who had nothing left of his original $110,000 LSP because it reminded him "of what he went through to get the money." Unable to disassociate the two, Survivors regarded the compensation as a kind of perverse dividend of their childhood misery:

> Many have the attitude that 'money equals shame.' Many feel they've sold their innocence, in other words, that they're prostituting themselves. How individuals have internalized abuse will determine how they deal with money.

> Money reminded recipients of the shame and humiliation of sexual abuse. These feelings resurfaced because Survivors linked the money with the shameful acts. Derogatory comments like 'arse money' re-victimized people.

Obviously, phrases such as "arse money," a label some Survivors levelled against the first group of former students to pursue and receive compensation, only added insult to injury, according to recipients and non-recipients. Combined with the shame already felt by recipients, the effect of these criticisms was to effectively re-traumatize Survivors. That said, such comments are apparently rare today.

Recipients who had chosen not to face their past often reacted angrily or sadly to their LSP. In one case, the recipient of over one million dollars was later seen getting burned with coffee during a dispute. Here too, questions were raised by recipients as to the appropriateness of people who are damaged emotionally, physically, and mentally receiving upwards of $100,000. As one recipient suggested, "Money doesn't mean you aren't still a victim, you have to let it go." Meanwhile, recipients who regarded themselves as "ready" for the money said they felt no emotion at news of the money's arrival. In their eyes it was a "paycheque," nothing more, and certainly no cause for excitement or happiness.

LSPs led to pressure and abuse from intimate circle

From infighting over payments to the financial and physical abuse of elders, it appears one's own intimate circle could sometimes pose the greatest risk to LSP recipients. Because they felt pressure from family and friends to share their compensation, recipients were reluctant to spend time with those closest to them. Elders who lived with families sometime bought things for everyone but themselves. Some tried to keep their LSPs a secret if they could help it, "otherwise they'd be knocking on my door all the time." But attempting to isolate one's self creates its own tensions, some recipients said, not to mention fights and bad feelings. One Survivor recalled a fellow recipient who apparently faced demands for thousands of dollars from family members. With their efforts spurned, the relatives shunned the recipient. The isolated individual reportedly died not long after.

Non-recipients shared numerous examples of how the ethic of sharing was sometimes abused within certain families. At the less intense end of the spectrum, participants note how "families have this sense of entitlement" to their parents' or grandparents' money. "People are sitting and waiting for it. It's become a family expectation" that recipients will hand over some or even all of an LSP to relatives. One recipient noted cases where children would get "spoiled" because of money spent on them when the LSPs first came in, then find the situation "especially hard when it ran out." Non-recipients speculated that others will "take advantage of Survivors' generosity" and the fact they like to help family out: "The $8,000 elders got, they comment that they gave it all to their kids." Some elders were allegedly taken advantage of by their children when they received their payments, although one recipient said it was confined to less than five per cent of cases where they lived. Elders who are forced to rely on young people for help can find themselves stuck, unable to say anything for fear of being abandoned.

Other recipients were scared to go to the bank by themselves because people they knew would be there to ask them for grocery or rent money. One participant noted on the pressure to make loans that were never paid back, and such behaviour by friends left some feeling "used." While some Survivors simply face pressure, others face much worse, according to non-recipients. From stories of recipients whose "children took their ATM cards and emptied their bank accounts" to "a man who took $5,000 from his mom's advance and blew it on slot machines," or the elder whose "kids [took] her entire $8,000 advance payment in one day," non-recipients told many tales of such financial abuse of elders.

One recipient raised the troubling possibility that such intense family demands on recipients' money may actually be a form of retaliation: "About 50 per cent of our group had family members who wanted a part of the compensation because the Survivors had inflicted physical and sexual abuse on them." It could also be the case that Survivors take it upon themselves to help their children out as a way of expressing their regret and guilt for the way they have treated their family in the past.

Non-recipients claimed that for all these negative LSP outcomes, outside help was often rebuffed: "You can't stop that tradition of sharing." As another noted, you can provide "lots of help to get Survivors the money, [but] no one's asked us to help with payments once they come in. It's seen as a family issue." But it may not be the family members "hounding the recipients for money" that prove hardest to reach, but recipients themselves: "Old people always want to do things for others. You can't tell them what to do. It's a personal thing. 'It's my business,' they tell us." However, recipients were reluctant to go against family. In fact, most will go out of their way to help their relatives, one non-recipient said, even if it means they themselves go without:

> I know someone who wants to use her money to rent a place for her grandkids. They won't work. She doesn't take care of herself and she's not well. We had to remove her from that house. Now she wants to go back. I try to encourage her to save it for travel to see family in the U.S. She lost it all. This will happen again. For me, I'm dreading it. What can you do?

Yet some recipients' relatives would only treat them well so long as there was enough money to go around, said non-recipients. As soon as the cash stopped flowing, so did whatever loyalty and attention Survivors once enjoyed. It was a pattern that would repeat itself with friends, romantic or otherwise. "The whole reserve's your friend 'til the money runs out," in the words of one non-recipient. Another non-recipient shared a theory that, with a shortage of housing in Aboriginal communities, adult children with nowhere else to go came to grow utterly dependent on their over-indulgent parents. "Granny's money is being taken by these young adult children and grandchildren," as one non-recipient put it. But the negative impact of money on families can extend even further into divisiveness. Infighting over LSPs can lead to adult children no longer speaking to parents, said non-recipients. One situation involved

> extended family and friends [who] borrowed money from recipients, up to tens of thousands of dollars, and never paid it back … The money had a fatal impact—people died. Families are broken up because of the money.

Thus, the original rupture to familial ties caused by residential school is echoed a generation later within the same extended family in a dispute over residential school compensation. That said, there were non-recipient accounts of families who took care of their older relatives, and elders' affairs were managed honestly on their behalf.

LSPs quickly and unwisely exhausted

Where non-recipients saw Survivors who were ill-equipped to handle their newfound wealth, they also witnessed the consequences. "People who got money did not spend it properly." "The problem is people do not use their money wisely." One estimate put the rate of this 'unwise' behaviour at "50 per cent" of recipients. Recipients noted the desire of some Survivors to spend their payments right away with no thought as to what they bought, much less how to manage it. A few Survivors originally tried to lock up their LSP money, but that lasted just a year before unemployment forced its withdrawal. One recipient spoke of watching friends commit suicide after they went broke, an indication to them of a lack of ready support services and counselling. Some communities witnessed similar behaviour with smaller cheques from other sources such as resource royalties, said recipients.

Hoping to see "something constructive done with the money," many non-recipients said it "seemed like it didn't last long," and in most cases, a negative outcome was attached. In the words of one non-recipient, "They couldn't spend it fast enough." Some took six months to exhaust their payment, others just a few weeks. "A good chunk of the community who got $50,000 to $80,000, it was gone in a month. Some still have the stuff they bought, [but] they probably can't account for the rest." Others were left with absolutely nothing, not even their original purchases:

> The people who got money bought stuff for houses and cars, but not healing. They sold that stuff off in the end. I can't think of anyone who got payments—around twelve people— who has anything left of their thousands.

> This year, some got the $8,000 advance payments and they're broke already.

> One guy needed food vouchers two months after his payment came in.

The results can often be more mixed, said non-recipients, as in the case of a recipient who bought a parent a house, then "took friends to the city, drove around in cars and limousines for two weeks, flew the two friends home, [then later] came home broke." Among the first and biggest ticket items to be acquired with LSP monies, automobiles were often seen as the most troublesome and least worthwhile of purchases: "A lot of people bought a new car, which loses its value quickly. No one invested in land or property." There were non-recipient reports of Survivors buying "cheap cars that broke down within a year," and elders using their $8,000 advance payments to get "crappy cars that last three months." In one extreme case, "one person bought five vehicles in a month, now he's walking." Would-be entrepreneurs thought they could start a business, bought the equipment, but stalled after they realized just how much extra time, know-how, and money were involved.

Again, things were not always black and white. One recipient, hoping for an education in forestry, found help to put some of the money aside, but promptly spent the rest of the LSP on alcohol. Another recipient, scared to drink up the entire LSP, deliberately put off receiving the compensation until the danger point had passed, eventually buying a computer. Many recipients found that they started with the best of intentions, but ended up doing something other than what they had originally planned. Some non-recipients believed that one's environment played a big part in accounting for their behaviour:

> Growing up in an alcoholic community and family, that played a part in bad investments some guys made. Back then, it's spend, spend, spend. If they got a chance to revisit that, they would do better.

> Most were never raised with the concept of saving. It's more like, 'you get your money, you spend it.'

Other non-recipients noted how lump sum payments change people, causing them to lose sight of the fact that material things do not last, ultimately leaving them empty-handed: "After our money is gone, then what? There's nothing but negative impacts." Alternatively, a few non-recipients suggested Survivors who had "nothing to show" for all the money they had spent from their 'first' LSP might know better the second time around. Indeed, one reported that elders who received CEP payments have spent it "more usefully" than they had with previous LSPs.

LSPs sparked resentment among other Survivors

There were two main reasons recipients gave as to how LSPs would generate resentment among Survivors: i) because some former students had received more money than their peers, and ii) because some Survivors had received no LSP at all. As mentioned earlier, those who did not obtain the amount of compensation they had hoped for made no secret of their disappointment, leading to community friction in some cases.

While some non-recipients recognized the potential harms that came with receiving an LSP, they also understood how, for some Survivors, not receiving an LSP carried its own effects: "Not getting a settlement hurt, as if what happened to us didn't matter as much as what others went through." As this comment illustrates, the same situation can be seen very differently depending on the vantage point of Survivors. On a related front, some individuals who never attended the schools felt left out simply because others had large sums of money and they did not, according to recipients.

Recipients' financial inexperience exposed them to predators

Recipients spoke of salespeople such as car dealers coming from nearby towns to try and persuade newly wealthy recipients to buy their wares. Pawn shops were only too eager to offer loans that amounted to double or more the original amount borrowed. One such store owner reportedly earned enough money off pawns and loans to take the entire family to Hawaii. According to some non-recipients, many LSP recipients have fallen prey to unscrupulous individuals. Such predation was an open secret:

> Everybody will be after us to sell us things. Vultures descended on the community because they knew people were getting advance payments. Loan sharks were lending recipients money before they got their payment. Some fall for this because of gambling addictions, alcohol, and drugs.

Non-recipients said loan sharks reportedly encouraged a number of recipients to spend their money "in advance" before the LSPs are handed out so "the money is spent before it arrives." Other non-recipients recalled the "car salespeople from Edmonton and Winnipeg" who came to their community and how "the pawn shop operators made thousands on our people." The reason elders "are very vulnerable to scam artists," some non-recipients say, "is because they're lonely and they want a friend." In anticipation of payments to come into the community, a non-recipient predicted that "We'll probably see prostitutes. The local bar is even talking about getting strippers. Every bad element will come in to exploit recipients."

One factor that may help to explain the susceptibility of recipients to scams, according to some participants, is a near-total absence of long-term planning or vision on the part of Survivors. With their "notion of compensation in the immediate term" only, most "elders are just happy to get the cash," and do not think too far ahead. Then again, just to have the money available for future considerations is an unfamiliar situation for most Survivors.

Indeed, according to most non-recipients, savings and investments by recipients were far from the norm among recipients. Once LSPs arrived in the communities, it quickly became evident that most Survivors were in a poor position to cope with or even comprehend the large sums of money they had received. "Most recipients were living on social assistance when they got their payment," recalled one non-recipient. The sudden influx of thousands of dollars, in some cases tens of thousands, overwhelmed people, a number of whom were "used to $400 or $500 a month or on welfare" or were homeless. Most Survivors were "never raised with this quantity of money," one non-recipient remarked, and thus they had "no real sense or perspective or concept of it." Working with limited education in many cases, "people did not keep the money in their pocket ... because they could not manage any money, let alone a large amount." One non-recipient summed it up this way: "After years of dependency, why would we be surprised" at recipients' difficulties with money?

Virtually no non-recipient begrudged the right of Survivors to their LSPs. "It's good in a way they got the money, [but it's] sad to receive such a lump of money with no training on how to save it. All they know is they need it."

For those recipients who might have sought financial training, help was not generally available, noted non-recipients. As for possible business ventures, one non-recipient claimed entrepreneurship has yet to take root across Aboriginal communities, and, at any rate, the LSPs were insufficient for starting a business. "What is there beyond the five years? Nothing."

Some non-recipients suggested that Survivors' unfamiliarity with money caused them to look upon LSPs as an almost random event like winning a bingo or a lottery. Many used the term 'windfall' to describe Survivors' attitudes toward their LSPs, suggesting an almost 'easy-come-easy-go' mentality among some Survivors. It is as if their compensation came 'by chance,' and not as a deserved outcome obtained through a deliberate course of action. A similar devaluation of the origins and significance of the LSP can also lead Survivors to grossly underestimate their situation in other ways, commented one non-recipient:

> Probably most Survivors would have taken $2,000 … [Because] they'd lost most of their sense of self-worth, they don't say 'I'm worth more than this.' They thought they were worth nothing, so how could they value money?

LSPs detracted from or were irrelevant to healing opportunities

Where non-recipients referred to lawyers promoting the availability and use of counselling to their clients, it appeared that such efforts went mostly nowhere: "$10,000 to $12,000 cheques for counselling were handed over to individuals. Some chose to self-medicate with it. This money could have been used for programs instead." Some non-recipients disagreed with the idea of the costs of such care coming out of recipients' own pockets: "They wanted counselling but did not want to pay for this themselves." Moreover, when counselling was made mandatory, some non-recipients felt such "coerced" counselling sessions simply did not work. Ultimately, some argued, "if people want to heal, they have to choose to take advantage of programs and services." One counsellor conveyed this anecdote:

> Initially, Survivors came to us because their lawyers referred them to us. Law firms had put aside five to ten thousand dollars for therapists. In the late nineties, this was the norm. Clients came here to access the remainder of their money. They had already got some money, [but would only get] the rest after counselling. I found it morally unethical to work with the clients under these circumstances. My colleague saw the people.

Meanwhile, some non-recipients recalled no effort by anyone to connect healing to the LSPs: "The money was a free-for-all. They were not shown how to heal with it." Others still saw no effect on healing one way or the other, even going so far as to question whether it was a practical option for most Survivors: "There is no healing now, so the money makes no difference. It's the last thing on their mind." One non-recipient laid out the basic challenge before anyone seeking to press healing upon Survivors:

> We can't force anyone to start healing and making a better life for themselves. I've worked in court. It's all First Nations [people] there, where individuals sign forms agreeing to treatment, then they take off … People do not follow through with due process to help themselves.

"Money does not heal, money brought more tragedy," concluded one non-recipient. Some firmly believe LSPs detracted from healing opportunities for Survivors, who lost more than they gained. In many cases, LSPs only added to the anguish of Survivors. As one non-recipient shared: "I actually wished my family didn't get the money."

Other concerns and comments

Among the other concerns with LSPs expressed by recipients, one recipient felt it was wrong for welfare authorities to cut a Survivor's monthly cheques off just because they had received a large one-time LSP, which in turn created a disincentive to invest the funds. Another said LSPs offered the mixed blessing of revealing people's true character: "I learned about people and how they change regarding money," a reference to one family's power struggle over a business founded with one member's LSP seed money. One recipient shared a fervent belief that these payments acted to silence and "shut down our resistance." Despite efforts to mobilize them, the participant lamented on the people's lack of activism regarding the unfairness of LSPs, and felt the payments "have made us complacent and unready to fight for our rights."

Barriers to Proposed Supports and Suggestions

Before listing the various barriers identified by participants, it should be said that a few non-recipients felt that nothing necessarily prevented the implementation of any suggested support related to LSPs.

Mental Health and Addictions

Among recipients, the most frequently referenced barriers to LSP-related interventions were mental health issues for Survivors, a legacy of their time in residential school. From fear and shame to self-isolation and silence, these manifestations of the pain of former students can make outreach challenging. Participants also identified Survivors' difficulties in showing emotion and affection as a barrier. A good number of LSP non-recipients also shared accounts of extremely private and silent Survivors who did not feel they needed help and refused to listen to anyone who suggested otherwise. Described as angry and stubborn, these recipients tend to isolate themselves and retreat. According to non-recipients, any approach about LSPs were met with terse responses like, "I suffered for this money, so I'll use it the way I want." On the other hand, some non-recipients blamed a lack of genuine outlets for Survivors who were withdrawn but needed to talk.

Like LSP recipients, non-recipients saw the lack of self-confidence and self-reliance in Survivors as a barrier. One counsellor described a "learned helplessness" among some Survivors that manifested as apathy and shame. Unable to consider, much less seek out options for themselves, paternalism has taught them to believe that they cannot make a difference in their own lives. Though it is not a normal practice to do so, the counsellor has tried to introduce modest budgeting principles and goals to nudge Survivors in the direction of helping themselves, but was concerned that large LSPs will derail their short-term goal-setting. In some cases, this dependency has made Survivors stay with lawyers that are not meeting their needs.

The prevalence of intergenerational abuses in some communities has kept people in a 'victimhood' mentality, said a non-recipient. This engrained identity eventually becomes an all-purpose excuse to justify any and all subsequent behaviour: "I went to residential school, therefore it gives me the right to do what I want." On a related front, one non-recipient described a fear of success among some Survivors:

> When I sobered up, I had three fears: failure, rejection, and success. I feared success because, growing up, I'd find a way to jeopardize it. We need to help people find growth, to move beyond being stuck. This takes years.

Many non-recipients saw addictions, and those who profit by them, as a serious impediment to action. Recipients also noted difficulties with alcoholism and addictions as additional layers of complexity in addressing the needs of Survivors. Such addictions make people more vulnerable, non-recipients argued, and impede their ability to see things clearly. Non-recipients felt sobriety is extremely important to handling LSPs properly, but many 'dry' communities in remote areas find that they are surrounded by liquor stores in neighbouring non-Aboriginal towns. Recipients echoed this concern along with the presence of drug dealers. The drug trade is not totally imposed from outside: many drug dealers who lived virtually next door to their clients made no secret of their trade. Some non-recipients questioned whether local authorities really cared, since dealers threaten anyone who tries to stem the flow of narcotics, and workers were afraid of retaliation. Furthermore, for young people, drug-running may be one of the few local and lucrative sources of income. According to some non-recipients, some residents faced addictions like drinking, smoking, gambling, and now, money—yet another substance of which there is never enough.

Funding Issues

A number of participants in the recipient group believed that funding, or the lack thereof, was a barrier, in particular the treatment of community-based entities. Members of one Survivor group felt that it was a discriminatory funding practice to not get reimbursed for travel or labour time like band councils. Another recipient felt that national organizations like the AHF only "take money for administration, not healing. If AHF continues, how can we ensure that those who are to get healing funds get them?"

Along with the consistent under-funding of Survivor programs and care identified by recipients, non-recipients discussed the politics of funding, where some individuals and communities were, in a sense, punished for success. Government funders assume that positive community project results suggest that there is no need for additional funding. One non-recipient felt that funders miss the fact that the more successful programs typically accept and receive clients from outside their area, entailing extra lodging, food, and labour costs. These costs were previously picked up by the community. When they ask for funds to make up the difference, their request is rejected. Such innovative facilities are thus forced to continually make something out of nothing even though they are thought to have everything.

On the flipside, some non-recipients perceived a lack of transparency and accountability for residential school-related projects. Another barrier was identified in the way governments were seen to be unwilling to fund intergenerational treatment, a barrier to a more expansive and inclusive view of residential school impacts.

Healing and Treatment

There were a cluster of barriers identified by LSP recipients in the areas of healing and treatment. Many felt that their community had a shortage of local healing facilities and opportunities, if any at all, explaining why some recipients perceived an over-reliance on the use of outside healing resources instead of local ones. Similarly, some recipients argued that there is now an excessive 'professionalization' of care, where at one time families could deal with their own problems, and "now only paid professionals" can legitimately handle matters of health and justice. "Everything was made someone else's responsibility. It started at residential school and still goes on today."

Some recipients believe there is an unwillingness to explore or fund alternative and unconventional forms of treatment, to the detriment of efforts to employ more innovative methods of supporting Survivors in healing. As well, sometimes elders with health problems presented a barrier to some LSP-related interventions, said recipients. Non-recipients identified a barrier when funders relegated cultural or community-based healing methods and traditional knowledge to the margins. One way they did this was by requiring Masters degrees for those who are working with Survivors.

Other non-recipients focused more generally on a lack of accessible, affordable, and discreet healing resources. To be forced to seek care outside one's community because of confidentiality concerns incurs additional expenses, sometimes prohibitively so. Others facing a lack of local, qualified, accessible health professionals were effectively in the same situation. Some non-recipients identified the inapplicability of addictions treatment methods to Survivors' needs as a barrier because this non-transferability has, in their eyes, yet to be widely or properly understood.

Meanwhile, some non-recipients bemoaned the shortage of healers who are themselves Survivors, and they made a case for healers who are truly empathetic. A lot of former students do not want to share their story with someone who is younger and has never attended residential school. Similarly, they noted that a lack of Aboriginal personnel (e.g., counsellors) can, in some cases, serve as a barrier to a deeper connection between helper and client.

Attitudes

A number of negative or unconstructive attitudes present their own barriers, according to LSP recipients. Two of the barriers were seen to operate at a wider level: community apathy toward the situation of Survivors, and a general stigma and insensitivity surrounding LSPs, such as labelling LSPs as 'blood money.' Some non-recipients felt that these negative attitudes toward LSPs as 'tainted' or 'selling-out' served to divide.

Recipients and non-recipients of LSPs both saw a barrier in the need individuals can have for secrecy and confidentiality. Some Survivors fear breaches in confidentiality just by virtue of being seen near a health provider's facility. As one recipient noted, some Survivors felt more comfortable working on their issues with strangers for fear of being judged by the people they know in their immediate surroundings, pointing to one instance where local resources are not necessarily the most desirable.

Other attitudinal barriers discussed by non-recipients included a lack of community spirit and co-operation. As one non-recipient remarked, "We only get together at funerals, baptisms, weddings, or occasional events. There's not enough fun gatherings, and we function too much in cliques." Consequently, problems are left entirely to the band council to solve. Other non-recipients feel that their people's communal spirit was lost at residential school:

> We're too individualistic now and have lost our values. We used to share moose meat. What's the difference between a one-thousand-pound moose and $28,000? The almighty dollar has broken down our relationships and community-mindedness.

Some non-recipients attested to a lack of unity in some locales among Survivors. Either because of religious differences or the over-individualistic tendencies criticized above, some communities feature a number of

Survivor groups/societies working either in isolation from one another or at cross-purposes, despite all of them having few resources. Such factionalism and divisions between Survivor groups have occasionally led to rumours and resentment, said recipients, not to mention fear and competition. Some communities featured as many as five Survivor groups. With money tight to begin with, some recipients implied that the money was being spread too thinly and efforts needlessly duplicated by having more than one group.

Family Dynamics

A barrier that came up often with recipients highlights the dynamics within and between families. So-called 'feuds' between families can sabotage cross-community efforts at education and co-operation. Meanwhile, tension and exploitation inside a family can isolate Survivors from any outside efforts to help. Non-recipients also mentioned family infighting and inter-family feuds as impediments to successful LSP interventions. They also raised a lack of parenting skills as a potential barrier.

Dependency

Some recipients believed that any lack of community self-sufficiency is, in a sense, self-imposed. One highlighted how communities possess "oodles of internal resources. We need to use and honour people from within the community." To their mind, local problems demand local solutions. To go outside for solutions only increases dependency. In fact, some recipients perceived an over-reliance on the involvement and approval of local government to get things done. They felt that entities like band councils and Indian and Northern Affairs Canada erect unnecessary barriers to community initiatives, and resent having to seek their approval before funding requests or loans can proceed. Meanwhile, some recipients blamed the lack of a vibrant local economy as a major barrier.

Governance Issues

Many recipients perceived their local government to be a barrier to action because of alleged corruption, ineptitude, and/or instability. This perception was echoed among non-recipients. Some recipients believed that this may have had something to do with the lack of Survivors active in their local governance bodies. Meanwhile, others are cynical and mistrustful of non-Aboriginal governments, which present a potential barrier to their involvement in any LSP-related intervention effort. Non-recipients who recalled an excessive bureaucracy surrounding treatment and Survivor programs feared that a similarly complicated administration would emerge for newer LSPs.

Accessibility and Information Issues

Under this set of identified barriers, both recipients and non-recipients mentioned the lack of easy Survivor access to transportation where they lived, especially for disabled Survivors. They also identified the challenges to communication presented by the rates of low to no literacy among Survivors. Elders who are illiterate cannot do things on their own like banking, and have been taken advantage of in some cases, said non-recipients. Others with only a low level of literacy often find overly formal legal and financial documents a challenge to understand.

That said, many recipients complained of the lack of readily available and accessible LSP information. In some quarters, fundamental questions and misunderstandings abound over the potential distribution of LSPs under the *Indian Residential Schools Settlement Agreement*. In one case, Survivors were operating under the very upsetting impression that only Aboriginal governments and Survivor societies were eligible to receive LSP monies, demonstrating how easy it was to misinterpret these matters. This only highlighted the need for clarity and precision in the language and concepts to be used in conveying information.

Non-recipients also keyed in on language as a barrier in cases where non-Aboriginal people were unable to speak Indigenous languages or where Aboriginal people faced challenges communicating in English, their second language. Either way, a formidable barrier exists to expressing important and/or intimate information to another party.

Finally, recipients also felt that the absence of local banking/financial institutions made community-based financial interventions around LSPs that much more difficult.

Mistrust

Given their experience in the courts and beyond, many recipients have become suspicious and wary when it comes to members of the legal profession. Some felt that lawyers do not always use language comprehensible to the grassroots. Other recipients accused law firms of threatening people should they attempt to switch legal counsel. Furthermore, there are the financial predators and scam artists who are only too ready to exploit Survivors' newfound LSP wealth, said recipients.

According to some non-recipients, the deep loss of respect for church authority coming out of residential schools now extended to all authority and, in extreme cases, has led to a lack of respect for everyone. Some people reportedly hesitated to participate in certain initiatives when outsiders ran them because they simply "don't trust white people." For this reason, some non-recipients argued that programs have to be implemented by more 'grassroots' caregivers. Meanwhile, other non-recipients reported full acceptance of outsiders where they live. In some cases, this was due to a belief that outside resources were more professional than what was locally available. Finally, some non-recipients rejected the entire LSP process because they knew people who have deliberately misrepresented what happened to them in school or outright lied about their attendance in order to qualify for large LSPs.

Mainstream media

Some non-recipients felt that the mainstream media tended to sensationalize the issues surrounding residential school compensation, choosing to focus on the "billions of dollars" in settlement costs at the expense of a greater, more nuanced understanding of the principles and people involved.

Aboriginal and Non-Aboriginal Resources

Both recipients and non-recipients suggested the following resources and assistance to Survivors, families, and communities given the advent of the next wave of LSPs.

Regional/national Aboriginal organizations

Non-recipients felt that regional and national Aboriginal political organizations (e.g., Assembly of First Nations, Federation of Saskatchewan Indian Nations) as well as those with a non-governmental social or economic mandate (e.g., Pauktuutit, Inuvialuit Regional Corporation) had a potential advisory role to play in ensuring the best possible outcomes for Survivors with their LSPs. Some non-recipients wanted to hear more from political leaders who were perceived as "dropping the ball" after they initially fought for LSPs, but then failed to follow through on helping people handle their payments. One non-recipient suggested the Aboriginal Peoples Party of Canada as a possible ally.

Voluntary or non-profit sector

There were frequent references to organizations and efforts in the not-for-profit, voluntary sector. From cultural and language programs to Friendship Centres to women's shelters, non-recipients looked to this sector for potential alliances and aid in dealing with LSPs. Educational partners that were referenced include the First Nations University of Canada. As well, many looked to the self-organized Survivor groups as resources. These ranged from local groups to provincial associations (e.g., Indian Residential School Society of Alberta) and beyond (e.g., National Residential School Survivors' Society). Recipients also proposed groups in the social services sector, ranging from Alcoholics Anonymous and AIDS groups to men's groups, and Friendship Centres. Other suggestions under this broad banner include the Aboriginal Family Services Circle Project and the Native Women's Association of Canada.

Resources in the health sector came up often among LSP recipients, from health centres to local departments of health, to the Justice Institute of British Columbia. The AHF was also recommended. There were also frequent calls among non-recipients for health and healing entities and individuals, including treatment centres at the local level and those more widely available, such as Four Worlds Development Project, University of Lethbridge, and Canadian Mental Health Association.

Non-recipients made special mention of the Aboriginal Healing Foundation, which was described by one person as the only group "Aboriginal people know and have confidence in." This same participant hoped that the AHF could help those communities trying to access support from other funders. It was also called upon to take a lead role in setting up LSP information meetings as well as serve as a clearinghouse for support agencies.

Governments: Non-Aboriginal

Some non-recipients were uneasy with looking to any non-Aboriginal government for help. "We fundamentally have to get control of our own lives first." Many of them named this category of government as a resource, and at all levels. It was said that since the Canadian government threatened parents who did not put children into residential school, it should be offering free resources to Survivors. Some non-recipients wanted to see neighbouring hamlets, towns, and/or cities more involved. A number of government-run or government-funded agencies at the provincial level were specifically identified by non-recipients, from hospitals and regional health authorities to child and family services, and departments of justice. The federal Indian Residential Schools Resolution Canada (IRSRC) office was also suggested by non-recipients. Governments at all levels were regularly mentioned by recipients as well. Although most supported local governmental involvement, some felt politicians should "stay away from it," lest they be seen as interfering or dictating "what people should do with their money." Another recipient issued a call out to "anyone with influence on the federal government [who can] expedite the process."

Governments: Aboriginal (First Nation, Métis, and Inuit)

Chiefs and councils came up often among non-recipients. While most felt that their band council should become involved and help their people, others were skeptical, even critical, about their government's level of interest or ability. Some non-recipients were careful to make a distinction between their government and the employees who administered and delivered services for the community. One recipient singled out the James Bay Cree as a model of local government.

Churches/religious societies

A number of non-recipients felt that an appeal for resources should be made to the institutional entities that run each of the various churches, mainly "because that's where abuse happened" and they should be held accountable. Some non-recipients recalled that church initiatives like the Anglican Church's Indigenous Healing Fund have been set up to help with community residential school projects.

Banks/financial

On the financial and management side, Aboriginal entities like Peace Hills Trust or the Toronto Dominion First Nations Bank of Canada were suggested by both recipients and non-recipients, and they wanted to see the active participation of expert financial advisors as part of any LSP intervention strategy. In fact, any large-scale body experienced in budgetary matters, such as land corporations, could have a role to play.

Legal/law enforcement

Be it individual lawyers or larger bodies such as the Indigenous Bar Association, both recipients and non-recipients saw a role to play for members of the legal sector, including members of the law enforcement branch such as the RCMP. That said, certain participants strongly opposed the RCMP's involvement, while others felt the force was being asked to do things other agencies should be doing.

Towards a Strategic Framework

This section attempts to summarize and analyze the rich and ready input participants provided to the survey, therefore, several important concepts and ideas are examined and discussed. The main purpose is to propose a strategic framework for dealing with lump sum payments complete with cross-cutting issues, strategic principles, strategic goals, and strategic interventions and recommendations.

Cross-cutting Issues

Class, age, gender, religion, geographic location, and culture (tradition/modernity) affect how LSPs are experienced in communities. Many participants were concerned about issues like unequal power relations in communities, tensions between generations, discrimination against women, poor access to services, and reconciling traditions and modern ways. By the same token, historic trauma, elder abuse, human resources and funding, and research surfaced as issues of significance across the board. Participants felt that history has been unkind and harmful to Survivors, families, and communities alike. Elders have been hardest hit, resources are scarce, and more evidence is needed.

Class differences

Survey participants believe there are class differences in communities, meaning that there are distinct haves and have-nots in communities. As one participant said, "Money is power, money is energy. Knowledge is power, knowledge is energy." Because resources, decision making, and power are concentrated in very few hands, relationships among leaders, workers, street people, and welfare recipients have become strained, an unwelcome situation when LSPs are made, according to the participants. Self-reliant individuals and families were also seen to be left out in these kinds of community struggles.

Many participants thought that greater diffusion of community power and control is required to meet the needs of Survivors who receive LSPs: "Workers or leaders should stand by their people. We're so isolated, so disassociated." Classic monopolies on authority and influence need to yield to more inclusive visions if things are to ever significantly improve, say community members.

> Leaders and chiefs now have their own businesses and take care of themselves, and people are afraid of confronting them. People, meanwhile, do not feel good enough and do not look after themselves materially and physically.

Some participants identified a tendency to pay Aboriginal people less than non-Aboriginal people for the same work: "White people get paid more at $500 a day, while our own workers get $300." They added that such pay inequity can occur even when the funder is Aboriginal.

Participants called for better communication between, and closer collaboration among, competing groups and levels of government around LSPs. They also sought the development of meaningful consultative mechanisms so impoverished individuals and those from the so-called wrong camp would be given fair and just opportunities to influence decision making and allocation of resources. In the words of one participant, "loyalty should be more important than royalty." For many who took part in this survey, the frustrating divisiveness of politics never goes away:

Power relations get in the way, including dirty politics, and we have too many people playing politics in the system. We're all working for recovery and healing, but sometimes you feel so alone. You need teamwork and adequate funds.

Given the scale of monies coming into the communities, community members are worried they may not be able to afford the status quo: "We have a lot of trouble with our own leaders today. We need advocates … We need to get a huge group together to talk about both sides of [LSPs]."

Age Divides

Intergenerational tensions are commonplace according to some participants who said that tensions between age groups are inevitable when poverty, scarce resources, and substance abuse are so prevalent. Some attributed intergenerational tensions to what may be termed 'extreme parenting' where parents overindulge youth with material goods while enabling their negative behaviour. One participant pointed out the phenomenon of missing parents, a situation that finds grandparents assuming the role of parents.

In anticipating LSPs, participants urged action that minded this gap in generations: "We're not dealing with one generation only here. We're dealing with youth, adults, and elders." Even though some participants recognize that "older people know how to spend their money," they are no less "concerned about elder abuse regarding compensation payments because it's out there." While many elders have bank accounts, "unfortunately their kids have access to these accounts" as well. Elder abuse was very much a recurring theme during the survey:

> There is elder abuse and financial abuse of elders. They get $1,100 old age pensions on the 27th of each month and they're broke in two weeks. Their kids take their money and groceries. Some are in denial and say they want to help their grandchildren, but they buy them junk food, etc.

Many feared such abuse would only "worsen," fearing that "there will be probably homicides too" when the LSP arrive.

Gender Inequality

The term *gender* refers to the differences between men and women (Status of Women Canada, 1998). These differences are usually learned, changeable, and shaped by cultural values and beliefs (Women's Health Victoria, n.d.), but are important to keep in mind nonetheless. Gender inequality occurs when there is a basic power imbalance between men and women. By many accounts, gender inequality has been an issue during compensation payments, but female participants who have felt excluded have chosen to speak out about it: "We women protested this process. We told them you're dealing with a whole different group."

During the interviews, both men and women disclosed and opposed the sexual discrimination, sexual abuse, and spousal violence women faced around LSPs. Participants also reported, "At least once a week, there are violent acts in our communities [like] suicide, gang rape, and violence." They pointed to the stubbornness of the problem: "I've worked with women for the last 20 years, and I know men are guilty of committing violent acts against women." These observations are supported by statistics showing that Aboriginal women face a higher victim rate of spousal violence than Aboriginal men or non-Aboriginal people (Statistics Canada, 2006). Other evidence concludes that women are burdened by the residential school legacy with higher rates of violent death from suicide and homicide, sexism, and disease (Dion Stout, Kipling, and Stout, 2001). Some participants detected a deeply anti-woman bias in the manner in which the entire residential school issue has been framed and pursued:

> My argument with them was that I got messed up at residential school, but their comeback was that it was all about men. They just about drove me to drinking, as there was no sensitivity to women and our issues.

Others feel that women continue to live with the effects of residential school in a distinctly gendered way: "Especially in the North, women are getting beaten, and they hang their heads in public while their husbands speak for them. We will live with the legacy of residential school 'til we die." Moreover, they feel this effect has extended to the LSP process itself: "Women are family keepers and caretakers, yet we were not compensated. They wasted all the money on men. This is the frustration of the women who were basically left out." In some cases, a woman whose spouse received an LSP could not always assume it would be of mutual benefit: "Money brought more tragedy. Men throwing away wives and children for younger women. This was not common, but it did happen." Nor have Survivors themselves always paid proper respect to women: "I went to another gathering on residential school. There was a lot of anger and disrespect for women there."

To address these concerns, some suggested that more care must be taken beforehand to include members of vulnerable sectors: "Women, elders, and youth need to be more involved in decision-making. All three groups are not being listened to and should be." According to participants, any solution to problems precipitated by LSPs must include women, whose experience and ability are valuable assets. "Women my age have carried a lot, a lot of abuse. A lot of times we ignore women though they are strong."

Religious Influences

Although participants expressed concerns about the residual and divisive effects of religious-based residential schools, some Survivor groups are establishing themselves along religious lines at the community level, such as Catholic or Anglican Survivor groups. Only time will tell how this emerging trend will evolve, but for the moment, these groups are organized enough to seek or receive funding for LSP-related activities.

Still, some people's loyalty to their faith has led to conflict with others: "I know grandfathers who abused granddaughters who tended to protest the fact we were pressing cases against the Church." In some locations, differences of religion can be a very real issue: "There's a lot of community put-down if, for example, you change from Catholic to Pentecostal." A religiously divided community faces an uphill challenge in rallying around Survivors: "Half of us on our reserve are Catholic, half are United Church. This divides us. We now have to learn to manage what little we get and be happy about it." Meanwhile, some want the churches to be the most legally responsible for what took place in the schools:

> The Catholic Church is the second biggest corporation in the world. Hold them accountable. It's criminal what they've done. They should be talking to the abused. Create a different reality in 2006, in other words, dialogue and talking circles.

Others feel that this legal responsiblity should cover the LSP process as well: "The government and church should pay all lawyer's fees."

But religion can obviously be a source of strength too: "My family are leaders and we're always active Anglicans. I also do sweat lodges [with] traditional medicines." In another case, a participant spoke of the power of weekly bible study: "We did a session on forgiveness, this was a big help in my healing journey."

Geographic Location

Communities in more remote areas must contend with limited access to certain facilities, services, and resources. In the case of managing LSPs, access to financial services such as full-service banks are not always available. These remote locales are 'off the radar' for the many funding and support organizations based in larger urban centres of the South, and are all too often neglected and forgotten. Accordingly, one recipient urged the Aboriginal Healing Foundation "to be more active in isolated communities to see our social problems and to do something about them." Properly factoring in such isolation may have to lead to LSP-related initiatives that "partner up with others … at the national level." This would help to offset the costs and facilitate access to resources that would otherwise be unavailable. At the same time, there is a silver lining in a community's isolation, which can act as a buffer to outside negative influence. "It may be a good thing we're isolated without a year-round road. We have a winter road for three months [only]."

Culture (Traditions and Modernity)

Some participants recommended holistic approaches when dealing with LSPs. One Survivor called for tradition-oriented actions like wearing regalia to court hearings, while another pressed for the power of the Creator over that of any helper organization or institution. The Survivor who recommended wearing traditional clothing as a form of resistance also insisted on the importance of keeping current on LSP policy developments and writing a daily journal even though he knew the written word is often denounced by community members on cultural grounds. Despite adopting a strong spiritual position, the second Survivor also reported a personal letter-writing campaign to a member of parliament and to government officials to express frustrations about LSPs. These examples show how traditions and modernity co-exist, illustrating the sheer pragmatism of many Survivors.

Some participants advocate a balanced approach: "Our traditional ways are powerful but we need to combine them with Western ways." Others are less optimistic about hanging on to the old teachings and values: "We can't rely on a traditional lifestyle, our caribou here is decreasing." However, a land-based set of ethics possesses sufficient flexibility to function within the context of modernity, so long as they are rooted in community. "Self-governing people want to use their own resources, [drawing on] their people and their own traditional knowledge." Survivors who have worked hard to retain/regain their spiritual and cultural ethos and protocols can play a pivotal role here. "Spiritual guidance could be provided by elders, and by cultural workers well versed in language and culture."

Historic Trauma

Unlike post-traumatic stress disorder, the term *historic trauma response* captures chronic trauma in one's lifetime as well as trauma across generations. Mounting evidence shows that Survivors of residential schools and their descendents are at high risk for suffering from historic trauma. What is often overlooked in the evidence is the multidirectional effects of unresolved trauma. For example, front-line workers who took part in the survey said that they frequently suffer from secondary trauma while working with Survivors and their families because they cannot separate themselves from the pain, grief, and loss they hear about.

Dr. Maria Yellow Horse Brave Heart, co-founder of the Takini Network, coined the term *historical trauma* and defined it as cumulative emotional and psychological wounding across generations, including one's own lifespan (Yellow Horse Brave Heart and Kills Straight, 2003), underscoring its rootedness in massive group trauma such as massacres, boarding (residential) school abuses, and intergenerational transfer of traumatic responses. Because this phenomenon has spilled over and within generations from abrupt changes other than the residential school legacy like disease epidemics, rampant substance abuse, and dislocations from the land, it has to be dealt with before healing can take place (Wesley-Esquimaux and Smolewski, 2004). Historic trauma responses to the cumulative wounds inflicted over several lifetimes have generated chronic symptoms ranging from depression and psychic numbing to hyperglycemia (high blood sugar) and substance abuse (Dion Stout and Kipling, 2003), causing poor health for Survivors, families, and communities.

For their part, Wesley-Esquimaux and Smoleswski (2004) drew on several disciplines to propose a model for historic trauma transmission (HTT) where constant social and cultural disruptions in communities cluster into traumatic events and into a disease. Meanwhile, Boyer (2006) decried the intergenerational effects of residential schools that continue to manifest themselves on city streets and in current statistics on Aboriginal women. Similarly, the Aboriginal Healing Foundation (1999) has raised a cautionary note about the lasting and normalizing effects of unresolved trauma.

Elder Abuse

Elder abuse was a problem participants had cited at numerous times in light of LSPs. According to an RCMP presentation, elder abuse takes the form of physical harm, financial exploitation, and neglect (Royal Canadian Mounted Police, n.d.). A study conducted on two Navaho reservations showed that financial dependency of adult children on their parents is a major risk factor for financial abuse of elders (Brown, 1999), and occurs due to high rates of unemployment and severe poverty. The study further noted that for such families, the only funds often available are the elders' monthly pensions, social security, or welfare cheques. Elders who are ill or disabled are increasingly dependent on younger generations and, as a result, are at risk for abuse, especially since their values and traditions often differ from those of younger family members. Patterns of violence that are transmitted from one generation to the next also contribute to elder abuse (Brown, 1999).

Human Resources and Funding

Scant capacity, skeletal infrastructure, and stretched finances pose constant challenges for communities at the best of times. According to survey participants, these resource constraints will be exacerbated by the influx of lump sum payments because these will likely cause an increased demand for services and support and more competition between groups and communities. As individuals and organizations increasingly compete for healing dollars and fundraising revenues, there is a growing sense that some of this competition is going to have to be turned into collaboration (Hodgson, n.d.).

The site visits where the survey was conducted were a reminder of the remoteness and isolation of the vast majority of communities. Participants said that this was a problem when important, trustworthy services are not within reach, and that they have to depend on outside, distant, and costly services. At the same time, they expressed strong ideas and interests in having enough resources to build the kind of capacity that will support a strategy for LSPs from inception to implementation.

Research

Brant Castellano defines research as an "activity intended to investigate, document, bring to light, analyse or interpret matters in any domain, to create knowledge for the benefit of society or of particular groups" (2004:99). Through research projects, the Aboriginal Healing Foundation (2006) has produced new knowledge for Aboriginal and non-Aboriginal organizations, researchers, media, and the general public to help promote and improve healing prospects for Survivors, families, and communities. Public education about the legacy of abuse at residential schools has also been integral to AHF's work, and it has been a stalwart supporter of reconciliation efforts.

Strategic Principles

These strategic principles are advanced to frame the solutions and recommendations participants put forward. Incorporating these principles encourages their application and cultivates comprehensive initiatives and the achievement of lasting outcomes. Fittingly, the fields of reference for these principles correspond with the three main actors in the LSP equation: Survivors, their families, and their communities. Each constituency possesses both unique and overlapping interests. To be effective, therefore, supporters of LSP recipients must think about the respective dynamics within and between each 'sub-group.' Such a separation, particularly in smaller communities, is relative. A Survivor is simultaneously a member of a family at the same she/he is part of the community; but, there will be occasions when what is workable for the family may not be so for a Survivor. Therefore, each realm must be addressed within every solution. The figure below helps illustrate how these nested groups both stand alone and interconnect:

Figure 4) Key Actors and LSP

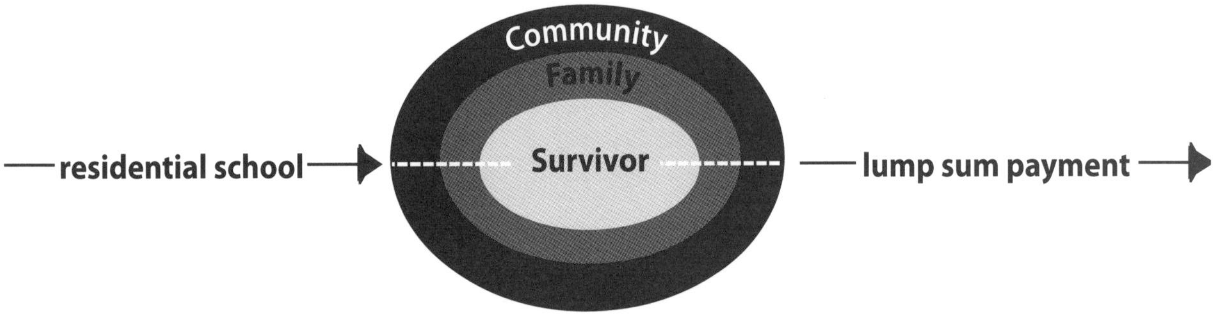

Much like these concentric circles, this discussion of support principles locates Survivors' interests at the center—precisely where most participants would say they belong.

Strategic Principle 1: Survivors' rights and autonomy are central

While stating that every individual Survivor is different may sound clichéd, this makes it no less true or vital. Any solution in this area must always respect the ultimate right of Survivors to make their own decisions, and many participants were at great pains to emphasize this:

> Why is this of interest to the Aboriginal Healing Foundation? What business is it of theirs? In the long run, it's none of our business. This smacks of the days of Indian agents, and control by others. This [report] will inspire resentment. Survivors will say, 'That's my money: I will spend it how I want. If I drink it all away to drown my sorrows, then that's what I will do to escape the pain of my memories.' How do we get people to spend wisely? Good luck: if you learn how, let me know.

Survivors are vigilant about their personal sovereignty. Those hoping to support Survivors must then respect and protect their autonomy and independence, however and wherever they may decide to spend their LSPs. Survivors who suspect they are being treated otherwise will only view efforts to help in the same paternalistic and authoritarian light of residential school:

> My organization works with Survivors, especially those who have been traumatized. I know one person who … invested his [LSP] in an RRSP and is sharing his money with his relatives. It is his choice. Who are we to tell people what to do with their money? For me, that money I'm getting is mine. Residential school took my language and culture. I abused myself for 27 years. I'm still an addict. I overeat. I gamble, sometimes too much. I have relationship problems. My marriage broke up.

This first principle of respect for Survivor autonomy suggests some basic guidelines for potential interventions, not least of which is to start where Survivors are at. As the above comment illustrates, no one knows more about Survivors' foibles and fallibility than Survivors themselves. Empathy goes a long way toward gaining their trust—a trust that could prove to be the single most critical factor to the success of any proposed support. Many participants understood that Survivors of abuse at residential school can be reluctant to go for treatment: "You can have plans, goals, strategies, individuals will still turn around and say 'It is none of your business.' But you still give them an opportunity to access services and programs." For some participants, it cannot be repeated enough: "It's really up to the individual. [We] can only offer solutions. People's choices are what's key." For those who would seek to assist Survivors, therefore, increasing or expanding their available options, and people's awareness thereof, should be a top priority.

Strategic Principle 2: Survivors are their own best resource

Survivor and/or elder groups are invaluable resources for former residential school students, according to participants, and they must be centrally involved in any effort to prevent elder abuse related to LSPs:

> Educate the elder committees—every community has one—about the payments and tell them about their options and choices. Include other Survivors in this. We have an Elder Day Program here, so we need to have someone go in and tell them about safety and security issues.

The degree of Survivor involvement should be utilized by communities as a constant litmus test for their work. Where and whenever possible, providers and supporters should endeavour to collectively meet and work with Survivors: "I would like to see this group meet as a group to discuss how the money can last. What do we want to happen?" Based in such a cooperative, peer-based structure, Survivors can operate from a position of greater strength and solidarity, making them less vulnerable to the potentially negative influences of outside forces.

Strategic Principle 3: The family has a rightful place at the table

According to one participant: "Everything starts at home, start your work there." While an individual's right to choose must be recognized, it is nonetheless understood that those choices are subject to influence, for better or worse, by members of a Survivor's intimate circle. As one participant emphasized, "There is no single, catch-all solution. We need to understand the dynamics of the individual and the family as a unit. Solutions need to address things at this level."

Accordingly, interventions should be ideally tailored to, and inclusive of, an LSP recipient's immediate family members. "Family-centred approaches are very important. Resolve the issues at home as much as possible. This would ward off bootleggers. Family members can help others make the best use of LSP money." For example, when inviting Survivors to sessions about LSPs, invitations should also be extended to the children, grandchildren, and/or any relatives they are in regular contact with as well. At these sessions, consideration ought to be given to "workshops on family dynamics, how to work with people in your family who are getting payments."

Families should be encouraged by whatever means to discuss the issue at home. Ultimately, it may be family talking to family that makes the difference.

> I spoke to my family members and told them not to tell our mother how to spend her money. My mother is 87 years old and needs dignity, and we need to respect her, [not] re-victimize her like residential school and INAC [Indian and Northern Affairs Canada].

The more vocal and dynamic members of a family circle will be more likely to be entrusted with looking after their relatives. In smaller communities, individuals fitting this profile are typically well-known: "Every one of our staff is related to someone." Recruiting their support and participation is essential:

> The more staff are connected to the actual community, the better they'll do. Encourage meetings at the family level. Target the members most able to talk to others, to say the stuff only family member[s] could say.

A family's complex interplay of interests means dealing with not just one generation but at least three: elders, adults, and youth. Some argued that it is the children who bear the brunt of negative LSP outcomes, which are only compounded by the 'ripple effect' of intergenerational traumas. Young people obviously have distinct needs and require similarly distinct approaches as part and parcel of an overarching intervention framework. Yet it is critical to remember that family dynamics go both ways: children and youth have the potential to exert a powerful influence upon their parents, so it would be important to capitalize on this. Communities may find that the most effective way to get to parents and grandparents is through their children as a source of ideas and inspiration. By generating settings and opportunities for that intergenerational dialogue to take place, youth are permitted to play a meaningful role in the life of their family, itself a potent source of healing.

Strategic Principle 4: The community is the natural catalyst

According to some participants, community healing is community-based. Ideas take root most deeply when they emerge from the people themselves. Initiatives developed by and for the community nurture and reinforce a sense of local ownership and responsibility over policy and programming. As a support principle, therefore, efforts targeted to supporting Survivors should strive to elicit wide community input and involvement: "The whole community will have to set plans." Where feasible, such participation should be generated by means of an open and public environment, not only to promote transparency, but also as more positive forms of peer pressure that respect the interests of Survivors. As well, brainstorming possibilities is often easier in groups: "We can help each other set goals. People who have had some experience with success are willing to share with others."

Some participants urged that if any employment opportunities arise from this work, "job postings should be filled by local people" so as to create lasting community capacity, not to mention to foster a greater buy-in. Community governments and administrations must also reach out to their citizens: "Aboriginal employees and leaders have to be more empathetic to their own. So many feel superior once they get positions of power. They need to train other Aboriginal people so they can become more self-sufficient." Moreover, by keeping people current on what is going on inside the community, one participant suggested that one should focus on coming up with solutions rather than by making outside events the center of attention, as there is a risk of getting people caught up in assigning blame.

For a number of participants, the one institution that is best placed to take an active role in the welfare of Survivors is the local government. To them, social issues often become political issues, necessitating the involvement of the local governing body. Many wished that their government would be more consistently vocal about the anticipated social and intergenerational effects of LSPs, particularly on elders:

> Have the leadership and politicians be more involved, and sharing some of their concerns about how well these payments have gone or not. They'll have to balance people's personal rights and sovereignty [with] their wellness. I'd like to see someone step up.

Closely connected with the work of politicians are the various programming and administrative staff employed by Aboriginal governments, thought to have their fingers on the pulse of everyday community life. They need to be prepared for what is coming. Indeed, it is their connections and experience, and, in the case of longer-serving employees, their institutional memory that together offer a potentially enormous resource for any community initiative. Fittingly, many recommendations originated within this sector.

Figure 5) Comprehensive LSP Strategic Framework

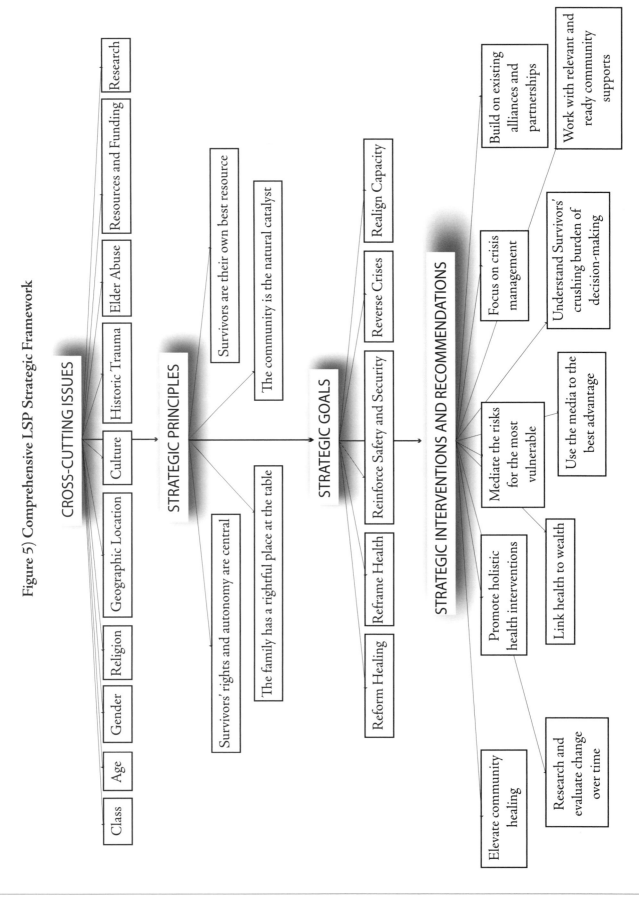

CROSS-CUTTING ISSUES

Class | Age | Gender | Religion | Geographic Location | Culture | Historic Trauma | Elder Abuse | Resources and Funding | Research

STRATEGIC PRINCIPLES

Survivors are their own best resource

The community is the natural catalyst

Survivors' rights and autonomy are central

The family has a rightful place at the table

STRATEGIC GOALS

Reform Healing | Reframe Health | Reinforce Safety and Security | Reverse Crises | Realign Capacity

STRATEGIC INTERVENTIONS AND RECOMMENDATIONS

Build on existing alliances and partnerships

Work with relevant and ready community supports

Focus on crisis management

Understand Survivors' crushing burden of decision-making

Use the media to the best advantage

Mediate the risks for the most vulnerable

Link health to wealth

Promote holistic health interventions

Elevate community healing

Research and evaluate change over time

Strategic Goals, Interventions, and Recommendations

This section details the five sets of strategic goals and interventions: reform healing, reframe health, reinforce safety and security, reverse crises, and realign capacity. These propose long-term solutions as well as immediate and practical recommendations for dealing with the impacts of LSPs.

Generally, the two most widely suggested types of support by LSP recipients were financial planning and self-directed healing. In the case of the former, many participants envisioned using more formal mechanisms and methods to assist LSP recipients that often carried an important role for local government. With the latter forms of support, recipients stated a preference for a more personal, more direct approach to helping Survivors, with their own resources playing as central a role in their care as anyone elses. These suggested interventions could be seen to fall along a continuum, with formal and informal interventions at either end. An analysis of non-recipient feedback, meanwhile, uncovered five broad streams of potential need and opportunity: prevention and preparation, advocacy and alliances, financial training and support, local capacity building, and the benefits of greater awareness and support generated through media and ceremony.

Strategic Goal: Reform Healing

The Canadian Institute for Health Information (2004) lists the legacy of residential schools as one of five key determinants of health for Aboriginal people. Meanwhile, NAHO (National Aboriginal Health Organization) states that "the goal of traditional medicine is to improve the quality of life with an emphasis on the healing journey" (2002:9). Furthermore, since 1999, "the Aboriginal Healing Foundation has been providing funding support to community-based initiatives that address the intergenerational legacy of physical and sexual abuse in Canada's Indian residential school system" (Aboriginal Healing Foundation, 2006:14). This strategic goal, therefore, underlines the importance of reducing exposure to harm when compensation payments are made. At the same time, it proposes some lasting solutions for bringing the Legacy to a close, a request that was frequently voiced by participants.

The healing movement has already gone some distance in reversing the historical wrongs at residential schools, and has been liberating individuals, families, and communities from the shackles of the residential school legacy. What is now needed is a radical shift in thinking that steers the healing paradigm from the pursuit of healing to being healed. Under a healed paradigm, Survivors break their once inextricable ties to a painful past in order to move on to a hopeful future of their own making.

Many Survivors see LSPs as a powerful tool for making this shift. For them, compensation payments are potentially cathartic and decolonizing partly because they foreground an improved sense of self, family, and community, herald better relations with governments, institutions, and other Canadians, and spur the resurgence of healthy communities. Most importantly, Survivors who felt that they had an upper hand over the legacy of residential schools said that they wanted to shed it as a proverbial excuse and enterprise.

There is a common misconception that the residential school legacy has left no one standing, but what became abundantly clear from the participants is that most Survivors and their families and communities are not in deep crises every moment of every day. Even though flashbacks and painful periods are still relatively common, many Survivors find reprieve by reasoning out problems with friends, family members, and/or counsellors/therapists, by distracting themselves with favorite activities, and/or by asking for divine intervention. In a similar vein, participants suggested that not enough attention is given to the strength of individuals and families and to the assets communities have.

It cannot be assumed that LSPs will secure and sustain better life outcomes for everyone, especially since some individuals, families, and communities may not possess the full capacity to deal with a sudden influx of money. Participants clearly predict that abuse, discrimination, exploitation, and death will result from LSPs, making it necessary to anticipate the most vulnerable times for at-risk groups like children, elders, street people, women, and the infirm.

Resilience

Many definitions of resilience exist in the mainstream. It is most easily understood as the "capacity to be bent without breaking and the capacity, once bent, to spring back" (Vaillant, 1993:284). This definition suggests that a resilient person manages to have a good life outcome with a steady job, long-term marriage, and lack of mental illness despite exposure to high-risk situations with emotional, mental, or physical distress (Rutter, 2001).

Meanwhile, the term *indigenous resilience* has recently surfaced, and is defined by Mason Durie, a Maori from New Zealand, as follows:

> Superimposed on adversity and historic marginalisation, indigenous resilience is a reflection of an innate determination by indigenous peoples to succeed. Resilience is the polar opposite of rigidity. It provides an alternate perspective to the more usual scenarios that emphasise indigenous disadvantage and allows the indigenous challenge to be reconfigured as a search for success rather an explanation for failure (2006:3).

This is an appropriate and useful definition for Survivors, families, and communities who prevail despite history having left them struggling with the Legacy for generations. Yet they prevail. When determined Survivors revisited the impact of the Legacy, they were unanimous in stating that LSPs could not erase their pain completely, and they would continue to act wilfully to move past this pain, overcome trauma from residential school, and move on with the rest of their lives.

Survivors are also speaking openly about problems associated with LSPs, and by sharing their stories and experiences with one another they are, in many cases, forming and benefiting from meaningful and productive partnerships and mentorships in their communities. Participants reported that they are convening family meetings around kitchen tables and are organizing public meetings in settings like community halls, schools, and offices to discuss, debate, and decide on LSPs.

STRATEGIC INTERVENTION TO REFORM HEALING:
Elevate community healing

Participants were clearly literate about traditional teachings that project healthy, democratic, and united communities. They used terms like "community," "healing," "traditions," and "culture" to make this point. These notions are consistent with the concept of civil society, which can involve three levels of activity: i) high-level advocacy such as the work of international Indigenous groups; ii) non-governmental organizations (NGOs) like the AHF; and iii) volunteer groups that provide services at the local level. On the one hand, civil society is defined as individual, corporate, and government citizens being responsible for one another (Torjman, 1997). On the other hand, this concept means that organizations are free to interact with one another, and free of interference from government or market forces (Swift, 1999). Barber asserts that the citizens of a strong democratic civil society "are active, responsible, engaged members of groups and communities that, while having different values and conflicting interests, are devoted to arbitrating those differences by exploring common ground, doing public work, and pursuing common relations" (1998:37). Many participants reported that communities have responded to LSPs in this very fashion.

Residential school apology

One participant wanted a ceremony hosted at the community level that included representatives from the institutions most responsible for residential schools, namely, the churches and the federal government, in order for them to deliver their respective apologies directly to Survivors for what happened. In this way, LSP recipients would see that the parties responsible for enabling the residential school abuse are also taking responsibility for the harms inflicted. An opportunity to question these institutional representatives, or simply address statements toward them, could potentially offer Survivors in attendance the deep sense of closure and reckoning they need with "a sense you've been heard, you can then let it go."

Community-wide ceremony

In some communities, ceremonies have been specially carried out for the purpose of honouring residential school students who had passed away. Seen as both culturally appropriate and therapeutic at the same time, such events allow people to both let Survivors go "in a good way" as well as release residual anger. It could be the case that a similar approach is needed to help process Survivors' emotions around LSPs and all this can represent. Along with the beneficial effect of raising awareness, such a ceremony would subtly send the message that it is a shared community concern that must be collectively owned by the community. By marking the occasion of the arrival of LSPs, it conceivably helps to set the stage for closure on the issues the payments initially give rise to as the community symbolically moves on together. Some community examples referenced in interviews included smudging, singing and drumming, healing and sharing circles (men's, women's, or mixed), demolition of known residential school properties, community-based hearings, give-aways, community feasts, round dances, and a residential school inquiry.

Civic engagement

Where governments will not or cannot provide a needed social service, voluntary associations often step in to fill the gap, and Aboriginal communities have many examples of such non-governmental assistance and support. Such NGOs may be informally self-funded through cash or in-kind community donations, or more formally supported through funds from one or more levels of government.

Many participants felt that some LSP recipients might relish the opportunity to support such civic-minded groups with a portion of their payment. In fact, as mentioned previously, some already have: one community managed to convince Survivors to dedicate five per cent of their payments toward local social initiatives. This sort of philanthropic exercise by Survivors, carried out individually or in concert, could be extended to any other program, facility, or cause. Be it an existing entity, or one created just for these LSP contributions, any NGO could be made a formal beneficiary. Governments at all levels might offer to match such aid as an additional inducement to give.

Survivors may elect to combine their contributions, either informally or as a formally incorporated foundation or endowment. Decisions to support any civil society group could be first delegated to a smaller committee of Survivors who would narrow down the field, then present a short list to the larger group for the ultimate determination.

Along with the aforementioned healing and education services, the following are other suggested candidates for LSP-based donations:

✓ men's groups	✓ women's groups
✓ health centre	✓ physical care providers
✓ foster homes	✓ therapists
✓ youth programs (e.g., groups, exchanges)	✓ youth centre
✓ youth workers	✓ Survivor-specific treatment
✓ full-time student counsellor	✓ counselling (individual, family and group)

RECOMMENDATIONS
Reform Healing | Elevate community healing

1. Address the call for a formal apology to recognize the legacy of residential schools and its effects on First Nation, Métis, and Inuit communities. The movement towards an apology could be strengthened by the support from the Aboriginal Healing Foundation and other national Aboriginal organizations, judges, lawyers, chiefs and councils, Survivor groups, Survivor advocates and champions, government departments, youth groups, and churches.

2. Hold ceremonies at local, regional, and national levels to mark the occasion of Canada-wide lump sum payments with an emphasis on their healing power for Survivors, families, and communities and on their potential to enhance reconciliation with other Canadians. The parties that can help to make

this happen are elders, Survivor groups and champions, community leaders, the Aboriginal Healing Foundation and other national Aboriginal organizations, governments at all levels, businesses, and churches.

3. Facilitate personal and collective donations by Survivors and communities who wish to give their lump sum payments to a worthy cause by helping them to identify the range of choices and by assisting them through the donation process. Governments at all levels, the Aboriginal Healing Foundation, donor experts, financial institutions, lawyers, Survivor groups, and community leaders can help Survivors who want to give to unconventional causes, while elders, community leaders, and Survivor groups lend their support to traditional and ceremonial give-aways.

> ## STRATEGIC INTERVENTION TO REFORM HEALING:
> ### Research and evaluate change over time

Assess impacts and conduct evaluations

With regard to LSPs, communities have to establish a process for comprehensive planning and preparedness and to assess and measure the final results. Such an exercise pays attention to practical steps, such as: monitoring problem areas; listing high-risk individuals; surveying traumas including deaths; developing a data base; determining what constitutes a crisis and the level of response needed; and providing accurate information (DeBruyn et al., 1994). Besides measuring population characteristics, organizational dynamics, and gaps in service, for example, performance measures will have to consider soft issues like trust, inclusion, and fairness and be matched with cultural rituals and ceremonies. Measures that matter to the community can have a positive influence on crisis responses, so they need to be integrated into LSP crises response frameworks.

Dialogue and action

The site visits showed that individuals and communities continue to preserve strong cultural identities, lifestyles, and values perhaps reflecting the national resurgence and healing movement that has taken place over the past two decades. Two instructive conceptions of healing need attention in this regard. First, it is "a process involving the grieving of significant losses in one's life that have inhibited growth and development and contributed to personal difficulties" (Mussell, 2005:11). Second, healing "involves efforts to rebuild the human foundations for healthy communities" (Mussell, 2005:5). Meanwhile, ceremonies and traditions have been seen as transformative enough to integrate into community health services and programs. Yet only anecdotes and testimonials have served to measure their effectiveness.

Gender-based analysis

Based on the input of participants, women are very involved in healing initiatives, a trend that deserves more attention and action. One ready tool for tracking this trend is gender-based analysis (GBA), which differentiates the overall health status of women relative to that of men. A gender lens will help to move toward a fuller assessment of the impact of healing policies, practices, and programs on both women and men and to seek redress for women who have often felt the brunt of the negative effects of LSPs. Research projects are needed to look at the relevance of GBA in communities and to adopt a culturally appropriate version of it to promote gender equity in healing initiatives.

The private sector

Presently, healing initiatives are not formally involved with the private/corporate sector, though private consultants are hired by communities and private sponsors support major healing conferences. Since the main function of the private sector is to sell goods in volume and to make a profit, it could be argued that such economic interests would give less attention to culture, community values, and traditional knowledge of Survivors, families, and communities. Even though some private companies have trouble working with concepts that cannot be priced, many of them support a social conscience and demonstrate an interest in working with communities. Applied research on the private sector's contributions to healing initiatives in communities would assist in uncovering real and potential benefits for these kinds of partnerships, especially with LSPs.

The voluntary/NGO sector in communities

Non-governmental organizations (NGOs) are no longer a sleeper issue in communities, yet little is known about their accomplishments and prospects in the area of healing. The voluntary sector (also called the 'non-profit sector,' 'third sector,' and most commonly the 'NGO sector') is involved in service provision, volunteerism, research, academia, and advocacy. The NGO sector is valued because it delivers services, is active and creative, holds knowledge, acts as a conscience, creates jobs and networks and often challenges the status quo. Since it is not profit-driven, it is perceived to be more trustworthy and closer to the community, in part, because it works with community volunteers and local boards. Research that links healing with the emerging voluntary sector in communities would help to determine how the latter shapes the former and would capture best practices.

Citizen engagement, social capital, and social cohesion

O'Connor states that citizen engagement "appears to govern a cluster of strategies aimed to increase participation by individual citizens and at the same time create political processes that can revive a sense of, and deliberation on common interests and public goods" (1998:16). At a practical level, and to achieve similar results, participants said they resorted to prayers, sweat lodge ceremonies, talking circles, storytelling, humour, drumming, and singing. Putnam defines social capital as "the features in our community life that make us more productive -a high level of engagement, trust and reciprocity" (1996:4). Survey participants recognized that dense networks are vital for connecting neighbours and organizations because they help to cultivate co-operation, equality, tolerance, and mutual benefits, though they often cited barriers in achieving these. Putnam also defines social cohesion as "the ties that bind," but as the participants indicated, personal, financial, and structural barriers sometime block trust and reciprocity. Participants also spoke openly about community conflicts that needed to be better understood and resolved. It is therefore important to conduct research on these key terms so they can be reinterpreted and redefined by communities, and be used in training sessions for community development.

Ceremony and spirituality

Time and time again, participants disclosed the significance of ceremony, culture, and faith to their own personal healing journeys. From taking part in sweats to engaging in language revival and traditional storytelling to regular Bible study, cultural and spiritual pursuits are themselves pathways to wellness. One participant spoke of seeing four therapists for deep depression before making a breakthrough with a medicine lady who relied on sweats and songs: "I don't know how, but it removed things no one else did."

To share one's shame aloud can be an act of heroism, and collective, culturally rooted activities may be among the most safe and effective means of nurturing such disclosure. That is why ceremony can often provide a profound opportunity for rooting LSPs within a larger frame of reference as the community is assembled together in common purpose and prayer.

One recipient's decision-making process began with a family-run sweathouse and pipe ceremony, where all 10 members prayed together on how the money might be best allocated. Some communities elected to hand out LSP cheques at the conclusion of a specially held sweat, although some worried about the pressure on elders at such events to reveal the amount they received. Confidentiality must therefore be preserved.

Room can also be made within ceremony for the inclusion of those who have brought harm to Survivors. A moving account was offered as to the power of a public apology delivered within the community itself by a senior church representative. This direct, "public acknowledgment of wrongs" helped Survivors move on with their own lives.

RECOMMENDATIONS
Reform Healing | Research and evaluate change over time

4. Prioritize impact assessments and evaluations by training front-line workers on the early detection of risks and impacts of LSPs and by collaborating with individuals who have expertise on tracking the effectiveness of interventions and on factoring in variables like gender, geography, and age. Front-line workers, Aboriginal and non-Aboriginal researchers and evaluators, Survivor groups, government departments, the Aboriginal Healing Foundation, and community leaders are well placed to do this work.

5. Study the emergence/resurgence of the voluntary sector in communities by examining mainstream concepts like citizen engagement and social cohesion and by adopting corresponding community concepts to promote community involvement around healing and LSPs and to sustain the formation of related support groups. Together, community leaders, Survivor groups, Survivor advocates and champions, and Aboriginal and non-Aboriginal researchers have the capacity to carry out such a study.

Strategic Goal: Reframe Health

Many participants were getting ready to receive LSPs by examining their options (sharing, spending, saving, or investing), and were also positioning themselves for a potentially life-changing experience that would see them past abject poverty and high-risk lives. They sincerely hoped that the compensation payments would help them realize their full human potential and productivity. Looking at health through an economic lens frames it as a resource that can be pressed against the Legacy and the socio-economic status it has compromised for Survivors, families, and communities.

Participants suggested that it was critically important to improve the socio-economic determinants of health if individuals, families, and communities are to make the best of LSPs and heal from the legacy of residential schools, making it just as important to highlight strategies and recommendations for maintaining and improving the health of Survivors, families, and communities against the backdrop of LSPs and a sustainable health system where spending has to shift to strategic investments. Thinking about health as a resource must first take root.

> ## STRATEGIC INTERVENTION TO REFRAME HEALTH:
> ### Promote holistic health interventions

Most health institutions, providers, and consumers now acknowledge how important holistic approaches are to health and healing. A renewed interest in the healing powers of ceremonies and traditions place these front and center in community programs and practices. Moreover, health disparities and mental health and addictions have to be considered if health and healing are to proceed in tandem and across the spectrum of care.

Health disparities

In 2004, Aboriginal leaders met with First Ministers to discuss measures to address health disparities one year after the *Health Care Renewal Accord* called for concerted action to reduce health gaps for Aboriginal people in Canada:

> First Ministers recognize that addressing the serious challenges that face the health of Aboriginal Canadians will require dedicated effort. To this end the federal government is committed to enhancing its funding and working collaboratively with other governments and Aboriginal peoples to meet the objectives set out in the Accord including the priorities established in the Health Reform Fund. Governments will work together to address the gap in health status between Aboriginal and non-Aboriginal Canadians through better integration of health services (Canadian Intergovernmental Conference Secretariat, 2003:7).

In December 2004, a seminal report stated that "Major health disparities exist in Canada, and the most important relate to socio-economic status, Aboriginal identity, gender and geographic location" (Public Health Agency of Canada, 2004:1). The same report concluded that "Better health enables more people to participate in the economy, reducing the costs of lost productivity" (Public Health Agency of Canada, 2004: vii). This echoed the emphasis placed by participants on reducing poverty through higher incomes, regular employment, and better education. The participants also expressed concern about the health effects LSPs were having on Survivors who were already dealing with health problems.

Mental health and addictions

Many participants were very concerned about LSPs because these can give rise to higher addiction rates, which tend to go hand-in-hand with mental health problems that sometimes end in violence and death. Aboriginal people generally experience disproportionate rates of mental illness and disorders, problems that are compounded by the effects of residential schools. Because mental health problems like major depression and substance abuse disorders are so intertwined, special efforts will have to be made to raise awareness about this complex health problem and the challenge of working with Survivors who suffer this double burden. Making mental health and addictions a priority will likely require a suitable knowledge base, sustainable funding frameworks, and best practices that have been tested in communities and ideally informed by the World Health Organization's definition of traditional medicine and healing:

> the sum total of the knowledge, skills and practices based on the theories, beliefs and experiences indigenous to different cultures, whether explicable or not, used in the maintenance of health, as well as in the prevention, diagnosis, improvement or treatment of physical and mental illnesses (2000:1).

Conventional methods of treatment for addictions and substance abuse do not readily carry over to the needs of former residential school students. What is needed instead, some suggest, is a more specialized form of care, one that categorizes Survivors' experiences under the heading of trauma and post-traumatic disorders. The hope here is that by framing "residential school syndrome" as the by-product of trauma, it could lead to more effective diagnoses and prognoses. The basic argument is that conventional therapy does not work for traumatized individuals. Alternative approaches that have reportedly produced promising results for trauma patients elsewhere, including eye movement desensitization and muscle work, may also benefit Survivors. According to what was heard from participants, these techniques are apparently covered by government health insurance plans in some jurisdictions.

Opportunities for healing

Among those participants who believed that LSPs presented Survivors with a great opportunity to help with their healing, some were unequivocal that it be based on Aboriginal traditions, free of "white" influence, and taking place inside community-based facilities with elders at the center. Some suggested a very specific path: "1. critical incident debriefing; 2. trauma recovery therapy; 3. spiritual or land-based care; and, 4. financial counselling." Others felt it best to enroll Survivors in "grief and loss outreach and recovery programs." One stressed that healing can only take place when and where entire families are treated.

Some believe that the costs of any such healing initiative must come not out of Survivors' payments per se, but as a special 'top-up' provided by government. Suggestions ranged from an extra 25 to 50 per cent; monies would then go to well-established and strictly accountable community-based care providers. Whether self-funded or partially subsidized, these healing processes could be facilitated by a variety of support personnel, from "qualified counsellors and psychiatrists" to victims advocates and social workers. Counselling especially had its champions among LSP recipient participants. "I should've had $10,000 for counselling while I was going through court case. Sharing my issues would've helped." Survivors must be allowed to "shop around" until they find a counsellor they are comfortable with and can trust. Male and female therapists whose experiences connect them with those of their clients are ideal. It was also implied that the more widely available therapy is, the more it will come to be utilized and accepted across the community. In addition, it was suggested that mental health support staff, in addition to being properly paid, have access themselves to self-care opportunities such as sharing circles.

Even as they spoke of the very real challenges LSPs pose for elders, participants often referred to the work ethic they were raised with and the value family members placed even on paltry amounts of money earned through hard work. The elders they referred to have long taught that too much can be taken for granted when money is plentiful. Most people will stay disenfranchised unless surpluses cement relationships, forge self-reliance, and improve productivity. The concept of culture has now narrowed to the extent that elders' teachings about money and productivity are being forgotten, making it imperative to reintegrate what elders have to say about these twin concepts culturally. This can be done by encouraging them to share relevant stories, by holding consultations about traditional approaches to money and work, and by conducting an exploratory study on this topic.

Land-based cultural and traditional activities

Many participants highlighted the positive contribution culture and tradition have to offer to any potential LSP-related intervention. A number promoted the revitalization and transmission of traditional knowledge in areas such as herbs and medicines, along with the related healing protocols. Others promoted drumming, dance, songs, language instruction, and teachings, especially for youth.

For a number of participants the land is healing, in every sense of the phrase. Many proposed that families work with elder relatives in using LSPs to fund regular trips out on the land. It was also suggested that healing therapies incorporate land-based principles and techniques whenever and wherever possible. Be it as guides or participants, elders who are asked to get involved in these outdoor excursions reportedly "start to glow because someone is paying attention to them. They feel useful rather than 'just sitting there like a blob' as some people perceive. It is about relationships, not money. A lot of us forget this." Away from the many distractions of technology, alcohol, and drugs, many Aboriginal people "come alive on the land" in a way they do not in more urban areas. The fact elders responded so positively to being integrated into community life rather than marginalized might hold lessons for interventions as a whole. It suggests that Survivors who use LSPs to purchase skidoos and motorboats are making a qualitatively different kind of purchase than those who buy automobiles.

Elders have the innate capacity to mobilize and influence others because they are seen to be legitimate, trustworthy, and credible sources of knowledge and skills. They are considered to be valuable community members because they help to validate, affirm, and evaluate community spirit in its everyday sense. While it can be argued that elders only serve a symbolic function, they still play a key role in allocating communal rights and responsibilities. The sad irony is that some fall victim to abuse when they come into money. A member of the RCMP had this to say about LSPs: "people were expressing concerns about how elders were taken advantage of by family members. Therefore money was not benefiting recipients as it was a disbursement in families."

Cultural competency

Cultural competency is a vital ingredient for safe, satisfactory, and sustainable programs. It is a conscious process that goes beyond cultural awareness and sensitivity, and fulfills people's expectations and preferences within the mainstream health system (Mutha, Allen, and Welch, 2002) and in community programming. Defining characteristics of cultural competency (Purnell and Paulanka, 1998) include:

+ developing awareness of one's own existence, sensation, thoughts, and environment without letting it have an undue influence on those from other backgrounds;

+ demonstrating knowledge and understanding of the client's culture;

+ accepting and respecting cultural differences; and,

+ adapting care so it is congruent with the client's culture.

When LSPs start flowing into communities in earnest, identifying 'problem' recipients is a potential pitfall, especially if the money is seen as a source of instability and problems. Front-line workers will need training to become culturally competent so they can meet the needs of all LSP recipients, including those who are hardest to reach:

> A lot of ADR recipients are drinking and on the street. They're neglected by counsellors and very traumatized since they were very young, five or six years old. I don't know what kind of schools they have for counsellors, but they need to be trained properly and they need to focus on the ground, on the street.

Becoming culturally competent will better prepare front-line workers to think through common problems like alcohol abuse, especially when the problem is presented as the oldest form of protest:

> I grew up very angry when I was a kid because residential school took my culture and hunting and trapping and language away. They took something away that belonged to me. This is why a lot of our people use substances to forget about it.

Front-line workers who are culturally competent will understand the crushing burden of decision making that individuals and families already face daily, let alone when the LSPs will arrive:

> In our culture, it is our way to share, to help our neighbor—anyone in need—through hard times and good times. All grandparents will give everything to their offspring. Today they are enabling them to do drugs, take alcohol. Grandparents cannot say no and have to shop this way too. They buy flour and baking powder to make bannock rather than fruits that would only last for a day. I can't help but think of this at lump sum payment time. How can we help youth understand this is not their money? In our society this is a problem especially when it comes to drugs and alcohol.

Since the end goal of cultural competence in health and healing initiatives is patient safety, front-line workers will have to deal with problems requiring remedial action. For example, while it is commendable in one sense that most mental health counselling is done by family and friends, this practice can also pose its own hazards: "My husband is gone because of residential school money. The only time he wanted to talk about this was when he was drinking. This is what I see in the street people who were once well-to-do."

RECOMMENDATIONS
Reframe Health | Promote holistic health interventions

6. Reduce health disparities for Survivors by weighing their poor health status and poverty against key health determinants like self-determination, income, employment, education, culture, and health services and by costing out the impact of lump sum payments in dollar terms. Health departments, governments at all levels, finance departments, front-line workers, Survivor groups, women's groups, elder coordinators, Aboriginal and non-Aboriginal health organizations, and local health committees will bring necessary commitment and knowledge to this process.

7. Couple mental health and addictions in programming to reflect this common cluster of health problems for Survivors and their families by reviewing related evidence, developing suitable funding frameworks, and integrating best practices like traditional medicine and healing. Health departments, governments at all levels, Survivor groups, health professionals, front-line workers, Elder groups and coordinators, and Aboriginal and non-Aboriginal researchers are well placed to support related initiatives.

8. Capture elders' teachings about money, self-reliance, and productivity to restore traditional approaches to money and work and to embed an economic dimension in the meaning of culture for the long-term benefit of Survivors, families and communities. Elders, Survivor groups, government departments, Aboriginal and non-Aboriginal organizations, Aboriginal and non-Aboriginal researchers, interpreters, elder coordinators, and community leaders will be instrumental in making this happen.

9. Integrate cultural competency into programs by providing training to front-line workers on issues like historic trauma, traditional knowledge, and resilience so they can influence program development for Survivors and their families, and help make programs safe, satisfactory, and sustainable for them. Front-line workers, post-secondary institutions, governments at all levels, health departments, health professionals, Aboriginal and non-Aboriginal non-governmental organizations with related expertise, and Survivor groups will be needed to do this work.

> **STRATEGIC INTERVENTION TO REFRAME HEALTH:**
> **Link health to wealth**

Local self-sufficiency

For one set of participants, healing must be integrated within a comprehensive, all-encompassing strategy for local economic development. LSPs offer a unique investment opportunity for seeding independently owned and operated enterprises: "We need to activate people's capacity to do things for themselves, without government." For some, it was vital that such initiatives stand free of government involvement and interference, including Aboriginal governments. Indeed, there were a few examples raised about some families or clusters of individuals who were contemplating pooling their resources to set up a business.

Financial counselling and planning

Time and time again, participants attested to a low rate of financial literacy among Survivors. As Aboriginal communities face an unprecedented influx of cash, having the necessary supports in place could prove to be the critical difference between constructive and destructive LSP outcomes.

Participants called for bank representatives to be brought into communities to advise Survivors of their options at a general meeting convened especially for that purpose. Broadly structured as an awareness-raising session about the potential risks and opportunities of large LSPs, the meeting would simply expose Survivors to what they might expect. With no forewarning of what is to come, it is easy to imagine many elders becoming overwhelmed. Some promoted the use of group talking sessions to exchange and compare people's thoughts and ideas about their money, adding it may be good to group people of a similar age together for these talks, as some elders are more comfortable in the company of other elders. At the very least, the meeting helps elders look 'beyond the dollar signs' to see that alternate visions do indeed exist. Lawyers can also have a role here; indeed, some participants reported that it was their legal counsel who urged them to plan and to engage in goal planning.

Moving from the general to the specific, participants wanted to see individual financial counselling offered to recipients. In these one-on-one sessions, advisors would educate and collaborate with Survivors on their investment options as well as the basics of short- and long-term budgeting. One participant said that counsellors must enable LSP recipients to reflect for themselves on the differences between their wants and their needs, so that they weigh the relative costs and benefits of different choices. These personal counselling sessions would ideally be scheduled as soon as possible after the cheques arrive. Aboriginal-owned financial institutions came up as potential resources for these sessions.

Care must be taken not to push Survivors because, in the end, it is their choice to make. One participant cautioned that "there should not be a prescribed pace for how the money is to be spent." Some expected a negative response to such an initiative by some of the more "stubborn" Survivors, but also believed that others would welcome the chance to have all their options placed in front of them.

One person hoped to see a bank located right in the community, assuming it would treat Aboriginal clients with more respect by not always putting holds on their cheques, for example. But one voice protested the involvement of banks, seeing them as "only interested in making money." Others said many government staff are knowledgeable about money and should participate in putting out packages of information on the subject.

Financial workshops

By far, the most frequently recommended course of action by community participants was to hold specially tailored financial workshops for Survivors. These can be stand-alone sessions or part of the general meetings previously recommended. As discussed earlier, consideration should be given to break-out sessions organized along generational or gender lines, among others. As for the content of these financial management and protection workshops, participants put forth a wide range of items:

✓ commercial banking	✓ savings/chequing accounts
✓ budgeting	✓ investment banking
✓ retirement funds	✓ pension plans
✓ education funds	✓ trust funds
✓ wills and estates	✓ protection against loan sharks
✓ choosing reliable financial advisors and advocates	

Workshop leaders must be careful to use accessible language and concepts aimed at an entry-level understanding. Some research beforehand to assess people's actual awareness levels around money matters is key. At the beginning stage, simply de-mystifying financial services and institutions would go a long way to alleviating Survivor confusion and anxiety. Freed of intimidation, they will be in a much better position to begin to address the business of making concrete financial plans.

Accordingly, the first intervention may be as straightforward as asking Survivors what their current plans are for their money. Ideally, this is a conversation that would be encouraged by and among multiple Survivors themselves; for anyone else to ask might arouse suspicion. As for the ideal people to deliver such financial education, preference was voiced in favour of Aboriginal entities such as Peace Hills Trust.

Some suggest these workshops be designed, where applicable, for delivery through local radio stations and newspapers, which offers an easy, economical way to reach across a wide area all at once. The AHF was also encouraged to consider making budgeting workshops for clients a mandatory component of any future project it funds.

Given the advanced age of many Survivors, it is not surprising that the fate of their money after they pass away was raised on a number of occasions, and the need for education on wills and estates was urged: "I hear that if there is no will, INAC gets all the funds. I'm thinking of my kids: I don't want to leave them with nothing if I die or any funeral costs beyond what Indian Affairs covers."

It was reported that some find the topic taboo and unsettling, it was felt that making plans now gives people a say in what happens. On a somewhat related front, there were questions about the potential fate of monies owed to former students who had received the advance payment but have since died; it was felt that the remainder of the LSP should go to their surviving family members.

Financial and business support services

Beyond educational measures, many Survivors will likely want to go beyond theory into practice and open various banking accounts and/or invest. To this end, communities should strive to create or invite appropriate support services from the financial sector. Care must be taken to scrutinize the track record of would-be advisors, especially of their dealings with Aboriginal clientele. Aspiring entrepreneurs require their own specialized resource people, and here too reputable consultants should be sought.

There was one strong note of dissension as far as involving banks, which were seen to be a cynical partner in LSP assistance: "In 2000, we approached banks to get loans for Survivors, and advice to invest—nothing. Now that there's money, we're a focus of their attention."

Emotional dimension attached to money

The phrase "financial counselling" came up often, and its multiple meanings and implications are apt here. As mentioned earlier, money can indirectly tap into potent emotional issues, thereby triggering anxiety or worse. Therefore, individuals hired to help with Survivors' finances should be prepared and trained to expect and work with these extra-monetary concerns as they arise:

> The band has to hire a professional person to do financial planning for us. They cannot be dependent on substance abuse. These professional people have to speak the language, know about flashbacks, and understand the vulnerability of Survivors. These persons have to know how to talk to alcoholics.

The goal, to quote one participant, is to empower LSP recipients: "I've got to manage money and not have it manage me." The emotional and psychological dimensions to money, such as the overriding concern of some Survivors as to where the money came from and whether they are deserving of it, must be built into any planned workshop. Thought must be given as to how a sense of ownership and legitimacy can be attached to this money in the minds of Survivors who might carry the burden of a "poverty consciousness."

Approached correctly with the appropriate supports, some felt that the nurturing of personal responsibility for one's money by Survivors could be actively linked to taking responsibility over one's life in general. Thus, money management becomes a catalyst for overall growth and health. *Money as crisis* versus *money as opportunity* are two very different starting positions, and some believe that choosing to emphasize the latter inspires communities to view Survivors as active participants who bear responsibility for their own healing and well-being. Consistent with the ultimate goal of moving away from dependency, this approach embodies the ideal of personal economic self-determination:

> We cannot simply hand over our money to the Northern stores, airlines, liquor stores, banks, and casinos. We're the generation that is saying, 'I'm not financially aware now.' We're smart enough to have the patience to build up our money. We're fed up with instant gratification. We can start practicing patience. We can set our own boundaries.

No longer willing to tolerate others' control over their lives, some elders are clearly exercising their prerogative to be in charge of what happens with their money. In fact, some Survivors have already initiated investments, often with the support and help of family members. Such examples ought to be recognized and promoted to their peers.

Investment pools or funds

Many participants lamented on the lack of a mandatory installment method for paying out LSPs, whereby recipients would obtain compensation only through smaller, monthly increments. Survivors would then potentially make better use of the money over time and be less subject to abuse. However, the majority who raised the idea also saw its inherently paternalistic and patronizing assumptions about Survivors. As a result, only a few imagined that LSP recipients would accept it.

Communities can encourage and help Survivors to set up the necessary services for themselves through a variety of investment vehicles. One LSP investment proposal envisioned recipients pooling a pre-set portion (the suggestion was 2%) of their payments into a collective Survivors' investment or savings fund. A steady income could then be derived through regular dividends or interest payments paid out over time.

RECOMMENDATIONS
Reframe Health | Link health to wealth

10. Support Survivors who are interested in entrepreneurship and in saving, investing, and pooling lump sum payments through timely and accessible counselling and training. Financial institutions including banks and financial advisors, governments at all levels, businesses, entrepreneurs, Survivor groups, Aboriginal and non-Aboriginal non-governmental organizations, interpreters, and health professionals could team up to provide training and counselling to Survivors as they work toward their economic aspirations.

11. Hold inclusive training workshops for Survivors and their families on topics of interest like wills and estates, pension plans, trust funds, and protection against loan sharks by providing breakout sessions based on age, literacy levels, sex, and level of risk and by using plain language, non-intimidating settings, and sensitive approaches. Governments at all levels, mental health counsellors, financial advisors, Survivor groups, interpreters, government departments, post-secondary institutions, Aboriginal and non-Aboriginal non-governmental organizations can convene in community halls, schools, elders' lodges, and in homes to conduct training workshops.

12. Promote socio-economic development as a key determinant of health by defining health as a resource in health promotion messages to Survivors, families, and communities and by promoting employment and education opportunities for Survivors, families, and communities especially those who live in remote, northern, and hard-to-reach urban areas. Governments at all levels, government departments, community leaders, women's groups, Survivor groups, youth groups, Aboriginal and non-Aboriginal non-governmental organizations, the high-tech industry, and economists could serve to meet these needs.

Strategic Goal: Reinforce Safety and Security

Costs associated with LSPs can quickly outweigh the benefits unless strategies are put into place to avoid the myriad of problems that can fall out from LSPs, including social and emotional upheaval. For some participants, being able to call on the traditional authority exercised by certain family members does not suffice when LSPs cause multiple and overwhelming problems. Policing remedies and emergency protection represent important ways of reinforcing safety and security, especially for elders who do not generally enjoy the same rights and health as other community members. It is the creation of strong community networks with RCMP involvement that casts the widest safety net.

STRATEGIC INTERVENTION TO REINFORCE SAFETY AND SECURITY:
Mediate the risks for the most vulnerable

RCMP

Residential school experiences often manifest themselves in violent behaviours, assaults, major driving offences, and high imprisonment rates that are strongly related to anger management difficulties, alcohol abuse, and a deep resentment toward authority figures such as police (Corrado and Cohen, 2003). This observation resonates with participants who also worry about problems that lump sum payments can generate like domestic violence, theft, harassment, and elder abuse and the role the RCMP can play. The RCMP officers who were interviewed noted on how they "can be of support to a certain degree only. We can only intervene when crimes are about to be committed." While the RCMP saw community ownership and leadership with the LSP issue as markers for success, they also subscribed strongly to inter-agency collaboration and building on community structures and processes already in place. As one participant recommended, "Educating RCMP and our social workers, these are two front-line groups people usually call for help, including churches." Like many other participants, RCMP members expressed a particular interest in the welfare of elders. One participant wanted special attention to be paid to the Survivors who choose to opt out of the settlement package.

Real and perceived capacity of elders

Elders possess many gifts gained from performing multiple cultural roles for communities over many years. As oral historians, teachers, ecologists, healers, and cultural workers they stress the integrity of traditions where the good of individuals and communities are virtually identical, and no rights or power are intrinsically superior. Nonetheless, they are now caught in the web of families and communities that have become increasingly complex, hierarchical, socially, and economically stratified, a phenomenon participants lamented repeatedly for everyone's sake, but most of all for elders.

With the advent of a new and major wave of LSPs, a special campaign should be launched to underscore the elders' vulnerability and to recommend how best to protect them as beloved and respected community resources while safeguarding their payments. RCMP members also suggested safeguards for elders receiving LSPs: "Potential elder abusers have to be educated. Some individuals are elderly and frail, and money should go to them or their caregivers."

Resources describing the unique contributions of elders have been developed before, but information should now sensitize families, communities, governments, and funding bodies to the needs and realities of elders in the context of compensation payments. Specifically, elders should continue to be given the prominent role of sharing traditional values, beliefs, practices, and rituals. A code of ethics should be established for those who work with elders, and steps should be taken to ensure that language interpretation is available to them.

Dedicated elder resources

Elders face the unique pressure of being held in high esteem because they are close to the spirit world and are seen to have a vital identification with community people. They demonstrate how individuals can become personally involved and morally committed to inward and outward balance through natural and supernatural laws. They also do household work, provide child care, shore up family operations, create art, and direct the affairs of their community. They possess survival genius because they have done battle with many forms of oppression and have attained a remarkable place in producing, translating, and sharing what they know.

Still, the spectre of elder abuse prompted an RCMP member to suggest "kids and elders need special protection," and added how important it is to allocate some LSPs to the well-being of elders. "There's such a need for extended care for elders here, why not put some of the money into this?" In order to provide elders resources like shelter and respite care, steps have to be taken to give them the first opportunity to engage in this process.

Elders' teachings on relationship between money and productivity

It is normal for families and communities to expect material and moral support from elders, which means the ripple effects of LSPs can be powerful. Elders carry the weight of intergenerational grief experienced in residential schools along with other forms of oppression; partly because of this, they often rest their faith in others for safety and security. Accordingly, an RCMP member proposed warning elders about fraudulent activities: "We can be part of remedial efforts and potential abuses like telephone frauds. Once the money is there, elders will be targets and they need to be made aware of dangers and breaches of how and what their recourses are at that point." Another pushed for outreach efforts: "There's going to be a financial commitment to communications information sessions. A budget has to be identified for transportation. Elders will have trouble getting there. Home visits may have to happen."

Intergenerational impacts

Typically, the lives of Survivors "affect the whole family," as the lingering effects of prior trauma suffered at residential school are directly or indirectly transmitted to the next generation. On more than one occasion, participants noted the frustration and anger of younger generations mistreated by parents who went through the schools. These young people were often left wondering, "Where is our money?" Expanding on how one views the impacts of residential schools necessarily requires an expansion in the nature of the response. Current interventions seem to rarely take these cyclical effects into account. Some participants were keen to recommend any intervention to factor in these intergenerational impacts. After all, as one LSP recipient put it, since "they will be taking care of us soon, we have got to take care of them now."

Refuge from harm

At some point, communities may only be able to do so much to intervene directly in situations where an LSP encourages to foster negative dynamics between family members. Recognizing these limitations, a few participants offered two options that take a more pragmatic, 'harm-reduction' approach to Survivors and youth at risk. In the former case, an idea was floated to essentially have elders be away on vacation at the same time the LSP cheques are due to arrive. Some communities already offer annual elders' excursions, often taking them on extended holidays. The net effect is to distance Survivors from any potential threats sparked by the LSPs' initial arrival. In the same vein, a 24-hour community safe house can be provided for youth and anyone else exposed to danger in the wake of the LSPs. If, as some suggest, a certain degree of bingeing is inevitable, young people, including children, could be offered a temporary, secure place in the interim. As well, a toll-free hotline should be put into place for youth, with care and attention paid to customizing its features, for example, using operators closer in age to potential callers would offer a peer-to-peer approach. This hotline could be supplemented with an online chat room as part of a special 'LSP-for-youth' website.

Bank cards, group purchases, and discount plans

One simple yet strikingly effective proposal to stop (or at least discourage) others taking advantage of elders focuses on bank cards, a.k.a. ATM cards. Seen as all too easy to abuse once the secret PIN code is inappropriately obtained or, more likely, voluntarily shared by "too trusting" elders, this threat can be quickly and easily removed either by choosing not to get a card in the first place or by destroying any and all existing cards. Pressure from relatives to get these cards is a factor that likely needs to be incorporated into family-oriented workshops.

Banks also bear a role and responsibility here, and staff should be trained and prepared. Without ATM cards, Survivors must physically go to the bank in person. Bank employees thus need to know how to spot and deal with the potential abuse of their clients in such situations. On one reported occasion, a bank manager made what he called the "risky" decision to not give money to an inebriated client. Prior arrangements may have to be made in anticipation of such circumstances.

For those Survivors who intend to spend their money on consumer goods such as furniture or on big-ticket items like vehicles, help can be provided through group purchases. As an example, one community has helped its elders replace old stoves, fridges, and couches through its "appliance program." Another variation suggested was to simply offer a discount with no card involved at the local gas station to people 65 years and older once LSPs were issued.

RECOMMENDATIONS
Reinforce Safety and Security | Mediate the risks for the most vulnerable

13. Adopt innovative and anticipatory measures to safeguard the well-being of at-risk groups by laying out banking and purchasing options for elders, women, youth, street people, and the infirm to avoid scams and frauds and by providing them with temporary refuge from harm, if necessary, along with children and those who opt out of the settlement agreement. Elder abuse, in all its manifestations, will have to be addressed on a priority basis when LSPs arrive. The RCMP will play a critical role in ensuring the safety and security of elders and others, together with their community networks of community leaders, lawyers, health professionals, front-line workers, and government departments, financial institutions, elder coordinators, and Survivor, elders, women, and youth groups.

14. Support the development of disability and injury prevention and awareness initiatives in communities in light of LSPs by recognizing the risk pile-up from drug and alcohol abuse, gambling, domestic

violence, motor vehicle accidents, suicides, homicides, child abuse, elder abuse, drownings, and gang violence. Replicating best practices for preventing injuries and disability when LSPs are paid will be as important as identifying the myriad of problems a sudden influx of money can cause. In partnership with community leaders, governments at all levels, government departments, front-line workers, health professionals, youth, elders, women, and Survivor groups, and the RCMP can help to raise awareness about disability and injury prevention through existing community-based programs.

STRATEGIC INTERVENTION TO REINFORCE SAFETY AND SECURITY:
Use the media to best advantage

Media campaigns

Sharing stories that depict an alternative future, or perhaps an alternative present, could matter a great deal to Survivors and conceivably help lead them to better outcomes when LSPs are paid. The ideal is a multi-media public service advertising (PSA) awareness campaign delivered at the national, regional, and community levels that would facilitate discussion on topics like the potential risks of elder abuse as a result of LSPs. The aim is to get people talking and thinking about how and why such abuse can occur, and what can be done to prevent it. Natural outlets for such public dialogue could be talk shows on radio and television, websites that allow for online discussion forums and/or opinion pieces, and newspaper 'Op/ Ed' sections. Aboriginal media will merit special attention, and an opportunity exists to work with them collectively through various Aboriginal media associations in designing and delivering PSA campaigns.

Fraud awareness

According to participants, any LSP education and awareness campaign ought to include a focus on how to recognize and avoid various forms and sources of fraud, including but not limited to:

✓ telephone solicitation	✓ credit card offers
✓ payday loan/cash advance high-interest rate outlets	✓ individual "loan sharks"
	✓ religious fundraisers
✓ pyramid schemes	✓ rent-to-own/layaway outfits
✓ new and used auto dealerships	✓ salespeople in general (e.g., furniture and appliance stores)

Recipients should also have access to information on what recourse is available should fraud happen to occur. Some participants suggested that communities might act to pre-empt fraud through restricting or monitoring access to any salespeople, working in tandem with police forces; for example, requiring visitors to report to the chief and council office when they first arrive. It was also recognized that sometimes it is fellow community members who are the perpetrators of such scams.

Target groups and direct messages

Any campaign hoping to win the favour and buy-in of LSP recipients is counterproductive if Survivors perceive a lack of confidence in their abilities. The starting point for any and all media campaigns must therefore be messages for Survivor empowerment, respect, and recognition. The following examples of PSA announcer copy give an idea of the messages that might be used:

> "It's your money. It's your right to choose how you spend it."

> "No one should tell you how to spend your money."

> "This is your money, no one should tell you what to do with it."

> "If you feel someone is trying to get at your money, there is help ..."

> "If you're feeling pressured, and want help, call this number ..."

> "If you want to learn more about how to make your settlement money last ..."

Offering self-initiated, positive, active options will directly address and speak to Survivors, and the aim is to always affirm and respect the right of Survivors to make the ultimate choice on how to utilize their LSPs. To do otherwise arouses suspicion that Survivors are being told what to do, a hangover from residential schools.

For many Survivors, the opportunity to invest some of their LSP in the well-being of their youngest family members is inherently attractive, and media campaigns should be specifically designed to appeal to and encourage this. One participant went so far as to suggest that Survivors who have children to think of are the most likely to consider spending their LSPs constructively, and should thus be the top priority for targeted messaging and programming. Campaigns must essentially deliver in a dozen different ways this message to Survivors: "Think of their future. Think of the next generation." This could be a tough sell according to research participants, who claim many Survivors live only for the moment.

RECOMMENDATIONS
Reinforce Safety and Security | Use the media to best advantage

15. Launch public service advertising campaigns through a variety of media outlets to promote the positive impact of lump sum payments and to decrease the negative effects, while depicting an alternative future for Survivors and creating opportunities for dialogue on issues like elder abuse. Aboriginal languages should be used where desirable and feasible. Aboriginal media is well positioned to lead these campaigns and to tailor them for specific audiences in collaboration with federal, provincial/territorial, and local governments, government departments, interpreters, elders, youth, and Survivor groups, the high-tech industry, Internet users, social marketers, and Aboriginal and non-Aboriginal media personalities.

16. Design media campaigns for minimizing frauds and scams, whether these come from inside or outside the communities, and use Aboriginal languages wherever possible. To deal with the home-grown variety, local media specialists and outlets will have to work with community leaders, interpreters, youth, Survivor groups, formal and informal law enforcement officers, mental health and addictions counsellors, and

government departments. Outside scams and frauds can be more sophisticated and destructive, therefore, the RCMP and lawyers will need to work alongside the aforementioned parties so that appropriate messages are sent out.

17. Develop media messages to educate children and youth about the legacy of residential schools and lump sum payments by identifying popular and relevant sources of information including the Internet, graphic novels, and music, and by using Aboriginal languages as much as possible. Survivor groups, local media specialists and outlets, community leaders, elders, teachers, youth groups, government departments, and the Aboriginal Healing Foundation will be needed to do this important work.

Strategic Goal: Reverse Crises

According to what some participants said, communities will have to consider the impact of LSPs seriously enough to assess their vulnerability and move into crisis management mode. Crisis response plans and protocols will determine their level of preparedness, and will have to employ the skills and resources that are available in the community. To intervene as effectively as possible concerning LSPs, prevention, planning, and preparation will have to occur simultaneously.

Communities will have to adjust to doing things in a short period of time before, during, and after the arrival of LSPs with new or renewed skills in crisis management, and will have to apply these and other preventative and preparatory approaches against a whole host of challenges. Reversing crises involves preventing and managing challenges that might otherwise overwhelm communities. A participant raised the spectre of crisis as follows: "Nobody committed suicide before lump sum payments, but afterwards when people did not get services suicides rose, substance abuse rose, family violence rose. More negative stories ensued than success stories."

> ### STRATEGIC INTERVENTION TO REVERSE CRISES:
> Focus on community crisis management

Business plans

Business-like approaches dictate strict mandates and elements for investment. Speaking more generally, participants repeatedly called for similar approaches. "Organizations cannot abuse their power and be trustworthy. Networking is important. Trust is important." In order to work then, crisis responses must be developed in an informed way (Lane et al., 2002), and exchanged through community networks. In addition, community-driven resources along with culturally appropriate tools have to be developed and implemented. A few participants called for mobile crisis units to deal with the potential fallout from LSPs. Communities need to pay attention to the prevalence and effectiveness of mobile crisis services (Geller, Fisher, and McDermitt, 1995), examine and measure the strengths and weaknesses of previous crisis responses, and extract the lessons learned once actual crises have passed.

Timing critical

"Start now, we know the cheques are coming," stressed one participant. With each passing day, awareness of the LSPs has only grown in Aboriginal communities. "Time is so short. We have to make people realize their responsibility, take charge of their lives, and help them make good use of their lump sum payment."

For some, the possibility of a negative fallout from millions of dollars potentially flowing into their communities means that it is most urgent to prepare people for the payments before they arrive. It is too little, too late by the time the money comes, and prevention is everything.

When it comes to who is planning what, one participant conveyed this reality: "Drug dealers, loan sharks, and the banks are all getting ready for the compensation money, but we're not getting ready for receiving our payments." Simply put, the time to take action and "set up an infrastructure" regarding LSPs is now. In the words of one participant, "You can create facilities, but it's up to individuals to utilize them." Although the outright elimination of elder abuse is a laudable goal, it may not be possible in most communities. The question therefore becomes whether a community should frame and commit its anti-abuse efforts to a 100 per cent success rate—the "zero-tolerance" approach—or if it should simply try to do its best to reduce the amount of harm inflicted and suffered. By conceptualizing the situation in more harm-reduction terms, communities will be much less pre-occupied with stopping abuse where it is clearly unstoppable and focus on offering timely information and support once the harm takes place. Choosing interventions with greater potential to make a difference is key.

Vulnerability and accountability

Crises can change communities by increasing their vulnerability (Corrado and Cohen, 2003), a situation ripe for increased monitoring and surveillance and improved accountability. Accountability is powerful and complex because it is shaped by increased expectations, risk management, and liability. "Have leadership and politicians be more involved and sharing some of their concerns as to how well or not these [LSPs] have gone. They'll have to balance people's personal rights and their wellness. I'd like to see someone step up." Leaders may be too removed to avoid political disenchantment: "I'm not sure if our leaders should be involved with [LSPs] because it would become a competition and they would lose sight of why they were doing it. The people would pay the price." To respond to such a strong lobby, crisis management frameworks will have to be developed by the leadership through dialogue, clear dollar commitments, choices and avenues for recourse, and careful planning and analysis. In the process, leaders will have to respect current federal, provincial, and territorial mandates in crisis management.

Information and communities

Participants felt that they have not been kept properly informed about LSPs, the latest proposed settlement in particular. Absent of this full information, Survivors have called for a meeting sponsored by the parties involved in the negotiation of the *Indian Residential Schools Settlement Agreement*. Details are sought on the proposed independent assessment process and its administration costs ("1,200 jobs is what we're hearing"). The AHF has also been asked to come before community people to explain its new proposed role and what it intends to do with the 125 million dollars that has been set aside for healing. "[AHF] told us there is no money for residential school Survivors, and now they're trying to get involved," said one participant, who called on the AHF to work with Survivors and set up a national LSP strategy, and to establish what is actually going on, "before people go too far and spin their wheels." Participants requested that they be sent all the information gathered in this report.

Education sessions for communities

For most small communities, making the most of limited resources is not only a virtue, it is a necessity. One tried-and-true way to reach the most people in the shortest period of time is to convene a general meeting. According to participants, while the format for a community-wide conversation about LSPs is up to each community, they should begin as soon as possible. Leading the way should be the local public sector in every branch and every department. One advantage of getting band government employees onside early is that most possess familial ties to a good part of the community. Inter-family tension, to the extent it may exist, can thus be somewhat mitigated. As one employee put it, "The fact that we on staff work across the family divide is key to building trust with community members." According to participants, these meetings should:

+ offer information detailing what help is available, both inside communities and outside;

+ allow people the opportunity to identify LSP issues, concerns, and questions;

+ share stories of "the good and the bad" of LSPs from previous recipients; and

+ raise people's awareness about LSPs in order to "de-stigmatize" the process.

Then there is the need to inform the community about elder abuse. Through a frank yet considerate discussion, the general meeting can engage what LSPs can sometimes do to families:

> Elders could benefit by exposure to information prior to the money's arrival about how their families may react to the payments, and what their specific options are to protect themselves and their money in the event of unhealthy and disrespectful behaviour. We want to have workshops for elders to warn them of potential abuse.

RECOMMENDATIONS
Reverse Crises | Focus on community crisis management

18. Develop crisis response plans, protocols, and practices immediately by setting up meetings, assessing community vulnerability, securing funds, identifying choices and avenues for action, and becoming familiar with existing federal and provincial/territorial mandates in crisis management. Local crisis management initiatives will have to be led by community leaders with support from other governments, Survivor groups, government departments, the RCMP, teachers, front-line workers, health professionals, and Aboriginal and non-Aboriginal non-governmental organizations with expertise.

19. Develop a communication plan for disseminating the Aboriginal Healing Foundation's national lump sum payment strategy as a way of sharing the communities' past, present, and future strategies for dealing with lump sum payments and of highlighting the communities' evolving position on the legacy of residential schools and healing. In partnership with government departments, national Aboriginal organizations, media specialists and outlets, and Survivor groups, the Aboriginal Healing Foundation will take the lead so that this report is distributed in a timely and sensitive fashion.

20. Fund education sessions specifically for Survivors, families, and communities about the truth and reconciliation process to help them understand its purpose, objectives, structure, composition, powers, parameters, and resources, and how it can make a difference in their healing journey beyond lump sum payments. The Aboriginal Healing Foundation and other national Aboriginal organizations, Survivor groups and champions, churches, all levels of governments, and government departments will have to collaborate on this process.

> **STRATEGIC INTERVENTION TO REVERSE CRISES:**
> Understand Survivors' crushing burden of decision-making

Trusted advisors and advocates

A toll-free number that Survivors could call any time of day with virtually any question about LSPs came up more than once among participants. But they also saw it as offering more than just information, and suggesting it could provide quick access to counselling as well. Overall, it could serve as a resource referral service for financial counselling/advisory, and not simply just for health. Participants repeatedly voiced the belief that a cohesive team approach is the best, most effective form of Survivor advocacy:

> Capitalize on the community's natural response to help one another. When a crisis hits at home, everyone pulls together. We need an emergency-response-plan-like initiative. We need a professional team of financial planners, therapists, addictions workers, etcetera, and we have to work fast and have a team in each province.

Two kinds of teams or cohorts were proposed by participants: a panel of trustees and an inter-agency committee. In the case of the latter, a number of people envisioned "cohesive, interdisciplinary approaches [to] the whole issue of lump sum payments. The mentality is here, we just need the opportunity." One said to "make sure there are services for disabled" participants. In another community,

> the inter-agency committee includes the RCMP, band council, alcohol and drug program workers, residential school workers, the local Roman Catholic Church and its workers, health and social services, school staff, and land corporation staff. We have to press this committee into action.

Other potential sources of expertise for such committees include nurses, trauma counsellors, sports and recreation people out on the land, banks, interpreters, translators, trappers, hunters, fishermen, drummers, dancers, musicians, and last, but by no means least, elders. Lawyers are potentially valuable assets as well, and some felt they not only had a special technical role to play in obtaining an LSP but a moral duty to their clients, many of whom confront poor living conditions every day. Legal advocates are seen to be in a privileged position to advise recipients on how to go about handling and understanding large lump sum payments. Special effort should be made to include youth and a strong degree of female representation on these committees. This team could play a big part in helping to develop an LSP orientation to let front-line workers know what they can expect, and to be potentially adapted for use at various professional development days.

In terms of a panel or group of trustees, one participant suggested that communities consider adopting a public approval process that would screen potential candidates nominated by government and the community at large. Inherent in their title, such advocates need to be someone Survivors can trust. A related concept is guardianship, where individuals who literally are unable to make a decision on their own to have someone officially appointed as their legal guardian. At least one community has explored this option.

Not every community can single-handedly afford the time or resources to mount these kinds of efforts, which is why an inter-community or regional approach often makes the most financial and logistical sense:

> We have to have a centralized team that is ready to travel across the country. We have to think about isolated communities. We'll need to partner up with others. I'm in [a very remote northern community], so I'll need a partner at the national level.

Survivors' sense of options

Many participants believed that maximizing Survivors' sense of choice about their LSPs is vital. "In the end it is going to be up to each individual to manage their money, but they'll need information and ideas." Something as simple as a printout of names and places to go for help would be a good start, some remarked. This list would be ideally handed out at "an information meeting that provides and explains the services out there" in areas like finances, spirituality, and culture. One person voiced a desire for employment agencies, "because we need jobs along with the payments." As well, many participants eagerly anticipate the information and recommendations that will ultimately come out of this report. A few delivered admonitions to the effect that this report must lead to something being done. Feeling 'surveyed to death,' Survivors "want feedback, and don't want to be left up in the air" yet again.

Greater opportunities to make more informed decisions effectively leads to greater independence for Survivors. To that end, it should be constantly affirmed that the ultimate choice is theirs to make. As part of this process, some participants felt that Survivors need to be reminded that, while looking out for loved ones is obviously important, it should be just as obvious of how essential it is that they look after their own needs too: "I'd tell people to find yourself. Understand what you're getting. Understand what you can do for you and your children. You can do something that works for you. Don't try to please everyone else first."

For some Survivors, the living legacy of residential school is a persistent and pernicious self-effacement and self-erasure. Seen in this context, messages of self-care and responsibility for one's own well-being may be fundamentally important. Some participants championed any form of individual healing that would serve to shore up Survivors' sense of "personal boundaries, so they can say 'no' to family members," and thus avoid becoming potential "enablers."

Fraud and scams awareness

Some participants were well aware that LSPs make Survivors highly attractive targets for scams and frauds. With a community's borders offering little to no protection, an effective way to stop most fraud is to increase the awareness and cautiousness of LSP recipients. This can take the form of straightforward advice: "Do not broadcast that you're getting money within a certain time, keep this information to yourself." In other cases, help may consist of urging Survivors to always consult a second opinion before agreeing to any purchase.

When buying a car, "Talk to a mechanic [first]. Draw on resource people like that who at least will help you buy a good car, and give you different answers." It was also suggested that someone inside each community be assigned to identify and know the operating methods of each and every scam artist in the surrounding area. One participant expressed concern over a neighbouring casino's effects on Survivors, who may be just as apt to surrender their LSP to a slot machine as they would any fraud.

Survivors' stake in care

"Survivors should be helping Survivors," was a recurring theme among participants. They believe Survivor care rests on the skills training of fellow Survivors, who should design and deliver services and programs at every level. Claiming that there is a lack of in-patient trauma centres, some believe that a dedicated facility for Survivor treatment is in order. To help make it economical, it was suggested that communities could band together to fund the creation and use of one centrally located centre for a region. One participant felt that adapting the innovative insights of post-traumatic stress disorder clinicians to the situation of Survivors has not been taken seriously enough, and a critical opportunity has been lost in the process.

No one knows a Survivor better than other Survivors, and local societies and groups across the country have been at the forefront of residential school student advocacy. Yet, despite widespread recognition that they should be at the heart and soul of healing efforts, many local Survivor organizations seem to constantly contend with funding issues. Consistently, participants urged interventions that draw on and bolster Survivor-led initiatives. Some went so far as to demand that the $125 million earmarked for the AHF to "go straight to Survivors." They also called for Assembly of First Nations National Chief Phil Fontaine to meet directly with Survivors on the ground for a "better sense of reality."

More specifically, participants thought it would be useful to gather together elders taken advantage of by their children with previous LSPs "so they can share their experiences." Such testimony can serve as cautionary words warning "future recipients what a payment can do to you unless you're ready." Such peer-based assistance may be especially effective when it is one-on-one.

RECOMMENDATIONS
Reverse Crises | Understand Survivors' crushing burden of decision-making

21. Establish mechanisms for Survivors to draw on given that lump sum payments may be a new arena of struggle for them by setting up talking circles, teams of advocates and advisors, networks between communities, information booths, and treatment programs and centres specifically for Survivors. All levels of governments, government departments, churches, Survivor groups, lawyers, front-line workers, and elders will be needed to move this agenda forward.

22. Provide early and continuous learning experiences for Survivors on the fundamentals of negotiation skills, problem solving, and anger management by emphasizing real life examples (e.g., homelessness, food insecurity, frauds, and scams), considering oral traditions, and encouraging positive lifestyle choices and behaviours. Survivor groups, elders, mental health and addictions counsellors/therapists, government departments, local governments, life skills trainers, educators, and Aboriginal and non-Aboriginal non-governmental organizations will be needed to help Survivors make the best everyday decisions about lump sum payments.

Strategic Goal: Realign Capacity

While relative success has been achieved in promoting capacity building at certain tables, participants remained concerned about the level of disruption LSPs will cause to service provision in communities. To drive this point home, they drew attention to trust issues, lack of outreach initiatives, the failure to pool resources, and the sheer volume of anticipated cases. However, they also provided insights into local skills and knowledge, and how these might be realigned to support the overall LSP strategy. Paid and unpaid human resources, culturally competent workers, and virtual linkages will help communities stay on top of capacity building when LSPs are distributed across the country, and this will be made possible by rethinking, repackaging, and redistributing community skills and knowledge. LSPs have the potential to bring about acute forces of change for communities, and at this extraordinary time they have to continue providing quality and accessible services in collaborative, low-cost ways.

> **STRATEGIC INTERVENTION TO REALIGN CAPACITY:**
> Build on existing alliances and partnerships

Virtual communities

Very few participants spoke directly about using technology to deal with LSPs. Still, their persistent message was that almost every facet of community life is governed by the ideals of connection and communication. The Internet has spawned an information age, producing not only modern forms of connectedness and a more informed public, but rapidly changing public services. It is also a buttress for hard-to-reach communities and a medium for discussing controversial subjects like the residential school legacy. Digital opportunity overtakes digital divide when sustainable capacity is built, and re-envisioning information as a public resource so that service delivery is improved and citizen engagement is increased (Crossing Boundaries National Council and KTA Center for Collaborative Government, 2006). Information and communication technology will allow communities to network and share success stories about LSPs. It holds tremendous promise when there is agreement about its significant potential to decrease social disparities, improve Aboriginal and non-Aboriginal relationships, and promote economic development in remote communities (Donna Cona, 2002).

Conceiving capacity from the ground up

Front-line workers who participated in the survey reported that they were subjected to steep learning curves when the residential school file was added to their workload or they were newly recruited to positions involving LSPs. In these kinds of situations, their capacity would flow from taking advantage of other's experiences, exchanging information, sharing activities, imitating successes, and targeting recruitment: "We need more than one therapist in the community, someone with the same background who's had our experience with violence." From one participant's perspective, traditional and local knowledge are critical elements for capacity building:

> The system degrades traditional knowledge in communities. Service providers have to readopt these in their front-line work and be a part of their job descriptions. Support front-

line workers through funds that are needed. Do away with selection criteria like, you have to have an M.A., especially since community people have the knowledge and skills required to work in communities. Do away with certain phrases the system uses sometimes: "it is my way or the highway."

From what was heard during the interviews, partnerships also promote capacity building even though not all potential partners come to the table with money, and building relationships is often time-consuming, costly, uneven, and political. High-caliber, committed volunteers have assisted in achieving significant program objectives while champions, including government employees, have helped to promote initiatives chosen by communities. Therefore, capacity has to be homegrown and spread out among informal and formal networks to prevent burnout and maintain good service levels when compensation payments are made.

Human resources and supports

Suggested advisors for LSP recipients came in a number of forms. For some, employees in local government can offer a great deal of support. Among the more notable are elders' workers, whose coordination of people's meals, fitness, transportation, and activities inside and outside the community make them well-positioned to help LSP recipients.

One participant told the story of becoming a Survivors' trustee. Although she had never sought out the role, her name was put forward by people in the community, who felt her experience as a fellow Survivor, along with her connections, made her well-qualified. To anyone who contemplates taking on such a role, she offered this advice:

> Everybody's related, so it's challenging. Pick someone everyone can go to. I did it as a volunteer. I'd go to people's houses at night, I'd travel all over, [even places] really hard to get to. You need someone who knows the area. Keep politics out of it, political neutrality is key. My priority was not taking advantage of people. I'd take them to the bank and sit with them, as they were intimidated to be there.

In her case, the trustee, with confidence, could refer Survivors to some financial professionals she knew. Combined with her credibility as a Survivor, her network enabled her to serve Survivors well, and her story serves as a case study in trusteeship.

Topping many participants' lists of recommended actions, among recipients and non-recipients alike, was the creation of a full-time position specifically for residential school Survivors, and "not a person who's already employed and has a lot [to] do already." Although some communities have created Elder Coordinator positions, each overseeing a host of seniors' needs, from housing to health to pensions, specialized residential school Survivor staff are now needed to focus primarily on issues and impacts extending from the LSP process. Participants in one community had discussed this idea with their local government, but promises to hire someone have gone unfulfilled.

RECOMMENDATIONS
Realign Capacity | Build on existing alliances and partnerships

23. Link communities through the Internet so that they can exchange lessons learned and best practices related to LSPs on macro issues like capacity building, good governance, and community development and micro issues like keeping costs down, reassigning human resources, maintaining safe communities, leveraging economic and healing opportunities, and improving relationships internally and externally. Stakeholders include governments, government departments, Survivor groups and champions, Internet users, the high-tech industry, youth, and front-line workers.

24. Identify and dedicate a community Survivor coordinator who can bring all paid and unpaid partners together on a regular and on an emergency basis to help meet the needs of Survivors, efficiently and effectively, by ensuring smooth and steady information sharing, service provision, and programming. Local governments, government departments, Survivor groups, and front-line workers will be needed to establish this staff position.

> ## STRATEGIC INTERVENTION TO REALIGN CAPACITY:
> ### Work with relevant and ready community supports

Family-oriented involvement

Many Survivors reported turning to family members for assistance with their LSP, and they recommended that all families be explicitly encouraged to be healthy allies to Survivors. Accordingly, some suggest that planning workshops be both "aimed and delivered at the family level," and not just to individual Survivors alone. One participant shared the story of collectively writing out a list of payment options as a family, including extended family members. A constructive, team effort that revealed all the things that could be done with an LSP, this exercise allowed them to literally "see it all on paper." Small in scale and family-controlled, to some, this should be seen as the optimal level of LSP intervention. "You don't need to grow huge."

A number of Survivors who had children and grandchildren spoke of the way they factored in their descendants' future well-being into the LSP decision-making process: "I'm thinking ahead for my grandchildren. My incentive was to have something for them. I did not do this because I observed others' misspending."

Group discussions

Though raising such matters may prove challenging, participants did put forth ideas on how to ensure all voices are heard and respected. Given that Survivors' experiences at residential school have effectively left them with a set of interests and needs separate and apart from others in their family and the community, some participants strongly believed that certain portions of any community LSP gathering need to be reserved for "meetings set up by age or gender." Advocates of these temporary breakout sessions felt that it is safer this way because it permits Survivors of the same generation or the same gender the opportunity to voice their opinions within a protected and privileged space. As one female participant noted, "We women protested this payment process. We told them you're dealing with a whole different group. Women are thinking things through logically, despite the phobias we picked up in residential school." However, another voice urged communities to stay away from large-scale meetings altogether because of corrosive dynamics between and within families: "There should be no big groups in the community hall. Families will get into conflict. Small groups are better, so people aren't intimidated. It should be based on voluntary association, the people Survivors trust, and not based on family."

Drawing on real-life examples and using actual Survivors as role models or spokespeople are obvious ways to help their fellow recipients literally see and hear how people just like them have come up with healthy ways to spend, save, or invest their LSPs. Participants argued that the best kind of role model would be "someone who went through the same experience as you, but who's already taken steps to healing. Anyone who's done that, who has that experience and knowledge, that's where healing comes from."

Community mobilization

As for the challenge of getting people to the meeting itself, participants said that it begins with letters to everybody and, if possible, food and door prizes should be offered. Access must also be taken into account, with a budget set aside for transportation for elders who would otherwise have trouble getting there. How you promote the meeting requires some care, cautioned one participant. It is vital that Survivors understand that the meeting is not about the disclosure of residential school experiences so as to avoid misunderstandings.

These kinds of meetings are already happening in some cases. Last year, volunteer organizers in one community solicited donations to bring in therapists, lawyers, and the RCMP. Promoted through posters and word-of-mouth, the daylong workshop drew over 200 individuals from inside and outside the community, many of whom had questions on this "hot topic." The people who attended the meeting were of all ages, including teens whose parents went to residential school. Six months in the making, the workshop was popular enough to spark a demand for another. Organizers have also been asked to set up workshops in other areas and help with other LSP-related matters.

RECOMMENDATIONS
Realign Capacity | Work with relevant and ready community supports

25. Deal with lump sum payment issues, concerns, and questions through family dialogue and action, and begin this process at the kitchen table through very practical measures like drawing up and costing workable options, identifying family spokespeople, working with role models, creating caring spaces, and recognizing the limits to family meetings. Survivors, parents, youth, elders, and clans can begin this process in the home or in offices with assistance from advocates and champions, front-line workers, and Survivor groups.

26. Take this opportunity to work with youth on lump sum payment-related projects to promote a sense of self, family, and community, build capacity and confidence, and implement forward-looking strategies in communities. In order to draw on the strengths and support of youth, they will have to be supported by governments, government departments, Survivor groups and champions, parent groups, educators, and Aboriginal and non-Aboriginal non-governmental organizations.

Priority Recommendations

In total, 26 concrete, doable recommendations are included in this report, but six surface as the most salient and urgent. Given the imminent distribution of the next wave of LSPs, the impacts of which may be sudden and of a high magnitude, priority recommendations are needed to offset the worst effects of this powerful force on Survivors, their families, and communities before, during, and after LSPs. These priority recommendations emphasize actions that are best taken in advance of LSPs as well as in tandem. They are proactive and co-active, driven by a common fear and ambivalence of LSPs, and based on a strong sense of mutual duty and obligation to help carve out a healed future even before the LSPs arrive. Though each community is free to rank the 26 recommendations as they choose, this report ranks six on a priority basis according to their corresponding strategic goals and strategic interventions:

Priority Recommendation 1
Reverse Crises | Focus on community crisis management

Develop crisis response plans, protocols, and practices immediately by setting up meetings, assessing community vulnerability, securing funds, identifying choices and avenues for action, and becoming familiar with existing federal and provincial/territorial mandates in crisis management.

Priority Recommendation 2
Reinforce Safety and Security | Use the media to best advantage

Launch public service advertising campaigns through a variety of media outlets to promote the positive impact of lump sum payments and decrease the negative effects, while depicting an alternative future for Survivors and creating opportunities for dialogue on issues like elder abuse. Aboriginal languages should be used where desirable and feasible.

Priority Recommendation 3
Reinforce Safety and Security | Mediate the risks for the most vulnerable

Adopt innovative and anticipatory measures to safeguard the well-being of at-risk groups by laying out banking and purchasing options for elders, women, youth, street people and the infirm to avoid scams and frauds and by providing them with temporary refuge from harm, if necessary, along with children and those who opt out of the settlement agreement.

Priority Recommendation 4
Reframe Health | Link health to wealth

Support Survivors who are interested in entrepreneurship and in saving, investing, and pooling lump sum payments through timely and accessible counselling and training.

Priority Recommendation 5
Realign Capacity | Build on existing alliances and partnerships

Identify and dedicate a community coordinator who can bring all paid and unpaid partners together on a regular and emergency basis to help meet the needs of Survivors, efficiently and effectively, by ensuring smooth and steady information sharing, service provision, and programming.

Priority Recommendation 6
Reform Healing | Elevate Community Healing

Address the call for a formal apology to recognize the legacy of residential schools and its effects on First Nation, Métis, and Inuit communities.

Concluding Remarks

The Lump Sum Compensation Payments Research Project has identified strategic goals and interventions, as well as community recommendations that may be helpful with respect to the imminent mass distribution of LSPs, including CEPs. Addressing the impact of past LSPs on Survivors, families, and communities including the social, economic, political and cultural benefits and costs of such payments, has been an integral part of the Research Project. The main LSPs discussed in this report included those that came from court-based litigation, the government-run ADR process, as well as the more recent payments issued in advance of the CEP under the *Indian Residential Schools Settlement Agreement.*

The task of compiling, summarizing, and analyzing information involved poring over very rich interview notes and making every effort to document the input of survey participants as faithfully as possible. The motivation behind this was to make sure their voices were expressed in research that is essentially groundbreaking. A thorough literature review preceded the key informant survey in this research project, which showed the lack of empirical research on the personal experiences of individuals (Aboriginal or otherwise) who had received either reparation-type or revenue-type monetary payments. Indeed, evidence has shown that there is very little attention to research devoted to the impact and use of LSPs by individual recipients.

Four strategic principles led, in turn, to five broad strategic goals to be promoted, secured, and acted upon at the local level: reform healing, reframe health, reinforce safety and security, reverse crises, and realign capacity. The strategic interventions branched into immediate and long-term solutions that can support and sustain healing through a momentous change. The cross-cutting issues discussed in this report included class differences, age divides, gender inequality, religious influences, geographic location, culture (traditions and modernity), historic trauma, elder abuse, human resources as well as funding and research.

Based on the participation of recipients and non-recipients, recommendations involving the design, construction, and implementation of a comprehensive LSP intervention strategy were developed. This research project underscored the urgency of developing strategies for efficient, culturally appropriate, and accessible supports for Survivors, families, and communities that are undergoing a potentially life-altering experience.

Aboriginal Healing Foundation
Lump Sum Compensation Payments Research Project

Project Background

In 1998, the Government of Canada established a Healing Fund that is administered by the Aboriginal Healing Foundation (AHF). AHF funds community-based, holistic healing projects that address the Legacy of physical and sexual abuse in residential schools. The "Legacy" includes the impacts Survivors, their families, descendents and communities continue to deal with. These effects include but are not limited to: family violence; drug, alcohol, and substance abuse; and loss of parenting and self-destructive behaviour.

The AHF also supports research that promotes and sustains healing and is concerned with effective program design/redesign and the implementation and evaluation of healing projects. It is important to note that the AHF is increasingly emphasizing Survivors' pragmatism, resilience, and coping skills when conducting research projects on the "Legacy" of residential schools. The AHF is also supporting corrective measures of the "Legacy" in collaboration with other Aboriginal organizations and government agencies.

AHF's interest in pursuing research on the experience of receiving lump sum compensation payments stems from the AHF, Health Canada and the RCMP's mutual interest in minimizing the negative impacts on individuals and communities with respect to the compensation packages that are being awarded to residential school Survivors.

On November 20, 2005 an Agreement-in-Principle was reached among several parties: the Federal Representative (the Honourable Frank Iacobucci); legal counsel for former students; legal counsel for the Churches; the Assembly of First Nations and other Aboriginal organizations. Subject to court approval, the Agreement-in-Principle proposes a final settlement package including a "Common Experience Payment" (or lump sum compensation payments) to be paid to every eligible former Indian residential school student. The settlement agreement (Agreement in Principle) contains certain terms and conditions, one of which allows eligible former residential school students who are 65 years of age and older to apply for an advance payment of $8,000 immediately.

The Indian Residential Schools Unit at the Assembly of First Nations (AFN) has taken the lead with respect to the resolution of the *Indian Residential Schools Settlement Agreement*. This agreement compensates for the wrongs of the past, while allowing for future healing and reconciliation.

For its part, the AHF has commissioned this Lump Sum Compensation Payments Research Project which aims to assess the impact that past large sum payments have had on recipients, their families, and communities; and prepare recommendations on strategic directions to address and mitigate potential negative impacts of the Common Experience Payments.

Project Goal

The goal of the Project is to provide information with respect to the impact of large sum payments on individuals, families, and communities to use as the basis for recommendations of strategic interventions that can be helpful to recipients of Common Experience Payments, their families, and communities. This Project will involve on-site visits and interviews with recipients of past residential school-related lump sum payments (litigation or out-of-court settlements) as well as key community stakeholders.

Project Purpose and Objectives

The first phase of the Lump Sum Compensation Payments Research Project involved a systematic review of relevant literature, and it showed that very minimal research has been conducted on reparation/revenue compensations to Aboriginal people and their personal experiences with such payments. This information gap helps to validate the importance of the Lump Sum Compensation Payments Research Project the AHF is conducting.

The purpose of the Lump Sum Compensation Payments Research Project is to gather information related to individual monetary payments that were made in the past in relation to residential school experiences; to gather recipients' and key stakeholders' insights regarding the positive and negative impacts of these lump sum compensation payments; and to assess what would be helpful with respect to the distribution of large sum payments like the Common Experience Payments.

Project Time Frame

On-site interviews will be conducted in communities where individual monetary payments (litigation or out-of-court settlements) have been made to Survivors in the past. These interviews will be conducted in the communities beginning the first week of November 2006 to early January 2007. The final report of the Survey findings will be submitted to the Aboriginal Healing Foundation at the end of January 2007.

Project Researchers

Madeleine Dion Stout and Rick Harp will be working on this Project. Madeleine is a Cree speaker from the Kehewin First Nation in Alberta and is a Survivor. She is a nurse and former professor at Carleton University in Ottawa. Rick is Cree, a writer, and a former host of APTN's National news and the program *Contact*. Rick's mother is a Survivor.

Lump Sum Compensation Payments Research Project:

Literature Review

(Phase One)

Prepared for

the Aboriginal Healing Foundation

by

Madeleine Dion Stout and Nadine Jodoin

May 31, 2006

Table of Contents

Introduction

On 20 November 2005, the federal government announced that an Agreement in Principle had been reached to address the damaging legacy of the Indian residential schools.[1] Parties involved in the Agreement include a federal representative, legal counsel for former students, legal counsel for the churches, the Assembly of First Nations, and other Aboriginal organizations. According to the Agreement in Principle, Survivors of residential schools will be awarded individual compensation packages from an overall amount of well over a billion dollars for the wrongs committed against them.

Central to the Agreement is the concept that every former residential school student (First Nation, Inuit, and Métis) is entitled to monetary compensation for the suffering caused by the loss of family, community, language, and culture regardless of whether or not physical or sexual abuse was suffered. Under the Agreement, each former residential school student will receive a *common experience payment* consisting of two parts: a lump sum payment of $10,000 for the first year of attendance or part thereof, plus an additional $3,000 for each year attended beyond the first year. Eligible former residential school students 65 years of age or older can apply for an advance payment of $8,000. Common experience payments will not be taxable nor will they be deducted from other benefits such as social assistance, welfare, or unemployment. Former students who have settled their claim through litigation or the alternate dispute resolution (ADR) process are still eligible for the common experience payment.[2]

The settlement package, along with the advance of the common experience payment for those over the age of 65, has been approved by Cabinet (May 2006). Approval by provincial superior courts is now needed for the agreement to be finalized. Once the document is approved by the superior courts, and after a 90-day opt-out period, common experience payments will be made to all former students.

According to the Aboriginal Healing Foundation (AHF), approximately 86,000 former residential school students (with an average age of 60) stand to receive an average individual compensation of $28,000. This represents a massive and sudden influx of money into Aboriginal communities across Canada.

Against this context, the AHF has commissioned a project, the *Lump Sum Compensation Payments Research Project*, which aims to: a) assess the impact that past lump sum payments have had on First Nation, Inuit, and Métis recipients as well as on communities both rural and urban; and b) prepare recommendations on strategic directions to address and mitigate the potential negative impacts of the upcoming common experience payments on recipients and communities. This literature review represents the first phase of the *Lump Sum Compensation Payments Research Project*. A second phase will involve on-site visits and interviews with recipients of past residential school-related lump sum payments (litigation or out-of-court settlements) as well as with key community stakeholders. The findings of the literature review will inform the questionnaires that will be developed for the second phase of the project.

---

[1]   The residential school "Legacy" includes the effects Survivors, their families, descendents, and communities continue to deal with. These effects include but are not limited to: family violence; drug, alcohol, and substance abuse; loss of parenting; and self-destructive behaviour.

[2]   In addition to the common experience payment, the Agreement also includes: funds for the Aboriginal Healing Foundation; the future creation of a $60 million truth and reconciliation commission, including the establishment of a national archive and research centre; $20 million for commemorative events; and an independent assessment process, which will be a new method of review and documentation for former students who claim they experienced sexual or physical abuse while at the schools.

Methodology

The purpose of the literature review was to examine key concepts as well as costs and benefits typically associated with large individual monetary payments, both at the level of the recipients and at the level of the communities where these individuals reside. The literature review explored the following questions: What personal benefits and/or costs are experienced by recipients of large monetary payments? How do the recipients of large monetary payments typically spend their money? What benefits and/or costs are felt by the communities where several recipients of large monetary payments reside? How effective are compensation payments as a redress strategy?

Although the original intent was to focus on the impact of past residential school-related compensation payments (through litigation or out-of-court settlements), the lack of literature in this area led to an expansion of the search strategy. As such, the consultants explored the literature on other reparation-type compensation payments (e.g., First Nation veterans, Hong Kong veterans, land claims, Japanese internment, Hepatitis C, and orphanage abuse).[3] The consultants also investigated the experiences of Aboriginal individuals who receive revenue-type monetary payments (e.g., casino per capita payments and natural resource-based royalties). The general literature dealing with the experience of individuals receiving large lump sum tax credits, lottery winnings, or inheritances was also investigated. The focus was on locating data and information on the experiences of *individual recipients* of large monetary payments and not on those of *group recipients* (e.g., First Nation communities). Finally, the consultants explored two additional and unrelated topics: the impact of sudden wealth and financial abuse in the Aboriginal elder population.

A systematic approach was used to search for relevant references in the academic peer-reviewed literature, grey literature,[4] and popular literature. The following databases and catalogues were searched for quantitative, qualitative, and descriptive papers and articles published in Canada and other countries (1980-present): First Nations Periodical Index; Australian Institute of Aboriginal and Torres Strait Islander Studies Library Catalogue; Native Health Database; Bibliography of Native North Americans; PsycINFO; SocINDEX; Academic Search Premier; Canada Reference Centre; and ProQuest.

Findings

The most striking finding of this literature review relates to the lack of empirical research pertaining to the personal experiences of individuals (Aboriginal or other) who receive either reparation-type or revenue-type monetary payments. The search located only one empirical research paper, a study that examined the psychological impact of lump sum payments awarded to former Japanese American internees. Otherwise, the findings presented in this section are mainly drawn from qualitative/descriptive papers and other writings from the grey or popular literature.

The findings from the literature search are presented under the following headings (representing the types of lump sum payments for which literature was located): residential school legacy payments; Japanese internment awards; resource-based royalties; casino per capita payments; tax credits; and sudden wealth.

---

[3]   *Reparation* refers to a scheme that provides payment (in cash or in kind) to a large group of claimants for remediation of, or compensation for, past injustices.

[4]   *Grey literature* (also called non-conventional literature) comprises scientific and technical reports, conference papers, internal reports, government documents, newsletters, fact sheets, and theses that are not readily available through commercial channels.

A separate section deals with financial abuse in the Aboriginal elder population. Appendix 1 presents an annotated bibliography of the main references.

Impact of Lump Sum Payments

Residential School Settlements and Awards

According to Indian Residential Schools Resolutions Canada (IRSRC), over 15,000 residential school Survivors have filed claims against the Government of Canada and the churches that operated the schools (either through litigation or the alternative dispute resolution (ADR) process) for physical, sexual, and cultural abuses. To date, a total of 2,605 claimants in litigation have settled out of court and 22 claims have been resolved by trial in British Columbia and Saskatchewan with individual awards estimated to range from $15,000 to more than $300,000 (Indian Residential Schools Resolution Canada [IRSRC], n.d.; Canadian Broadcasting Corporation, 2001). To date, the IRSRC has received a total of 3,767 applications of which 805 have been resolved for a total amount of $41.7 million through the ADR process. From these statistics, we can infer that close to 3,500 Aboriginal residential school Survivors have received some form of compensation.

The literature search did not retrieve any empirical research studies addressing the impact of these payments on residential school Survivors or on the communities in which they reside. The information presented below was drawn exclusively from the popular literature (mainly newspapers).

Approximately 230 plaintiffs have received out-of-court settlements between $25,000 and $150,000 each because of sexual abuse suffered at the Gordon Indian Residential School (Saskatchewan) (Macleans, 2000). The literature search located three newspaper articles (Tibbetts, 1998; Foot, 2000; Warick, 2004) describing the experience of several individuals who received out-of-court settlements for sexual abuse suffered at the Gordon residential school. The point is made several times that money won by First Nation plaintiffs is often shrouded in shame and victims feel guilty for accepting money for being sexually abused. In that respect, some First Nation individuals have been ridiculed for taking residential school settlements, which is considered 'dirty' by other First Nation people. Another point made in the newspaper stories is that the money received did not help with the healing process of recipients and was not the solution that recipients expected. Finally, the settlement money was typically spent very quickly on drinking and partying, cars, clothes, and/or plainly given away to friends, family members, and even strangers on the street. One Survivor interviewed indicated that he cleaned out his new bank account as fast as he could because of the taunting about his tainted cash. Another spent his money quickly because he did not know how to handle it.

A fourth newspaper article reports on the need for tailored financial services for Survivors of residential schools who have received monetary settlements or awards. Taillon (2004) reports that the Royal Bank of Aboriginal Banking is taking the lead in British Columbia and has initiated a financial planning program specifically tailored for Survivors who have received monetary settlements or awards. The program was developed to help those people coming into a large sum of money who may have difficulty managing it to their best advantage and who need sound advice on which to base their financial decisions. Brochures, presentations, and handouts have been developed specifically for Aboriginal individuals receiving residential school settlements.

Japanese Internment Compensation

During the Second World War, roughly 22,000 Japanese Canadians were forcibly evacuated from the west coast and resettled in other parts of the country. In 1988, then Prime Minister Brian Mulroney acknowledged the wartime wrongs and announced compensation of $21,000 for each of the 13,000 survivors, $12 million for a Japanese community fund, and $24 million to create a Canadian race relations foundation, to ensure such discrimination never happens again. In the same year, the U.S. government issued a formal apology to the survivors of U.S. Japanese internment camps and awarded $20,000 in symbolic redress to each of the 60,000 surviving internees.

The search did not retrieve any literature dealing with the impact of the financial compensation on Japanese Canadians. One academic empirical research study dealing with the psychological reactions to redress among Japanese Americans was located.

Nagata and Takeshita (2002) examined the psychological impact of redress (financial compensation and apology from the government) on second-generation (*Nisei*) Japanese American former internees. The respondents, all of whom had been interned during the War, rated the degree to which the receipt of redress, nearly 50 years after their incarceration, was associated with eight different areas of personal impact including: the *Nisei's* sense of faith in the government; feeling of general relief; a sense of relief from specific internment-related hardships in each of three areas (economically, emotionally, and physically); a sense of closure; the reduction of negative feelings about their past incarceration; and their increased willingness to talk to others about the internment. Second, the study explored factors that were hypothesized to contribute to the diversity in redress reactions among the study's respondents.

The findings of the study highlighted two key points. First, the findings provided empirical support for the beneficial impact of the redress to Japanese American former internees. Redress was seen by *Nisei* former internees as having had a generally positive impact on their lives. The highest impact ratings occurred on increased faith in government, followed by a sense of closure and emotional relief. The lowest impact ratings were on physical relief and reduced negative feelings about their incarceration.

The second key point illustrated by the study is that significant diversity exists among the *Nisei* regarding the degree of positive impact of redress. As such, women and older respondents had reported higher levels of positive redress impact. *Nisei* with lower income levels perceived redress as having a greater impact than *Nisei* with higher incomes. Finally, former internees who expressed a stronger preference for and comfort with fellow Japanese Americans also showed more positive impacts from redress.

Natural Resources Compensation and Royalties

The literature search retrieved a few articles/descriptive studies pertaining to the impact of resource-related cash compensation and/or royalties on Aboriginal recipients (in the countries of Australia and Papua New Guinea).

Kate George (2003) reports on the impact of the Harding River Dam (that supplies the water needs of the ongoing development associated with resource industries) on the Yinjibarndi and Ngarluma peoples of the Pilbara region (northwest Australia). George writes that there is little, if any, capacity within the groups to plan for the best long-term use of a lump sum amount in a manner that will make inroads into their social and economic marginalization. Rather, periodic cash handouts are more often than not seen to be spent hastily with little thought for the future. The author writes that this spending pattern exacerbates negative stereotyping of Aboriginal people who are seen by the mainstream population as struggling to manage and improve themselves when given the opportunity. Note that George's comments are made in the context of an editorial and are not based on empirical findings.

O'Faircheallaigh (1986) examines the economic impact of the Ranger Uranium Mine Project (Northern Australia) on Aboriginal people during the period 1979–1985. The principal aim of the study was to provide detailed information on the use of royalty-related payments made to traditional owners through the Gagudju Association (representing the interests of the owners). In the case of the Ranger project, royalty payments were made in cash to all adult members (children's payments were lodged in a Children's Trust Fund to remain until the child reaches the age of 18) through the association, although the author stresses that those per capita incomes were well below the Australian average. The author concludes that royalty payments have permitted a modest increase in the incomes of Gagudju Association members. Potential negative impacts of royalty payments (e.g., disunity and jealousy within Aboriginal communities) were minimized by the fact that all members (including children) received identical cash distributions. The author does not describe how individual association members spent their royalty payments.

In another study of the effects of monies paid out under the Ranger and Nabarlek agreements (uranium mining in Northern Australia), Kesteven (1983) offers an account of the uses to which mining revenues have been put into:

+ *Consumption.* Kesteven writes that Aboriginal beneficiaries of compensation/royalty payments appeared to have a limited set of material objectives, which include: vehicles (by far the number one priority), clothes, food, bedding, and alcohol. She also notes that women's material aspirations may be more limited than men's.

+ *Financial gifts.* Beneficiaries were seen to give some of their mining money away. The author explains that it is expected by kin, and is not necessarily to the disadvantage of the person giving the money away, as it can be a means of indebting others and thus gaining status ('social credit'). About half of the beneficiaries report using part of their money to finance ceremonies.

+ *Investment.* In the case of the Nabarlek royalty recipients, this option was severely limited due to a lack of knowledge about investments and interest rates, a general lack of interest in financial matters, and a lack of financial professional capacity within communities. At the time the study was conducted, the recipients of cash payments had to rely on friends and casual contacts for financial advice.

In his description of the compensation agreement related to the Porgera gold mine of Papua New Guinea, Banks (1996) acknowledges that very little is known about how recipients of compensation have used their money. Between August 1987 and the end of September 1994, a total of 8,453 compensation claims were paid, worth US$30.2 million, and averaging US$3,574 per claim. Claims were rarely paid to one individual, but rather to a family or sub-clan group as the recognized owners of the land or buildings being compensated for. It was then up to the family or sub-clan to decide how the money was to be distributed to individuals. Banks makes two points related to how the money was spent by the members of the Porgeran community. First, much of the money has been redistributed by the recipients to family and friends, either as straight handouts or as contributions to ceremonial exchange. Second, the bulk of the money was consumed, and much of it in a highly visible way. Banks estimates that 65–75 per cent of the compensation money was consumed directly, redistributed and consumed, or redistributed outside Porgera. Another 20–25 per cent had been invested in local business ventures of which the majority have failed.

Banks also reports on the following impact of compensation payments: tensions in the community, within families, and between generations over distribution and leadership; younger people getting a share of the compensation money and feeling little need to go to school to improve themselves; and insufficient ability to invest or start sustainable businesses due to the high distribution and consumption rate. Socially destructive habits such as gambling, drinking, and using drugs are now widespread within the community.

A few key points can be summarized from these studies and papers. An obvious benefit of direct cash compensation and royalties can be seen as an increase in the person's income. However, there appears to be limited individual capacity for effective financial planning regarding the best long-term use of cash payments and a tendency to spend rather than save or invest monies received. Direct consumption on material goods (e.g., cars), distribution to family members or friends, and financing of ceremonies account for how the income is generally spent. Negative impacts of cash payments at the community level are also described, including tensions in the community over the distribution of funds, increased socially destructive habits (e.g., gambling, drinking, and using drugs), and young people who feel little need to pursue an education.

Casino Per Capita Payments

Under the *Indian Gaming Regulatory Act* (IGRA), which provides the regulatory framework for Indian gambling in the U.S., American Indian tribes must use casino revenues for specific purposes such as government, social services, and charitable works. After gambling revenues are allocated towards these purposes, tribes may make per capita payments to members. Of the 224 American Indian tribes operating casinos, 73 of them distribute per capita payments to their members (National Indian Gaming Association, n.d.). Per capita remittances from tribal gambling, in some cases, can be as large as $500,000 annually for each member (Kelley, 2001).

In Canada, the provincial governments are the sole legal providers and regulators of gambling and First Nations conduct gambling activities according to provincial regulations. This leads to great provincial variation in how First Nation casinos are operated and how their revenues are distributed. Generally, casino-generated revenues are divided between the host First Nation, the casino operator, the province, and various First Nations Development Funds. First Nations Development Funds are revenue sharing agreements that act as mechanisms to redistribute revenues from reserves that operate large-scale and profitable gambling operations to other reserves within the province. No province in Canada currently allows First Nations to grant per capita payments to band members from casino operations (Kelley, 2001).

Although there is a plethora of research studies and papers describing the economic and social impact of gaming revenues on communities and states/provinces, literature dealing with the impact of per capita payments on individual recipients is virtually non-existent. One reference was found in Kelley (2001) who writes: "in a review of revenue allocation for on-reserve casinos in the US, it was found that in some cases tribes whose members received per capita payments achieved little long-term improvement" (Anders, 1997: 233–234).[5]

Two articles were found describing efforts to provide financial education or planning services to recipients of per capita payments. One article describes the efforts of local schools in North Carolina to provide financial training to students who are eligible to receive lump sum payments from the revenues of Harrah's Cherokee Casino & Hotel. Cavanagh (2004) explains that all enrolled members of the Eastern Band of the Cherokee

---

[5]   The consultants are currently awaiting a copy of this chapter.

(adults and children) receive yearly per capita payments. Unlike the adults, young people receive their money once they have finished school or have turned 21. Although the goal of the per capita payments was to provide young adults with a financial head start as well as an incentive to graduate, community members are now noticing that the young people spend their money rather quickly. The schools are now developing and implementing a financial curriculum related to saving, budgeting, and investing per capita funds.

Another article announces that a financial services company in the United States (Benecorp LLC) has designed a plan specifically to assist tribes and their tribal members in long-range planning and maximization of their per capita payments. The founder of the company explained that this was done after recognizing that there was a financial planning and wealth management void in the fast growing, higher income Native American community who are receiving per capita payments (National Indian Gaming Association, 2005).

Tax Credits

The literature search located a few citations discussing the consumption behaviour of low-income recipients of lump sum tax credit payments in the United States. The Earned Income Tax Credit (EIC or EITC) is a US federal program that supplements the earnings of low-income working individuals and families. For the 2005 taxation year, the maximum EIC amount a qualifying worker with one child can receive is $2,662. For two or more children under one's care, the maximum amount is $4,400 (Tax Credit Resources, 2006). A number of states offer a state-level earned income credit for their residents, which is in addition to the federal government's Earned Income Credit. The majority of qualifying individuals and families receive the EIC as a lump sum payment.

Research has shown that people see their lump sum EIC payments as different from periodic income and, as a result, they spend it on different things. Most families begin planning what they will do with the money long before it arrives (Romich and Weisner, 2001).

Evidence suggests that lump sum EIC payments and tax refunds have a direct impact on consumption and household development. In terms of consumption, recipients of EIC credits and tax refunds often report using such lump sum payments to purchase items for their children, catch up on bills, purchase furniture and appliances, purchase or use as a down payment towards cars and homes, or pay for education expenses (Romich and Weisner, 2001; Smeeding, Phillips, and O'Connor, 2000). Romich and Weisner (2001) also report that although many families in their study had hoped to save a portion of their money, 68 per cent did not have cash savings left from their most recent EIC payment two months later. In conclusion, it appears that the EIC lump sum payment can help low-income families with basic expenses while promoting long-term household development by helping families manage larger purchases such as furniture, cars, and homes (Beverly, 2002; Romich and Weisner, 2001).

Sudden Wealth

The consultants did not find any reference to the term 'sudden wealth syndrome' in the academic literature; however, the term has been discussed and described in at least three major newspaper articles (Lee, 2004; Mandal, 2000; Dunn, 2000) and there are numerous web pages devoted to the topic.

Being flooded with a sudden fortune (earned, inherited, or won) can be highly stressful and sometimes even traumatizing. The term 'Sudden Wealth Syndrome' has been used to describe a cluster of issues and symptoms sometimes exhibited by people benefiting from a large financial windfall. Some of the signs include a marked increase in anxiety, impulse buying, social isolation, moodiness, money-related ruminations, and excessive guilt that inhibit decision-making and undermines pleasure. People suffering from sudden wealth syndrome experience distress or impairment that is in excess of what would ordinarily be expected from what appears to be a positive source of stress. These symptoms, attitudes, or behaviours usually persist over a noticeable period of time and can lead to troubling crises in relation to significant others at home or at work.

Dr. Steven J. Danish, interviewed for a Boston Globe newspaper article (Lee, 2004), has counselled lottery winners for years, and mentions that almost all his patients have had serious problems after collecting their winnings. After the initial shock passes, a sense of guilt often grows. Giving or leaving money to family often proves to be the biggest source of stress for lottery winners.

Sudden wealth syndrome is not really about the money, but about the cataclysmic changes that the money brings into one's life. Unfortunately, statistics show that as much as 70 per cent of financial windfall recipients end up losing it all to investment scams, unsound business investments, donations to family and friends, or reckless spending on themselves or others (National Endowment for Financial Education, 2002). Perhaps one of the biggest mistakes commonly made is not consulting a financial advisor for guidance.

Elder Financial Abuse

Potential financial abuse of elderly Aboriginal individuals is very relevant in light of the Agreement in Principle and the release of common experience payments. A short synopsis of the literature on this topic is presented below.

Financial abuse refers to the misuse of an older adult's money or belongings by a relative or a person in a position of trust (Swanson, 1999). There are no statistical data on the incidence and prevalence of elder abuse (including financial abuse) in the Aboriginal population of Canada (Dumont-Smith, 2002). However, qualitative information can be derived from various reports produced in the last few years. For example, the Canadian Panel on Violence Against Women (as cited in Dumont-Smith, 1997) reported on incidents of older Aboriginal individuals becoming targets for financial abuse by their own family members who take their money away on pension day. Empirical research has demonstrated that neglect and financial/material exploitation were the most typical manifestations of elder mistreatment in the American Indian population (Brown, 1989; Maxwell and Maxwell, 1992).

The connection between elder abuse and neglect and risk and protective factors in Aboriginal populations is complex. Poor socio-economic conditions characteristic of many communities (e.g., poverty, poor housing and over-crowding, drug and alcohol problems of abusers) inevitably lead to tension within families. Brown (1999) speaks specifically about the financial dependency of adult children on their parents as a major risk factor for financial abuse in the American Indian population. Adult children are experiencing high rates of unemployment and severe poverty and the monthly checks from pensions, Social Security, or welfare that the elderly receive are often the only funds available to the elder person's family. This breakdown in community economic life sets the stage for financial exploitation of the elderly by adult family members.

Another risk factor for elder abuse relates to the increasing physical dependency of elders on the younger generation due to multiple diseases, mental health problems, and physical disabilities. Elders may also be at risk for abuse as they continue to experience a loss in their respectful standing and traditional role within the immediate and extended family structures, and as the younger generation continues to adopt values and lifestyles contrary to those of the older generation. Patterns of violence that are transmitted from one generation to the next also contribute to elder abuse (Brown, 1999; Carson and Hand, 1999).

It is important to realize that what is defined as abuse by the majority population can often be understood as the norm by Aboriginal people. Although many researchers have found elder abuse to be present among American Indians, American Indians themselves often do not believe that they have been abused. There is a commonly held notion that the Native American culture emphasizes equal sharing of family resources, and that the use of an elder's money by other family members is "expected" as a cultural responsibility and not necessarily viewed as exploitation (Brown, 1999). This may prevent some elders from perceiving financial exploitation by adult children as abuse.

Conclusion

A few caveats are important to mention before presenting a summary of the findings from this literature review. First, very little research attention has been devoted to the topic of lump sum payments, whether pertaining to the impact that such payments have on individual recipients or how the recipients use the payments. This is the case for both reparation payments as well as other kinds of lump sum payments. Second, very few of the retrieved references are grounded in empirical research; many come from the popular media and present anecdotal data. Third, many of the findings arise from countries other than Canada, are not specific to Aboriginal people, and/or are related to lump sum income payments (and not reparation compensation).

While keeping these limitations in mind, we present a cursory summary of the main findings and issues that were highlighted by the literature review:[6]

- *Personal impact of monetary compensation.* There is indication that a large and sudden monetary windfall can bring significant and stressful changes in the individual's personal life and mental well-being as well as in their relationships with family members and others outside the family unit. The stress experienced by recipients is most likely brought on by the significant changes that the money brings and not caused by the money itself.

- *Impact of compensation payments at the community level.* There are hints in the literature that a large influx of money in a community can have a negative impact on socially destructive habits (e.g., drinking, gambling). Experience has shown that when a community comes into large amounts of money, problems such as alcohol abuse, assaults and robberies, and fraud often develop for which communities and RCMP/police need to prepare and plan for (Morin, 2006; The Vancouver Sun, 1998).

- *Use of lump sum payments.* Some evidence suggests that recipients of lump sum payments view the money as different from periodic income and, as a result, spend it in a different manner, with recipients often planning how to spend the money long before it arrives. Evidence arising from the Aboriginal and mainstream populations also suggests that lump sum payments tend to be consumed or distributed quickly, with limited saving or investing. In the case of reparation payments, settlement money was often spent on drinking, cars, clothes, or given away. Aboriginal recipients of income-related payments use their income on direct consumption of material goods (e.g., cars, clothes, food, alcohol), distribution to family members or friends, and the financing of ceremonies. In the general population, lump sum tax credits are spent on items for children, payment of bills, and the purchase of furniture, appliances, cars, and homes.

---

[6]   These themes and issues will be explored further during the second phase of the *Lump Sum Compensation Payments Research Project,* which will consist of on-site visits and interviews of Aboriginal recipients of past lump sum payments (litigation or out-of-court settlements) related to residential schools.

- *Attitudes within the Aboriginal community towards compensation payments.* There is anecdotal evidence that negative attitudes exist within the Aboriginal community toward settlements awarded for sexual abuse suffered at residential schools. Survivors of one residential school have reported being ridiculed and taunted for taking settlement money, which was considered 'dirty' by other First Nation people. Victims have voiced feeling guilty for accepting money for being sexually abused.

- *Effectiveness of compensation as a redress and healing strategy.* There appears to be differences in how redress impacts healing, depending on the type of compensation, the type of duress suffered, and/or the group receiving the compensation. Redress has been reported as having a positive impact on the lives of Japanese Americans who were interned during the Second World War. This group has reported an increased faith in government, a sense of closure, and emotional relief following redress. Within that group, however, diversity regarding the degree of positive impact was reported by individuals receiving the same compensation package. In the case of Japanese American former internees, there were women, older respondents, and individuals with lower income levels who have reported higher levels of positive redress impact. Anecdotal evidence suggests that settlement awards for past sexual abuse suffered at residential schools did not positively impact on the healing of recipients.

- *Availability and use of professional financial advice.* There is evidence that recipients of large lump sums of money often do not have the knowledge and skills to manage their money effectively. In addition, sound and tailored financial advice is often not available to recipients of large sums of money. This can have a negative impact on how money is utilized or distributed. Various institutions are becoming more and more aware of this fact and are developing and tailoring their financial advice programs.

- *Financial abuse of compensation recipients.* No evidence was found that directly links financial abuse to the receipt of large monetary lump sum payments. However, the limited data on elder abuse in the Aboriginal population suggests that the potential for financial abuse following receipt of the common experience payments does exist. Older Aboriginal adults are susceptible to financial abuse for a variety of reasons, including the poor socio-economic conditions characteristic of many remote communities, which inevitably lead to tensions within the family (e.g., poverty, poor housing and over-crowding, and drug and alcohol problems of abusers).

In conclusion, the fact that minimal research has been conducted on this topic (especially in the area of reparation compensation within the Aboriginal population) validates the importance of the *Lump Sum Compensation Payments Research Project*, which will assess the impact that past lump sum payments have had on Aboriginal recipients and communities in order to inform recommendations to address and mitigate the potential negative impact of the upcoming common experience payments.

References

Anders, G. (1997). Estimating the economic impact of Indian casino gambling: A case study of Fort McDowell Reservation. In W. Eadington and J. Cornelius (eds.), Gambling: Public Policies and the Social Sciences. Reno, NV: Institute for the Study of Gambling and Commercial Gambling: 233–234.

Banks, G. (1996). Compensation for Mining: Benefit or Time-Bomb? The Porgera Gold Mine. In R. Howitt, J. Connell, and P. Hirsch (eds.), Resources, Nations and Indigenous Peoples: Case Studies from Australasia, Melanesia, and Southeast Asia. Melbourne, AU: Oxford University Press: 223–235.

Beverly, S.G. (2002). What social workers need to know about the earned income tax credit. Social Work 47(3):259–266.

Brown, A. (1999). Patterns of abuse among Native American elderly. In T. Tatara (ed.), Understanding Elder Abuse in Minority Populations. Philadelphia, PA: Brunner/Mazel: 143–159.

————— (1989). A Survey on Elder Abuse at One Native American Tribe. Journal of Elder Abuse & Neglect 1(2):17–37.

Canadian Broadcasting Corporation (2001). Ottawa Moves Ahead on Residential School Settlements. CBC News, 30 October 2001. Retrieved on 27 March 2006 from: www.cbc.ca

Carson, D.K. and C. Hand (1999). Dilemmas surrounding elder abuse and neglect in Native American Communities. In T. Tatara (ed.), Understanding Elder Abuse in Minority Populations. Philadelphia, PA: Brunner/Mazel: 161–184.

Cavanagh, S. (2004). Hitting the jackpot. Education Week 23(30):30–33.

Dumont-Smith, C. (2002). Aboriginal Elder Abuse in Canada. Ottawa, ON: Aboriginal Healing Foundation.

————— (1997). Hear their stories – 40 Aboriginal women speak. Ottawa, ON: The Native Women's Association of Canada.

Dunn, A. (2000). Fairy tale falls short for rich. Los Angeles Times, March 14, 2000, part A.

Foot, R. (2000). Natives ridiculed for taking residential school settlements: Money received in sex abuse lawsuits considered 'dirty' by other natives. National Post (April 26, 2000), A5.

George, K. (2003). Exclusive rights: Ongoing exclusion in resource rich remote Aboriginal Australia. Australasian Psychiatry 11(Suppl 1):S9–S12.

Indian Residential Schools Resolution Canada (no date). Indian Residential School Statistics. Retrieved on 27 March 2006 from: www.irsr-rqpi.gc.ca/english/statistics.htm

Kelley, R. (2001). First Nations gambling policy in Canada. Calgary, AB: Canada West Foundation.

Kestevan, S. (1983). The effects on Aboriginal communities of monies paid out under the Ranger and Nabarlek Agreements. In N. Peterson and M. Langton (eds.), Aborigines Land and Land Rights. Canberra, AU: Australian Institute of Aboriginal Studies: 358–384.

Lee, J. (2004). Windfall not always a blessing, psychologists say, Boston Globe, July 10, 2004. Retrieved on 27 March 2006 from: www.boston.com/yourlife/health/mental/articles /2004/07/10/windfall_not_always_a_blessing_psychologists_say/

Maclean's (2000). Abuse of Trust, June 26, 2000. Retrieved on 20 May 2006 from: www.macleans.ca/topstories/article.jsp?content=36179#continue

Mandal, V. (2000). Growing ranks of the suddenly rich afflicted with illness all their own, National Post, Saturday August 19, 2000. Retrieved on 27 March 2006 from: www.ncf.carleton.ca/~aj624/toomuch.html

Marshall, C. (1994). The impact of royalty payments on Aboriginal communities in the Northern Territory. In P. Jull, M. Mulrennan, M. Sullivan, G. Crough, and D. Lea (eds.), Surviving Columbus; indigenous peoples, political reform and environmental management in North Australia. Casuarina, AU: North Australia Research Unit, Australian National University: 123–128.

Maxwell, E.K. and R.J. Maxwell (1992). Insults to the body civil: Mistreatment of elderly in two Plains Indian Tribes. Journal of Cross-Cultural Gerontology 7:3–23.

Morin, M. (2006). Personal communication with Cst. M. Morin, Program/Policy Analyst, Community, Contract and Aboriginal Policing Services National Aboriginal Policing Services on 24 March 2006.

Nagata, D.K. and Y.J. Takeshita (2002). Psychological reactions for redress: Diversity among Japanese Americans interned during World War II. Cultural Diversity and Ethnic Minority Psychology 8(1):41–59.

National Endowment for Financial Education (2002) Financial Psychology and Lifechanging Events: Financial Windfall. Brochure, revised 2004. Greenwood Village, CO: National Endowment for Financial Education.

National Indian Gaming Association (2005). Benecorp introduces CapNet7 Per Capita Maximization Plan. Indian Gaming 15(1):79.

——— (no date). Library: Indian Gaming Facts. Retrieved on 27 March 2006 from: www.indiangaming.org/library/indian-gaming-facts/index.shtml

O'Faircheallaigh, C. (1986). The economic impact on Aboriginal communities of the Ranger Project: 1979–1985. Australian Aboriginal Studies 2:2–14.

Romich, J.L. and T.S. Weisner (2001). How families view and use lump-sum payments from the earned income tax credit. In G.J. Duncan and P.L. Chase-Lansdale (eds.), For Better and for Worse: Welfare Reform and the Well-Being of Children and Families. New York, NY: Russell Sage Foundation: 201–221.

Smeeding, T.M., K.R. Phillips, and M. O'Connor (2000). The earned income tax credit: Expectation, knowledge, use, and economic and social mobility. National Tax Journal 53(4, Part 2):1197–1209.

Swanson, S.M. (1999). Abuse and neglect of older adults. The National Clearinghouse on Family Violence. Ottawa, ON: Health Canada.

Taillon, J. (2004). Money management skills can be learned. Raven's Eye 7(9):11–13.

Tax Credit Resources (2006). Retrieved on 19 May 2006 from: www.taxcreditresources.org

The Vancouver Sun (1998). Police prepare for aftermath of native compensation deal: Fort St. John RCMP say a big influx of cash can also bring problems in its wake. The Vancouver Sun (March 12, 1998), A3.

Tibbetts, J. (1998). Victims blow compensation money: Future no brighter for most who collected settlements. Sun Times (December 28, 1998), A1.

Warick, J. (2004). Money Didn't Help. Leader Post (August 9, 2004), D5.

Yunupingu, G. (1999). Royalties paid for essentials others take for granted. Land Rights Queensland. Retrieved on 27 March 2006 from: www.faira.org.au/lrq/archives/199912/stories/royalties-paid-story.html

Appendix 1

Annotated Bibliography

Residential School Legacy Payments

Foot, R. (2000). Natives ridiculed for taking residential school settlements: Money received in sex abuse lawsuits considered 'dirty' by other natives. National Post (April 26, 2000), A5.

Mr. Ben Pratt, 44, received an out-of-court settlement of about $46,000 in the late 1990s after he sued the federal government for the sexual abuse he suffered at the hands of a convicted abuser while attending the Gordon's Indian Residential School in the 1960s. In a report on the legacy of church-run residential schools, published in the Anglican Journal, Mr. Pratt says the money being won by native plaintiffs who have sued for their abuse is shrouded in shame. Around 7,000 natives are suing the federal government and Canada's mainstream Christian churches for the abuse they say they suffered in residential schools in the decades following the Second World War. While many former students claim they were sexually abused -- and a handful of people have been compensated following the criminal conviction of their abusers -- others are suing for their loss of language and culture.

Taillon, J. (2004). Money management skills can be learned. Raven's Eye 7(9):11–13.

British Columbia is taking the lead in terms of the numbers of Aboriginal people who are settling their residential school claims against churches, government, and individuals. Once they have a rather large sum of cash in hand, some people have difficulty managing it to their best advantage and want to turn to someone who can give them sound advice on which to base their financial decisions. The Royal Bank of Aboriginal Banking has stepped up to help in this unique situation.

Tibbetts, J. (1998). Victims blow compensation money: Future no brighter for most who collected settlements. Sun Times (December 28, 1998), A1.

The day Robert Pratt got his compensation cheque for being raped at an Indian residential school, he stuffed about $20,000 in his pants pocket and went on the biggest drinking binge of his life. More than 200 men who attended the school have collected out-of- court settlements from the federal government ranging from about $20,000 to $200,000 for the sexual abuse they suffered as small children at the hands of a dorm supervisor. Another 200 Gordon lawsuits are yet to be settled. The Gordon reserve hugs a winding, pot-holed road running about 20 kilometers through a desolate section of rural Saskatchewan. There are no stores, no businesses, and few jobs. The nearest community is Punnichy, which doesn't have much more than a bar, a general store or two and a bingo hall. Stories abound on the reserve of 1,200 about how people squandered their money. While just about everybody bought a vehicle, there was one man who bought seven, one for every day of the week. And there's the group that traveled 100 kilometers south to Regina the day they collected their money, rented the top floor of a swanky hotel and partied the night away. All of this has left federal officials wondering how to deal with the 2,000 people -- and counting -- across the country who have filed lawsuits against the Indian Affairs department.

Warick, J. (2004). Money Didn't Help. Leader Post (August 9, 2004), D5.

William Starr would send Ben Pratt back to his room around 3 or 4 a.m. Everyone in the dorm knew what Starr had been doing to Pratt, but no one teased him because many of them were also victims. At school, Pratt was labeled a troublemaker. Pratt's late nights and stress from by Starr's abuse caused him to sleep through many of his classes. The settlement money received for sexual abuse didn't solve Pratt's problems. He gave away money to casual friends and other hangers-on who were only friendly after he got the money. Pratt also harbored enormous guilt, feeling like a prostitute for accepting money for being sexually abused. In less than a year, the money was gone. He declared bankruptcy several years ago and is now $40,000 in debt.

Japanese Americans Internment Compensation Payments

Nagata, D.K. and Y.J. Takeshita (2002). Psychological reactions for redress: Diversity among Japanese Americans interned during World War II. Cultural Diversity and Ethnic Minority Psychology 8(1):41–59.

The psychological reactions of second-generation (Nisei) Japanese Americans to receiving redress from the U.S. government for the injustices of the World War II internment were investigated. The respondents, all of whom had been interned during the war, rated the degree to which the receipt of redress nearly 50 years after their incarceration was associated with 8 different areas of personal impact. Results indicated that redress was reported to be most effective in increasing faith in the government and least effective in reducing physical suffering from the internment. Women and older respondents reported more positive redress effects. In addition, lower levels of current income, and attitudinal preference for Japanese Americans, and pre-redress support for seeking monetary compensation each increased the prediction of positive redress effects. Findings are discussed in relation to theories of social and retributive justice.

Resource-Related Compensation and Royalties

Banks, G. (1996). Compensation for Mining: Benefit or Time-Bomb? The Porgera Gold Mine. In R. Howitt, J. Connell, and P. Hirsch (eds.), Resources, Nations and Indigenous Peoples: Case Studies from Australasia, Melanesia, and Southeast Asia. Melbourne, AU: Oxford University Press: 223–235.

This chapter focuses on the general issue of compensation at Porgera (including relation), and specifically on two aspects of compensation. These are, first, the negotiation and implementation of compensation and relocation agreements between the company and the Porgeran community, and second, the way in which local people have responded to the material benefits which have flowed from these agreements.

George, K. (2003). Exclusive rights: Ongoing exclusion in resource rich remote Aboriginal Australia. Australasian Psychiatry 11(Suppl 1):S9–S12.

This editorial discusses a paper which concentrated on sourcing jobs for Aboriginal people in the private sector of which the mining industry and associated major contractors are by far the largest potential employers. Since colonization and settlement in north-west Australia, the contest for land has been the central influence in defining relationships and dialogue between Aboriginal groups and non-Aboriginal interests. It focuses on the Pilbara region of Western Australia. Ordinarily, development should be expected to positively impact on all social groups in the region, but this has not happened in the Pilbara. Aboriginal people have not been active participants in this development that has, rather, been a major contributor to the ongoing social and economic exclusion of Aboriginal people. Where benefits are provided under an Agreement, the full legacy of ongoing disenfranchisement, lack of access to appropriate education and exclusion of Aboriginal people becomes apparent. There is little capacity within groups to plan for the best long-term use of a lump sum amount in an amount that will make inroads into the current social and economic marginalization.

Kestevan, S. (1983). The effects on Aboriginal communities of monies paid out under the Ranger and Nabarlek Agreements. In N. Peterson and M. Langton (eds.), Aborigines Land and Land Rights. Canberra, AU: Australian Institute of Aboriginal Studies: 358–384.

Much publicity has been given to the facto that Aborigines will be receiving sums of money as a result of signing agreements with mining companies for the mining of uranium ore in the Alligator Rivers region. This paper describes the effects of monies paid out under the Ranger and Nabarlek Agreements on Aboriginal communities (Australia). The paper is based on two years' fieldwork in the Alligator Rivers region, as part of a project to monitor the social impact of uranium mining on Aboriginal communities in the Northern Territory.

Marshall, C. (1994). The impact of royalty payments on Aboriginal communities in the Northern Territory. In P. Jull, M. Mulrennan, M. Sullivan, G. Crough, and D. Lea (eds.), Surviving Columbus; indigenous peoples, political reform and environmental management in North Australia. Casuarina, AU: North Australia Research Unit, Australian National University: 123-128.

This book chapter outlines the types of royalties payable under the Aboriginal Land Rights (Northern Territory) Act with particular reference to the Mereenie – Palm Valley royalty structures. The book chapter also sets out recommendations for improved management of royalty payments.

O'Faircheallaigh, C. (1986). The economic impact on Aboriginal communities of the Ranger Project: 1979–1985. Australian Aboriginal Studies 2:2–14.

This article attempts to answer a number of questions pertaining to the economic impact of the Ranger Project on Aboriginal communities including: How significant are the benefits generated for Aboriginal people by modern, capital-intensive mining projects of the type developed in north-Australia? Are these projects in fact likely to fulfill the expectations of Aborigines who support the controlled exploitation of mineral resources on their lands? The principal aim of the article is to provide detailed information on the use of royalty-related payments made to traditional owners, represented by the Gagudju Association, as a result of Ranger's operations. It also examines briefly two other areas of impact, employment and training opportunities for Aborigines and changes in their access to social and other services resulting from the establishment of Ranger, and its township, Jabiru.

Yunupingu, G. (1999). Royalties paid for essentials others take for granted. Land Rights Queensland. Retrieved on 27 March 2006 from: http://www.faira.org.au/lrq/archives/199912/stories/royalties-paid-story.html

This paper denies accusations that mining royalties to Gagudju people in Kakadu have been wasted. The paper argues that royalties are small compared to government funding but government services are poor. Finally, the author argues that royalties are used for essential services.

Casino Revenues

Cavanagh, S. (2004). Hitting the jackpot. Education Week 23(30):30–33.

For as long as many young people in North Carolina can remember, the local Indian casino has been luring the outsiders in: newlyweds, retirees, sightseers, and snowbirds, from Chattanooga and Charlotte, Asheville and Atlanta. They roar up the steep mountain switchbacks, park their pickups and chartered buses, and hit it big or bottom out at the slots and digital blackjack, where that fabled jackpot is just one wager away. But just a few miles down the road, students at Cherokee middle and high schools have a more surefire opportunity to pocket hefty winnings – without ever setting foot in the casino.

Earned Income Tax Credit

Beverly, S.G. (2002). What social workers need to know about the earned income tax credit. Social Work 47(3):259–266.

Over the past decade, the federal earned income tax credit (EIC or EITC) has become the largest antipoverty program in the United States. For the 2002 tax year, working families with children can receive as much as $4,140 in EITC benefits. Although families may arrange to receive benefits throughout the year (through their paychecks), most receive a lump sum after filing federal income taxes. Research suggests that many families use the credit to purchase big-ticket items, to move, to pay for educational expenses, or to set aside savings. Thus, the credit may promote long-term household development as well as help families with basic expenses. Research also suggests that EITC encourages work among single-parent families, an outcome that is consistent with one goal of welfare reform. Social workers can be involved in outreach efforts that help low-income workers claim EITC benefits and inform them about advance-payment options. Social workers can also support efforts to increase EITC benefits for larger families and link tax refunds to saving programs.

Romich, J.L. and T.S. Weisner (2001). How families view and use lump-sum payments from the earned income tax credit. In G.J. Duncan and P.L. Chase-Lansdale (eds.), For Better and for Worse: Welfare Reform and the Well-Being of Children and Families. New York, NY: Russell Sage Foundation: 201–221.

In this chapter, the authors draw on intensive qualitative data to provide a detailed description of how families view and spend their EITC. Drawing on economic theory, the authors examine ways to frame the lump sum versus advance payment trade-off, concluding that an augmented form of basic life-cycle consumption hypothesis best predicts the observed behavior. The sample is a subset (n=42 families) of 1,357 households that volunteered for the New Hope project, a community-initiated antipoverty program. Results and discussions are discussed in relation to EITC awareness, spending discipline, taxes, and post-check consumption.

May 8, 2006

CANADA, as represented by the Honourable Frank Iacobucci

-and-

PLAINTIFFS, as represented by the National Consortium

and the Merchant Law Group

-and-

Independent Counsel

-and-

THE ASSEMBLY OF FIRST NATIONS and INUIT REPRESENTATIVES

-and-

THE GENERAL SYNOD OF THE ANGLICAN CHURCH OF CANADA,

THE PRESBYTERIAN CHURCH OF CANADA,

THE UNITED CHURCH OF CANADA AND

ROMAN CATHOLIC ENTITIES

INDIAN RESIDENTIAL SCHOOLS

SETTLEMENT AGREEMENT

[Reformatted; table of contents and original page numbers removed]

May 8, 2006

Indian Residential Schools
Settlement Agreement

WHEREAS:

A. Canada and certain religious organizations operated Indian Residential Schools for the education of aboriginal children and certain harms and abuses were committed against those children;

B. The Parties desire a fair, comprehensive and lasting resolution of the legacy of Indian Residential Schools;

C. The Parties further desire the promotion of healing, education, truth and reconciliation and commemoration;

D. The Parties entered into an Agreement in Principle on November 20, 2005 for the resolution of the legacy of Indian Residential Schools:

(i)   to settle the Class Actions and the Cloud Class Action, in accordance with and as provided in this Agreement;

(ii)   to provide for payment by Canada of the Designated Amount to the Trustee for the Common Experience Payment;

(iii)   to provide for the Independent Assessment Process;

(iv)   to establish a Truth and Reconciliation Commission;

(v)   to provide for an endowment to the Aboriginal Healing Foundation to fund healing programmes addressing the legacy of harms suffered at Indian Residential Schools including the intergenerational effects; and

(vi)   to provide funding for commemoration of the legacy of Indian Residential Schools;

E. The Parties, subject to the Approval Orders, have agreed to amend and merge all of the existing proposed class action statements of claim to assert a common series of Class Actions for the purposes of settlement;

F. The Parties, subject to the Approval Orders and the expiration of the Opt Out Periods without the Opt Out Threshold being met, have agreed to settle the Class Actions upon the terms contained in this Agreement;

G. The Parties, subject to the Approval Orders, agree to settle all pending individual actions relating to Indian Residential Schools upon the terms contained in this Agreement, save and except those actions brought by individuals who opt out of the Class Actions in the manner set out in this Agreement, or who will be deemed to have opted out pursuant to Article 1008 of *The Code of Civil Procedure of Quebec*;

H. This Agreement is not to be construed as an admission of liability by any of the defendants named in the Class Actions or the Cloud Class Action.

THEREFORE, in consideration of the mutual agreements, covenants and undertakings set out herein, the Parties agree that all actions, causes of actions, liabilities, claims and demands whatsoever of every nature or kind for damages, contribution, indemnity, costs, expenses and interest which any Class Member or Cloud Class Member ever had, now has or may hereafter have arising in relation to an Indian Residential School or the operation of Indian Residential Schools, whether such claims were made or could have been made in any proceeding including the Class Actions, will be finally settled based on the terms and conditions set out in this Agreement upon the Implementation Date, and the Releasees will have no further liability except as set out in this Agreement.

ARTICLE ONE
INTERPRETATION

1.01 Definitions

In this Agreement, the following terms will have the following meanings:

"**Aboriginal Healing Foundation**" means the non-profit corporation established under Part II of the *Canada Corporations Act*, chapter C-32 of the Revised Statutes of Canada, 1970 to address the healing needs of Aboriginal People affected by the Legacy of Indian Residential Schools, including intergenerational effects.

"**Agreement in Principle**" means the Agreement between Canada, as represented by the Honourable Frank Iacobucci; Plaintiffs, as represented by the National Consortium, Merchant Law Group, Inuvialuit Regional Corporation, Makivik Corporation, Nunavut Tunngavik Inc., Independent Counsel, and the Assembly of First Nations; the General Synod of the Anglican Church of Canada, the Presbyterian Church in Canada, the United Church of Canada and Roman Catholic Entities, signed November 20, 2005;

"**Appropriate Court**" means the court of the province or territory where the Class Member resided on the Approval Date save and except:

a) that residents of the provinces of Newfoundland and Labrador, Nova Scotia, New Brunswick and Prince Edward Island will be deemed to be subject to the Approval Order of the Superior Court of Justice for Ontario;

b) International Residents will be deemed to be subject to the Approval Order of the Superior Court of Justice for Ontario;

"**Approval Date**" means the date the last Court issues its Approval Order;

"**Approval Orders**" means the judgments or orders of the Courts certifying the Class Actions and approving this Agreement as fair, reasonable and in the best interests of the Class Members and Cloud Class Members for the purposes of settlement of the Class Actions pursuant to the applicable class proceedings legislation, the common law or Quebec civil law;

"Business Day" means a day other than a Saturday or a Sunday or a day observed as a holiday under the laws of the Province or Territory in which the person who needs to take action pursuant to this Agreement is situated or a holiday under the federal laws of Canada applicable in the said Province or Territory;

"Canada" or **"Government"** means the Government of Canada;

"CEP" and **"Common Experience Payment"** mean a lump sum payment made to an Eligible CEP Recipient in the manner set out in Article Five (5) of this Agreement;

"CEP Application" means an application for a Common Experience Payment completed substantially in the form attached hereto as Schedule "A" of this Agreement and signed by an Eligible CEP Recipient or his or her Personal Representative along with the documentation required by the CEP Application.

"CEP Application Deadline" means the fourth anniversary of the Implementation Date;

"Church" or **"Church Organization"** means collectively, The General Synod of the Anglican Church of Canada, The Missionary Society of the Anglican Church of Canada, The Dioceses of the Anglican Church of Canada listed in Schedule "B", The Presbyterian Church in Canada, The Trustee Board of the Presbyterian Church in Canada, The Foreign Mission of the Presbyterian Church in Canada, Board of Home Missions and Social Services of the Presbyterian Church in Canada, The Women's Missionary Society of the Presbyterian Church in Canada, The United Church of Canada, The Board of Home Missions of the United Church of Canada, The Women's Missionary Society of the United Church of Canada, The Methodist Church of Canada, The Missionary Society of The Methodist Church of Canada **and the Catholic Entities listed in Schedule "C".**

"Class Actions" means the omnibus Indian Residential Schools Class Actions Statements of Claim referred to in Article Four (4) of this Agreement;

"Class Members" means all individuals including Persons Under Disability who are members of any class defined in the Class Actions and who have not opted out or are not deemed to have opted out of the Class Actions on or before the expiry of the Opt Out Period;

"Cloud Class Action" means the *Marlene C. Cloud et al. v. Attorney General of Canada et al.* (C40771) action certified by the Ontario Court of Appeal by Order entered at Toronto on February 16, 2005;

"Cloud Class Members" means all individuals who are members of the classes certified in the Cloud Class Action;

"Cloud Student Class Member" means all individuals who are members of the student class certified in the Cloud Class Action;

"Commission" means the Truth and Reconciliation Commission established pursuant to Article Seven (7) of this Agreement;

"**Continuing Claims**" means those claims set out in Section I of Schedule "D" of this Agreement.

"**Courts**" means collectively the Quebec Superior Court, the Superior Court of Justice for Ontario, the Manitoba Court of Queen's Bench, the Saskatchewan Court of Queen's Bench, the Alberta Court of Queen's Bench, the Supreme Court of British Columbia, the Nunavut Court of Justice, the Supreme Court of the Yukon and the Supreme Court of the Northwest Territories;

"**Designated Amount**" means one billion nine hundred million dollars ($1,900,000,000.00) less any amounts paid by way of advance payments, if any, as at the Implementation Date.;

"**Designated Amount Fund**" means the trust fund established to hold the Designated Amount to be allocated in the manner set out in Article Five of this Agreement;

"**DR Model**" means the dispute resolution model offered by Canada since November 2003;

"**Educational Programs or Services**" shall include, but not be limited to, those provided by universities, colleges, trade or training schools, or which relate to literacy or trades, as well as programs or services which relate to the preservation, reclamation, development or understanding of native history, cultures, or languages.

"**Eligible CEP Recipient**" means any former Indian Residential School student who resided at any Indian Residential School prior to December 31, 1997 and who was alive on May 30, 2005 and who does not opt out, or is not deemed to have opted out of the Class Actions during the Opt-Out Periods or is a Cloud Student Class Member;

"**Eligible IAP Claimants**" means all Eligible CEP Recipients, all Nonresident Claimants and includes references to the term "Claimants" in the IAP.

"**Federal Representative**" means the Honourable Frank Iacobucci;

"**IAP Application Deadline**" means the fifth anniversary of the Implementation Date:

"**IAP Working Group**" means counsel set out in Schedule "U" of this Agreement.

"**Implementation Date**" means the latest of :
(1)   the expiry of thirty (30) days following the expiry of the Opt-Out Periods; and
(2)   the day following the last day on which a Class Member in any jurisdiction may appeal or seek leave to appeal any of the Approval Orders; and
(3)   the date of a final determination of any appeal brought in relation to the Approval Orders;

"**Independent Counsel**" means Plaintiffs' Legal Counsel who have signed this Agreement, excluding Legal Counsel who have signed this Agreement in their capacity as counsel for the Assembly of First Nations or for the Inuit Representatives or Counsel who are members of the Merchant Law Group or members of any of the firms who are members of the National Consortium;

"**Independent Assessment Process**" and "**IAP**" mean the process for the determination of Continuing Claims, attached as Schedule "D";

"**Indian Residential Schools**" means the following:

(1)   Institutions listed on List "A" to OIRSRC's Dispute Resolution Process attached as Schedule "E";

(2)   Institutions listed in Schedule "F" ("Additional Residential Schools") which may be expanded from time to time in accordance with Article 12.01 of this Agreement; and,

(3)   Any institution which is determined to meet the criteria set out in Section 12.01(2) and (3) of this Agreement:

"**International Residents**" means Class Members who are not resident in a Canadian Province or Territory on the Approval Date.

"**Inuit Representatives**" includes Inuvialuit Regional Corporation ("IRC"), Nunavut Tunngavik Inc. ("NTI") and Makivik Corporation; and may include other Inuit representative organizations or corporations.

"**NAC**" means the National Administration Committee as set out in Article Four (4) of this Agreement;

"**NCC**" means the National Certification Committee as set out in Article Four (4) of this Agreement;

"**Non-resident Claimants**" means all individuals who did not reside at an Indian Residential School who, while under the age of 21, were permitted by an adult employee of an Indian Residential School to be on the premises of an Indian Residential School to take part in authorized school activities prior to December 31, 1997. For greater certainty, Non-resident Claimants are not Class Members or Cloud Class Members;

"**OIRSRC**" means the Office of Indian Residential Schools Resolution Canada;

"**Opt Out Periods**" means the period commencing on the Approval Date as set out in the Approval Orders;

"**Opt Out Threshold**" means the Opt Out Threshold set out in Section 4.14 of this Agreement;

"**Other Released Church Organizations**" includes the Dioceses of the Anglican Church of Canada listed in Schedule "G" and the Catholic Entities listed in Schedule "H", that did not operate an Indian Residential School or did not have an Indian Residential School located within their geographical boundaries and have made, or will make, a financial contribution towards the resolution of claims advanced by persons who attended an Indian Residential School;

"Oversight Committee" means the Oversight Committee set out in the Independent Assessment Process attached as Schedule "D";

"Parties" means collectively and individually the signatories to this Agreement;

"Personal Credits" means credits that have no cash value, are transferable only to a family member who is a member of the family class as defined in the Class Actions or the Cloud Class Action, may be combined with the Personal Credits of other individuals and are only redeemable for either personal or group education services provided by education entities or groups jointly approved by Canada and the Assembly of First Nations pursuant to terms and conditions to be developed by Canada and the Assembly of First Nations. Similar sets of terms and conditions will be developed by Canada and Inuit Representatives for Eligible CEP Recipients having received the CEP who are Inuit. In carrying out these discussions with the Assembly of First Nations and Inuit Representatives, Canada shall obtain input from counsel for the groups set out in Section 4.09(4)(d), (e), (f) and (g);

"Personal Representative" includes, if a person is deceased, an executor, administrator, estate trustee, trustee or liquidator of the deceased or, if the person is mentally incompetent, the tutor, committee, Guardian, curator of the person or the Public Trustee or their equivalent or, if the person is a minor, the person or party that has been appointed to administer his or her affairs or the tutor where applicable;

"Person Under Disability" means

    (1)   a minor as defined by that person's Province or Territory of residence; or

    (2)   a person who is unable to manage or make reasonable judgments or decisions in respect of their affairs by reason of mental incapacity and for whom a Personal Representative has been appointed;

"Pilot Project" means the dispute resolution projects set out in Schedule "T" of this Agreement;

"RACs" means the Regional Administration Committees as set out in Article Four of this Agreement;

"Releasees" means, jointly and severally, individually and collectively, the defendants in the Class Actions and the defendants in the Cloud Class Action and each of their respective past and present parents, subsidiaries and related or affiliated entities and their respective employees, agents, officers, directors, shareholders, partners, principals, members, attorneys, insurers, subrogees, representatives, executors, administrators, predecessors, successors, heirs, transferees and assigns the definition and also the entities listed in Schedules "B", "C", "G" and "H" of this Agreement.

"Trustee" means Her Majesty in right of Canada as represented by the incumbent Ministers from time to time responsible for Indian Residential Schools Resolution and Service Canada. The initial Representative Ministers will be the Minister of Canadian Heritage and Status of Women and the Minister of Human Resources Skills Development, respectively.

1.02   Headings

The division of this Agreement into Articles, Sections and Schedules and the insertion of a table of contents and headings are for convenience of reference only and do not affect the construction or interpretation of this Agreement. The terms "herein", "hereof", "hereunder" and similar expressions refer to this Agreement and not to any particular Article, Section or other portion hereof. Unless something in the subject matter or context is inconsistent therewith, references herein to Articles, Sections and Schedules are to Articles, Sections and Schedules of this Agreement.

1.03   Extended Meanings

In this Agreement, words importing the singular number include the plural and *vice versa*, words importing any gender include all genders and words importing persons include individuals, partnerships, associations, trusts, unincorporated organizations, corporations and governmental authorities. The term "including" means "including without limiting the generality of the foregoing".

1.04   No Contra Proferentem

The Parties acknowledge that they have reviewed and participated in settling the terms

of this Agreement and they agree that any rule of construction to the effect that any ambiguity is to be resolved against the drafting parties is not applicable in interpreting this Agreement.

1.05   Statutory References

In this Agreement, unless something in the subject matter or context is inconsistent therewith or unless otherwise herein provided, a reference to any statute is to that statute as enacted on the date hereof or as the same may from time to time be amended, re-enacted or replaced and includes any regulations made thereunder.

1.06   Day For Any Action

Where the time on or by which any action required to be taken hereunder expires or falls on a day that is not a Business Day, such action may be done on the next succeeding day that is a Business Day.

1.07   When Order Final

For the purposes of this Agreement a judgment or order becomes final when the time for appealing or seeking leave to appeal the judgment or order has expired without an appeal being taken or leave to appeal being sought or, in the event that an appeal is taken or leave to appeal is sought, when such appeal or leave to appeal and such further appeals as may be taken have been disposed of and the time for further appeal, if any, has expired.

1.08   Currency

All references to currency herein are to lawful money of Canada.

1.09   Schedules

The following Schedules to this Agreement are incorporated into and form part of it by this reference as fully as if contained in the body of this Agreement:

Schedule A   – CEP Application Form
Schedule B   – Dioceses of the Anglican Church
Schedule C   – Roman Catholic Entities
Schedule D   – Independent Assessment Process
Schedule E   – Residential Schools
Schedule F   – Additional Residential Schools
Schedule G   – Anglican Releasees
Schedule H   – Catholic Releasees
Schedule I   – Trust Agreement
Schedule J   – Commemoration Policy Directive
Schedule K   – Settlement Notice Plan
Schedule L   – Process Flow Chart
Schedule M   – Funding Agreement between the Aboriginal Healing Foundation and Canada
Schedule N   – Mandate for Truth and Reconciliation Commission
Schedule O-1 – The Presbyterian Church Entities in Canada Agreement
Schedule O-2 – The Anglican Entities Agreement
Schedule O-3 – The Catholic Entities Church Agreement
Schedule O-4 – The United Church of Canada Agreement
Schedule P   – IAP Full and Final Release
Schedule Q   – Treasury Board Travel Directive
Schedule R   – No Prejudice Commitment Letter
Schedule S   – National Certification Committee Members
Schedule T   – Pilot Projects
Schedule U   – IAP Working Group Members
Schedule V   – Agreement Between the Government of Canada and the Merchant Law Group
                    Respecting the Verification of Legal Fees

1.10   No Other Obligations

It is understood that Canada will not have any obligations relating to the CEP, IAP, truth and reconciliation, commemoration, education and healing except for the obligations and liabilities as set out in this Agreement.

ARTICLE TWO
EFFECTIVE DATE OF AGREEMENT

2.01   Date when Binding and Effective

This Agreement will become effective and be binding on and after the Implementation Date on all the Parties including the Class Members and Cloud Class Members subject to Section 4.14. The Cloud Class Action Approval Order and each Approval Order
will constitute approval of this Agreement in respect of all Class Members and Cloud

Class Members residing in the province or territory of the Court which made the Approval Order, or who are deemed to be subject to such Approval Order pursuant to Section 4.04 of this Agreement. No additional court approval of any payment to be made to any Class Member or Cloud Class Member will be necessary.

2.02   Effective in Entirety

None of the provisions of this Agreement will become effective unless and until the Courts approve all the provisions of this Agreement, except that the fees and disbursements of the NCC will be paid in any event.

ARTICLE THREE
FUNDING

3.01   CEP Funding

(1)   Canada will provide the Designated Amount to the legal representatives of the Class Members and the Cloud Class Members in trust on the Implementation Date. The Class Members and the Cloud Class Members agree that, contemporaneous with the receipt of the Designated Amount by their legal representatives, the Class Members and Cloud Class Members irrevocably direct the Designated Amount, in its entirety, be paid to the Trustee.

(2)   The Parties agree that the Designated Amount Fund will be held and administered by the Trustee as set out in the Trust Agreement attached as Schedule "I" of this Agreement.

3.02   Healing Funding

On the Implementation Date Canada will transfer one hundred and twenty-five million dollars ($125,000,000.00) as an endowment for a five year period to the Aboriginal Healing Foundation in accordance with Article Eight (8) of this Agreement. After the Implementation Date the only obligations and liabilities of Canada with respect to healing funding are those set out in this Agreement.

3.03 Truth and Reconciliation Funding

(1)   Canada will provide sixty million dollars ($60,000,000.00) in two instalments for the establishment and work of the Commission. Two million dollars ($2,000,000.00) will be available on the Approval Date to begin start-up procedures in advance of the establishment of the Commission. The remaining fifty-eight million dollars ($58,000,000.00) will be transferred within thirty (30) days of the approval of the Commission's budget by Canada. After the date of the final transfer, Canada will have no further obligations or liabilities with respect to truth and reconciliation funding except as set out in this Agreement.

(2)   Canada will appoint an interim Executive Director to begin start-up procedures for the Commission. The interim Executive Director may make reports to the NCC. The interim Executive Director will be appointed as soon as practicable after the Approval Date. That appointment will remain effective until the appointment of the Commissioners. Canada will assume responsibility for the salary of the Executive Director Position during this interim period.

3.04 Commemoration Funding

The funding for commemoration will be twenty million dollars ($20,000,000.00) for both national commemorative and community-based commemorative projects. The funding will be available in accordance with the Commemoration Policy Directive, attached as Schedule "J". For greater certainty, funding under this Section 3.04 includes funding previously authorized in the amount of ten million dollars ($10,000,000) for commemoration events. This previously authorized amount of ten million dollars ($10,000,000) will not be available until after the Implementation Date. After the Implementation Date the only obligations and liabilities of Canada with respect to commemoration funding are those set out in this Agreement.

3.05 IAP Funding

Canada will fund the IAP to the extent sufficient to ensure the full and timely implementation of the provisions set out in Article Six (6) of this Agreement.

3.06 Social Benefits

(1)   Canada will make its best efforts to obtain the agreement of the provinces and territories that the receipt of any payments pursuant to this Agreement will not affect the quantity, nature or duration of any social benefits or social assistance benefits payable to a Class Member or a Cloud Class Member pursuant to any legislation of any province or territory of Canada.

(2)   Canada will make its best efforts to obtain the agreement of the necessary Federal Government Departments that the receipt of any payments pursuant to this Agreement will not affect the quantity, nature or duration of any social benefits or social assistance

benefits payable to a Class Member or a Cloud Class Member pursuant to any social benefit programs of the Federal Government such as old age security and Canada Pension Plan.

3.07   Family Class Claims

The Parties agree and acknowledge that the programmes described in Sections 3.02, 3.03 and 3.04 will be available for the benefit of the Cloud Class Members and all Class Members including the family class defined in the Class Actions.

ARTICLE FOUR
IMPLEMENTATION OF THIS AGREEMENT

4.01   Class Actions

The Parties agree that all existing class action statements of claim and representative actions, except the Cloud Class Action, filed against Canada in relation to Indian Residential Schools in any court in any Canadian jurisdiction except the Federal Court of Canada (the "original claims") will be merged into a uniform omnibus Statement of Claim in each jurisdiction (the "Class Actions"). The omnibus Statement of Claim will name all plaintiffs named in the original claims and will name as Defendants, Canada and the Church Organizations.

4.02   Content of Class Actions

(1)   The Class Actions will assert common causes of action encompassing and incorporating all claims and causes of action asserted in the original claims.

(2)   Subject to Section 4.04, the Class Actions will subsume all classes contained in the original claims with such modification as is necessary to limit the scope of the classes and subclasses certified by each of the Courts to the provincial or territorial boundaries of that Court save and except the Aboriginal Subclass as set out and defined in the *Fontaine v. Attorney General of Canada*, (05-CV-294716 CP) proposed class action filed in the Ontario Superior Court of Justice on August 5, 2005 which will not be asserted in the Class Actions.

4.03   Consent Order

(1)   The Parties will consent to an order in each of the Courts amending and merging the original claims as set out in Section 4.01 and 4.02 of this Agreement.

(2)   For greater certainty, the order consented to in the Ontario Superior Court of Justice will not amend or merge the Cloud Class Action.

4.04 Class Membership

Class membership in each of the Class Actions will be determined by reference to the province or territory of residence of each Class Member on the Approval Date save and except:

(a) residents of the provinces of Newfoundland and Labrador, Nova Scotia, New Brunswick and Prince Edward Island, and;

(b) International Residents, who are be deemed to be members of the Ontario Class.

4.05 Consent Certification

(1) The Parties agree that concurrent with the applications referred to in Section 4.03, applications will be brought in each of the Courts for consent certification of each of the Class Actions for the purposes of Settlement in accordance with the terms of the Agreement.

(2) Consent certification will be sought on the express condition that each of the Courts, pursuant to the applications for consent certification under Section 4.05(1), certify on the same terms and conditions; including the terms and conditions set out in Section 4.06 save and except for the variations in class and subclass membership set out in Sections 4.02 and 4.04 of this Agreement.

4.06 Approval Orders

Approval Orders will be sought:

(a) incorporating by reference this Agreement in its entirety;

(b) ordering and declaring that such orders are binding on all Class Members, including Persons Under Disability, unless they opt out or are deemed to have opted out on or before the expiry of the Opt Out Periods;

(c) ordering and declaring that on the expiry of the Opt Out Periods all pending actions of all Class Members, other than the Class Actions, relating to Indian Residential Schools, which have been filed in any court in any Canadian jurisdiction against Canada or the Church Organizations, except for any pending actions in Quebec which have not been voluntarily discontinued by the expiry of the Opt Out Period, will be deemed to be dismissed without costs unless the individual has opted out, or is deemed to have opted out on or before the expiry of the Opt Out Periods.

(d) ordering and declaring that on the expiry of the Opt Out Periods all class members, unless they have opted out or are deemed to have opted out on or before the expiry of the Opt Out Periods, have released each of the defendants and Other Released Church Organizations from any and all actions they have, may have had or in the future may acquire against any of the defendants and Other Released Church Organizations arising in relation to an Indian Residential School or the operation of Indian Residential Schools.

(e) ordering and declaring that in the event the number of Eligible CEP Recipients opting out or deemed to have opted out under the Approval Orders exceeds five thousand (5000), this Agreement will be rendered void and the Approval Orders set aside in their entirety subject only to the right of Canada, in its sole discretion, to waive compliance with Section 4.14 of this Agreement.

(f) ordering and declaring that on the expiration of the Opt Out Periods all Class Members who have not opted out have agreed that they will not make any claim arising from or in relation to an Indian Residential School or the operation of Indian Residential Schools against any person who may in turn claim against any of the defendants or Other Released Church Organizations.

(g) ordering and declaring that the obligations assumed by the defendants under this Agreement are in full and final satisfaction of all claims arising from or in relation to an Indian Residential School or the operation of Indian Residential Schools of the Class Members and that the Approval Orders are the sole recourse on account of any and all claims referred to therein.

(h) ordering and declaring that the fees and disbursements of all counsel participating in this Agreement are to be approved by the Courts on the basis provided in Articles Four (4) and Thirteen (13) of this Agreement, except that the fees and disbursements of the NCC and the IAP Working Group will be paid in any event.

(i) ordering and declaring that notwithstanding Section 4.06(c), (d) and (f), a Class Member who on or after the fifth anniversary of the Implementation Date had never commenced an action other than a class action in relation to an Indian Residential School or the operation of Indian Residential Schools, participated in a Pilot Project, applied to the DR Model, or applied to the IAP, may commence an action for any of the Continuing Claims within the jurisdiction of the court in which the action is commenced. For greater certainty, the rules, procedures and standards of the IAP are not applicable to such actions.

(j) ordering and declaring that where an action permitted by Section 4.06(i) is brought, the deemed release set out in Section 11.01 is amended to the extent necessary to permit the action to proceed only with respect to Continuing Claims.

(k) ordering and declaring that for an action brought under Section 4.06(i) all limitations periods will be tolled, and any defences based on laches or delay will not be asserted by the Parties with regard to a period of five years from the Implementation Date.

(l)   ordering and declaring that notwithstanding Section 4.06(d) no action, except for Family Class claims as set out in the Class Actions and the Cloud Class Action, capable of being brought by a Class Member or Cloud Class Member will be released where such an action would be released only by virtue of being a member of a Family Class in the Class Actions or the Cloud Class Action.

4.07   Cloud Class Action Approval Order

There will be a separate approval order in relation to the Cloud Class Action which will be, in all respects save as to class membership and Section 17.02 of this Agreement, in the same terms and conditions as the Approval Orders referred to herein.

4.08   Notice

(1)   The parties agree that the NCC will implement the Residential Schools Class Action Litigation Settlement Notice Plan prepared by Hilsoft Notifications and generally in the form attached as Schedule "K".

(2)   The NCC will develop a list of counsel with active Indian Residential Schools claims and who agree to be bound by the terms of this Agreement, before the Approval date, which will be referenced in the written materials and website information of the notice program.

(3)   The legal notice will include an opt out coupon which will be returnable to a Post Office Box address at Edmonton, Alberta.

(4)   There will be a "1-800" number funded by Canada which will provide scripted information concerning the settlement. The information will convey a statement to the effect that although there is no requirement to do so, Class Members may wish to consult a lawyer.

4.09   National Certification Committee

(1)   The Parties agree to the establishment of a NCC with a mandate to:

a)   designate counsel having carriage in respect of drafting the consent certification documents and obtaining consent certification and approval of this Agreement;

b)   provide input to and consult with Trustee on the request of Trustee;

c)   obtain consent certification and approval of the Approval Orders in the Courts on the express condition that the Courts all certify on the same terms and conditions.

d)   exercise all necessary powers to fulfill its functions under the Independent Assessment Process.

(2)   The NCC will have seven (7) members with the intention that decisions will be made by consensus.

(3)   Where consensus can not be reached, a majority of five (5) of the seven (7) members is required.

(4)   The composition of the NCC will be one (1) counsel from each of the following groups:

    a) Canada;
    b) Church Organizations;
    c) Assembly of First Nations;
    d) The National Consortium;
    e) Merchant Law Group;
    f) Inuit Representatives; and
    g) IndependentCounsel

(5)   The NCC will be dissolved on the Implementation Date.

(6)   Notwithstanding Section 4.09(4) the Church Organizations may designate a second counsel to attend and participate in meetings of the NCC. Designated second counsel will not participate in any vote conducted under Section 4.09(3).

4.10   Administration Committees

(1)   In order to implement the Approval Orders the Parties agree to the establishment of administrative committees as follows:

    a) one National Administration Committee ("NAC"); and

    b) three Regional Administration Committees ("RACs").

(2)   Notwithstanding Section 4.10(1) neither the NAC nor the RAC's will meet or conduct any business whatsoever prior to the Implementation Date, unless Canada agrees otherwise.

4.11   National Administration Committee

(1)   The composition of the NAC will be one (1) representative counsel from each of the groups set out at section 4.09(4):

(2)   The first NAC member from each group will be named by that group on or before the execution of this Agreement.

(3)   Each NAC member may name a designate to attend meetings of the NAC and act on their behalf and the designate will have the powers, authorities and responsibilities of the NAC member while in attendance.

(4)   Upon the resignation, death or expiration of the term of any NAC member or where the Court otherwise directs in accordance with 4.11(6) of this Agreement, a replacement NAC member will be named by the group represented by that member.

(5)   Membership on the NAC will be for a term of two (2) years.

(6)   In the event of any dispute related to the appointment or service of an individual as a member of the NAC, the affected group or individual may apply to the court of the jurisdiction where the affected individual resides for advice and directions.

(7)   The Parties agree that Canada will not be liable for any costs associated with an application contemplated in Section 4.11(6) that relates to the appointment of an individual as a member of the NAC.

(8)   No NAC member may serve as a member of a RAC or as a member of the Oversight Committee during their term on the NAC.

(9)   Decisions of the NAC will be made by consensus and where consensus can not be reached, a majority of five (5) of the seven (7) members is required to make any decision. In the event that a majority of five (5) members can not be reached the dispute may be referred by a simple majority of four (4) NAC members to the Appropriate Court in the jurisdiction where the dispute arose by way of reference styled as *In Re Residential Schools*.

(10)   Notwithstanding Section 4.11(9), where a vote would increase the costs of the Approval Orders whether for compensation or procedural matters, the representative for Canada must be one (1) of the five (5) member majority.

(11)   There will not be reference to the Courts for any dispute arising under Section 4.11(10).

(12)   The mandate of the NAC is to:

    (a) interpret the Approval Orders;

    (b) consult with and provide input to the Trustee with respect to the Common Experience Payment;

    (c) ensure national consistency with respect to implementation of the Approval Orders to the greatest extent possible;

(d) produce and implement a policy protocol document with respect to implementation of the Approval Orders;

(e) produce a standard operating procedures document with respect to implementation of the Approval Orders;

(f) act as the appellate forum from the RACs;

(g) review the continuation of RACs as set out in Section 4.13;

(h) assume the RACs mandate in the event that the RACs cease to operate pursuant to Section 4.13;

(i) hear applications from the RACs arising from a dispute

related to the appointment or service of an individual as a member of the RACs;

(j) review and determine references from the Truth and Reconciliation Commission made pursuant to Section 7.01(2) of this Agreement or may, without deciding the reference, refer it to any one of the Courts for a determination of the matter;

(k) hear appeals from an Eligible CEP Recipient as set out in Section 5.09(1) and recommend costs as set out in Section 5.09(3) of this Agreement;

(l) apply to any one of the Courts for determination with respect to a refusal to add an institution as set out in Section 12.01 of this Agreement;

(m) retain and instruct counsel as directed by Canada for the purpose of fulfilling its mandate as set out in Sections 4.11(12)(j),(l) and(q) and Section 4.11(13) of this Agreement;

(n) develop a list of counsel with active Indian Residential Schools claims who agree to be bound by the terms of this Agreement as set out in Section 4.08(5) of this Agreement;

(o) exercise all the necessary powers to fulfill its functions under the IAP;

(p) request additional funding from Canada for the IAP as set out in Section 6.03(3) of this Agreement;

(q) apply to the Courts for orders modifying the IAP as set out in Section 6.03(3) of this Agreement.

(r) recommend to Canada the provision of one additional notice of the IAP Application Deadline to Class Members and Cloud Class Members in accordance with Section 6.04 of this Agreement.

(13) Where there is a disagreement between the Trustee and the NAC, with respect to the terms of the Approval Orders the NAC or the Trustee may refer the dispute to the Appropriate Court in the jurisdiction where the dispute arose by way of reference styled as *In Re Residential Schools*.

(14) Subject to Section 6.03(3), no material amendment to the Approval Orders can occur without the unanimous consent of the NAC ratified by the unanimous approval of the Courts.

(15) Canada's representative on the NAC will serve as Secretary of the NAC.

(16) Notwithstanding Section 4.11(1) the Church Organizations may

designate a second counsel to attend and participate in meetings of the NAC. Designated second counsel will not participate in any vote conducted under Section 4.11(9).

4.12 Regional Administration Committees

(1) One (1) RAC will operate for the benefit of both the Class Members, as defined in Section 4.04, and Cloud Class Members in each of the following three (3) regions:

a) British Columbia, Alberta, Northwest Territories and the Yukon Territory;

b) Saskatchewan and Manitoba; and

c) Ontario, Quebec and Nunavut.

(2) Each of the three (3) RACs will have three (3) members chosen from the four (4) plaintiff's representative groups set out in Sections 4.09(4)(d),(e),(f) and (g) of this Agreement.

(3) Initial members of each of the three (3) RAC's will be named by the groups set out in sections 4.09(4)(d),(e),(f) and(g) of this Agreement on or before the execution of this Agreement and Canada will be advised of the names of the initial members.

(4) Upon the resignation, death or expiration of the term of any

RAC member or where the Court otherwise directs in accordance with 4.12(7) of this Agreement, a replacement RAC member will be named by the group represented by that member.

(5) Membership on each of the RACs will be for a two (2) year term.

(6)   Each RAC member may name a designate to attend meetings of the RAC and the designate will have the powers, authorities and responsibilities of the RAC member while in attendance.

(7)   In the event of any dispute related to the appointment or service of an individual as a member of the RAC, the affected group or individual may apply to the NAC for a determination of the issue.

(8)   No RAC member may serve as a member of the NAC or as a member of the Oversight Committee during their term on a RAC.

(9)   Each RAC will operate independently of the other RACs. Each RAC will make its decisions by consensus among its three members. Where consensus can not be reached, a majority is required to make a decision.

(10)   In the event that an Eligible CEP Recipient, a member of a RAC, or a member of the NAC is not satisfied with a decision of a RAC that individual may submit the dispute to the NAC for resolution.

(11)   The RACs will deal only with the day-to-day operational issues relating to implementation of the Approval Orders arising within their individual regions which do not have national significance. In no circumstance will a RAC have authority to review any decision related to the IAP.

4.13   Review by NAC

Eighteen months following the Implementation Date, the NAC will consider and determine the necessity for the continuation of the operation of any or all of the 3 RACs provided that any determination made by the NAC must be unanimous.

4.14   Opt Out Threshold

In the event that the number of Eligible CEP Recipients opting out or deemed to have opted out under the Approval Orders exceeds five thousand (5,000), this Agreement will be rendered void and the Approval Orders set aside in their entirety subject only to the right of Canada, in its sole discretion, to waive compliance with this Section of this Agreement. Canada has the right to waive compliance with this Section of the Agreement until thirty (30) days after the end of the Opt Out Periods.

4.15   Federal Court Actions Exception

The Parties agree that both the *Kenneth Sparvier et al. v. Attorney General of Canada* proposed class action filed in the Federal Court on May 13, 2005 as Court File Number: T 848-05, and the *George Laliberte et al v. Attorney General of Canada* proposed class action filed in the Federal Court on September 23, 2005 as Court File Number: T-1620-05, will be discontinued without costs on or before the Implementation Date.

ARTICLE FIVE
COMMON EXPERIENCE PAYMENT

5.01 CEP

Subject to Sections 17.01 and 17.02, the Trustee will make a Common Experience Payment out of the Designated Amount Fund to every Eligible CEP Recipient who submits a CEP Application provided that:

(1)   the CEP Application is submitted to the Trustee in accordance with the provisions of this Agreement;

(2)   the CEP Application is received prior to the CEP Application Deadline;

(3)   the CEP Application is validated in accordance with the provisions of this Agreement; and

(4)   the Eligible CEP Recipient was alive on May 30, 2005.

5.02 Amount of CEP

The amount of the Common Experience Payment will be:

(1)   ten thousand dollars ($10,000.00) to every Eligible CEP Recipient who resided at one or more Indian Residential Schools for one school year or part thereof; and

(2)   an additional three thousand ($3,000.00) to every eligible CEP Recipient who resided at one or more Indian Residential Schools for each school year or part thereof, after the first school year; and

(3)   less the amount of any advance payment on the CEP received

5.03 Interest on Designated Amount Fund

Interest on the assets of the Designated Amount Fund will be earned and paid as provided in Order in Council P.C. 1970-300 of February 17, 1970 made pursuant to section 21(2) of the Financial Administration Act as set out in the Trust Agreement attached as Schedule "I".

5.04 CEP Application Process

(1)   No Eligible CEP Recipient will receive a CEP without submitting a CEP Application to the Trustee.

(2)   The Trustee will not accept a CEP Application prior to the Implementation Date or after the CEP Application Deadline.

(3) Notwithstanding Sections 5.01(2) and 5.04(2) of this Agreement, where the Trustee is satisfied that an Eligible CEP Recipient is a Person Under Disability on the CEP Application Deadline or was delayed from delivering a CEP Application on or before the CEP Application Deadline as prescribed in Section 5.04(2) as a result of undue hardship or exceptional circumstances, the Trustee will consider the CEP Application filed after the CEP Application Deadline, but in no case will the Trustee consider a CEP Application filed more than one year after the CEP Application Deadline unless directed by the Court.

(4) No person may submit more than one (1) CEP Application on his or her own behalf.

(5) Where an Eligible CEP Recipient does not submit a CEP Application as prescribed in this Section 5.04 that Eligible CEP Recipient will not be entitled to receive a Common Experience Payment and any such entitlement will be forever extinguished.

(6) The Trustee will process all CEP Applications substantially in accordance with Schedule "L" attached hereto. All CEP Applications will be subject to verification.

(7) The Trustee will give notice to an Eligible CEP Recipient of its decision in respect of his or her CEP Application within 60 days of the decision being made.

(8) A decision of the Trustee is final and binding upon the claimant and the Trustee, subject only to the CEP Appeal Procedure set out in Section 5.09 of this Agreement.

(9) The Trustee agrees to make all Common Experience Payments as soon as practicable.

5.05   Review and Audit to Determine Holdings

(1) The Trustee will review the Designated Amount Fund on or before the first anniversary of the Implementation Date and from time to time thereafter to determine the sufficiency of the Designated Amount Fund to pay all Eligible CEP Recipients who have applied for a CEP as of the date of the review.

(2) The Trustee will audit the Designated Amount Fund within twelve (12) months following the CEP Application Deadline to determine the balance held in that fund on the date of the audit.

5.06   Insufficiency of Designated Amount

In the event that a review under Section 5.05(1) determines that the Designated Amount Fund is insufficient to pay all Eligible CEP Recipients who have applied, as of the date of the review, to receive the Common Experience Payment to which they are entitled, Canada will add an amount sufficient to remedy any deficiency in this respect within 90 days of being notified of the deficiency by the Trustee.

5.07   Excess Designated Amount

(1)   If the audit under Section 5.05(2) determines that the balance in the Designated Amount Fund exceeds the amount required to make the Common Experience Payment to all Eligible CEP Recipients who have applied before the CEP Application Deadline by more than forty million dollars ($40,000,000.00), the excess will be apportioned *pro rata* to all those who received a Common Experience Payment to a maximum amount of three thousand dollars ($3,000.00) per person in the form of Personal Credits.

(2)   After the payment of the maximum amount of Personal Credits to all Eligible CEP Recipients who have received the CEP, including payment of all administration costs related thereto, all excess funds remaining in the Designated Amount Found will be transferred to the National Indian Brotherhood Trust Fund (NIBTF) and to the Inuvialuit Education Foundation (IEF), consistent with applicable Treasury Board policies, in the proportion set out in Section 5.07(5). The monies so transferred shall be used for educational programs on terms and conditions agreed between Canada and NIBTF and IEF, which terms and conditions shall ensure fair and reasonable access to such programs by all class members including all First Nations, Inuit, Inuvialuit and Métis persons. In carrying out its discussions with NIBTF and IEF, Canada shall obtain input from counsel for the groups set out in Section 4.09(d), (e), (f) and (g).

(3)   If the audit under Section 5.05(2) determines that the balance in the Designated Amount Fund exceeds the amount required to make Common Experience Payments to all Eligible CEP Recipients who have applied before the CEP Application Deadline by less than forty million dollars ($40,000,000.00), there will be no entitlement to Personal Credits, and the excess will be transferred to the NIBTF and IEF in the proportions set out in Section 5.07(5) for the same purposes and on the same terms and conditions set out in Section 5.07(2).

(4)   Any and all amounts remaining in the Designated Amount Fund on January 1, 2015 will be paid to the NIBTF and the IEF in the proportions set out in Section 5.07(5) for the same purposes and on the same terms and conditions set out in Section 5.07(2).

(5)   Funds in the Designated Amount Fund shall be transferred to the NIBTF and the IEF respectively proportionately based on the total number of Eligible CEP Recipients other than Inuit and Inuvialuit who have received the CEP in the case of the NIBTF and the total number of Inuit and Inuvialuit Eligible CEP Recipients who have received the CEP in the case of the IEF.

5.08   CEP Administrative Costs

(1)   It is agreed that Canada will assume all internal administrative costs relating to the CEP and its distribution.

(2)   It is agreed that all internal administrative costs relating to the Personal Credits and their distribution will be paid from the Designated Amount Fund.

5.09   CEP Appeal Procedure

(1)   Where a claim made in a CEP Application has been denied in whole or in part, the applicant may appeal the decision to the NAC for a determination.

(2)   In the event the NAC denies the appeal in whole or in part the applicant may apply to the Appropriate Court for a determination of the issue.

(3)   The NAC may recommend to Canada that the costs of an appeal under Section 5.09(1) be borne by Canada. In exceptional circumstances, the NAC may apply to the Appropriate Court for an order that the costs of an appeal under Section 5.09(1) be borne by Canada.

ARTICLE SIX
INDEPENDENT ASSESSMENT PROCESS

6.01   IAP

An Independent Assessment Process will be established as set out in Schedule "D" of this Agreement.

6.02   IAP Application Deadline

(1)   Applications to the IAP will not be accepted prior to the Implementation Date or after the IAP Application Deadline.

(2)   Where an Eligible IAP Claimant does not submit an IAP Application as prescribed in this Section 6.02(1) that Eligible IAP Claimant will not be admitted to the IAP and any such entitlement to make a claim in the IAP will be forever extinguished.

(3)   All applications to the IAP which have been delivered prior to the IAP Application Deadline will be processed within the IAP as set out in Schedule "D" of this Agreement.

6.03   Resources

(1)   The parties agree that Canada will provide sufficient resources to the IAP to ensure that:

   a)   Following the expiry of a six month start-up period commencing on the Implementation Date:

   (i)   Continuing Claims which have been screened into the IAP will be processed at a minimum rate of two-thousand five-hundred (2500) in each twelve (12) month period thereafter; and

(ii)   the Claimant in each of those two-thousand five hundred (2500) Continuing Claims will be offered a hearing date within nine months of their application being screened-in. The hearing date will be within the nine month period following the claim being screened-in, or within a reasonable period of time thereafter, unless the claimant's failure to meet one or more of the requirements of the IAP frustrates compliance with that objective.

b)   Notwithstanding Section 6.03(1)(a), all IAP claimants whose applications have been screened into the IAP as of the eighteen (18) month anniversary of the Implementation Date will be offered a hearing date before the expiry of a further nine month period or within a reasonable period of time thereafter, unless the claimant's failure to meet one or more of the requirements of the IAP frustrates compliance with that objective.

c)   All IAP claimants screened-in after the eighteen (18) month anniversary of the Implementation Date will be offered a hearing within nine (9) months of their claim being screened in. The hearing date will be within the nine month period following the claim being screened-in, or within a reasonable period of time thereafter, unless the claimant's failure to meet one or more of the requirements of the IAP frustrates compliance with that objective.

d)   For greater certainty, all IAP Applications filed before the expiration of the IAP Application Deadline will be processed prior to the six (6) year anniversary of the Implementation Date unless a claimant's failure to meet one or more of the requirements of the IAP frustrates compliance with that objective.

(2)   In the event that Continuing Claims are submitted at a rate that is less than two-thousand five hundred (2,500) per twelve month period, Canada will be required only to provide resources sufficient to process the Continuing Claims at the rate at which they are received, and within the timeframes set out in Section 6.03 (1)(a) and (b) of this Agreement.

(3)   Notwithstanding Article 4.11(11), in the event that Continuing Claims are not processed at the rate and within the timeframes set out in Section 6.03(1)(a) and (b) of this Agreement, the NAC may request that Canada provide additional resources for claims processing and, after providing a reasonable period for Canada's response, apply to the Courts for orders necessary to permit the realization of Section 6.03(1).

6.04   Notice of IAP Application Deadline

One additional notice of the IAP Application Deadline may be provided on the recommendation of the NAC to Canada.

ARTICLE SEVEN
TRUTH AND RECONCILIATION AND COMMEMORATION

7.01   Truth and Reconciliation

(1)   A Truth and Reconciliation process will be established as set out in Schedule "N" of this Agreement.

(2)   The Truth and Reconciliation Commission may refer to the NAC for determination of disputes involving document production, document disposal and archiving, contents of the Commission's Report and Recommendations and Commission decisions regarding the scope of its research and issues to be examined. The Commission shall make best efforts to resolve the matter itself before referring it to the NAC.

(3)   Where the NAC makes a decision in respect of a dispute or disagreement that arises in respect of the Truth and Reconciliation Commission as contemplated in Section 7.01(2), either or both the Church Organization and Canada may apply to any one of the Courts for a hearing *de novo*.

7.02   Commemoration

Proposals for commemoration will be addressed in accordance with the Commemoration Policy Directive set out in Schedule "J" of this Agreement.

ARTICLE EIGHT
HEALING

8.01   Healing

(1)   To facilitate access to healing programmes, Canada will provide the endowment to the Aboriginal Healing Foundation as set out in Section 3.02 on terms and conditions substantially similar to the draft attached hereto as Schedule "M".

(2)   On or before the expiry of the fourth anniversary of the Implementation Date, Canada will conduct an evaluation of the healing initiatives and programmes undertaken by the Aboriginal Healing Foundation to determine the efficacy of such initiatives and programmes and recommend whether and to what extent funding should continue beyond the five year period.

8.02   Availability of Mental Health and Emotional Support Services

Canada agrees that it will continue to provide existing mental health and emotional support services and agrees to make those services available to those who are resolving a claim through the Independent Assessment Process or who are eligible to receive compensation under the Independent Assessment Process. Canada agrees that it will also make those services available to Common Experience Payment recipients and those participating in truth and reconciliation or commemorative initiatives.

ARTICLE NINE
CHURCH ORGANIZATIONS

9.01   The Parties agree that the Church Organizations will participate in this Agreement as set out herein and in accordance with the Agreements between Canada and the Church Organizations attached hereto in Schedules "O-1", The Presbyterian Church Agreement, Schedule "O-2", The Anglican Entities Agreement, Schedule "O-3", The Catholic Entities Agreement and Schedule "O-4", The United Church of Canada Agreement.

ARTICLE TEN
Duties of the Trustee

10.01   Trustee

In addition to the duties set out in the Trust Agreement, the Trustee's duties and responsibilities will be the following:

a)   developing, installing and implementing systems and procedures for processing, evaluating and making decisions respecting CEP Applications which reflect the need for simplicity in form, expedition of payments and an appropriate form of audit verification, including processing the CEP Applications substantially in accordance with Schedule "L" of this Agreement;

b)   developing, installing and implementing systems and procedures necessary to meet its obligations as set out in the Trust Agreement attached as Schedule "I" hereto;

c)   developing, installing and implementing systems and procedures for paying out compensation for validated CEP Applications;

d)   reporting to the NAC and the Courts respecting CEP Applications received and being administered and compensation paid;

e)   providing personnel in such reasonable numbers as are required for the performance of its duties, and training and instructing them;

f)   keeping or causing to be kept accurate accounts of its activities and its administration of the CEP, including payment of compensation under the CEP, preparing such financial statements, reports and records as are required by the NAC and the Courts, in form and content as directed by the Courts and submitting them to the Courts so often as the Courts direct;

g)   receiving and responding to all enquiries and correspondence respecting the validation of CEP Applications, reviewing and evaluating all CEP Applications, making decisions in respect of CEP Applications, giving notice of its decisions in accordance with the provisions this Agreement and communicating with Eligible CEP Recipients, in either English or French, as the Eligible CEP Recipient elects;

h) receiving and responding to all enquiries and correspondence respecting payment of compensation for valid CEP Applications, and forwarding the compensation in accordance with the provisions of this Agreement and communicating with Eligible CEP Recipients, in either English or French, as the Eligible CEP Recipient elects;

i) administering Personal Credits in accordance with Section 5.07 of this Agreement;

j) maintaining a database with all information necessary to permit the NAC and the Courts to evaluate the financial viability and sufficiency of the Designated Amount Fund from time to time, subject to applicable law; and,

k) such other duties and responsibilities as the Courts may from time to time by order direct.

ARTICLE ELEVEN
RELEASES

11.01 Class Member and Cloud Class Member Releases

(1) The Approval Orders will declare that in the case of Class Members and Cloud Class Members:

a) Each Class Member and Cloud Class Member has fully, finally and forever released each of the Releasees from any and all actions, causes of action, common law, Quebec civil law and statutory liabilities, contracts, claims and demands of every nature or kind available, asserted or which could have been asserted whether known or unknown including for damages, contribution, indemnity, costs, expenses and interest which any such Class Member or Cloud Class Member ever had, now has, or may hereafter have, directly or indirectly arising from or in any way relating to or by way of any subrogated or assigned right or otherwise in relation to an Indian Residential School or the operation of Indian Residential Schools and this release includes any such claim made or that could have been made in any proceeding including the Class Actions or the Cloud Class Action whether asserted directly by the Class Member or Cloud Class Member or by any other person, group or legal entity on behalf of or as representative for the Class Member or Cloud Class Member.

b) The Class Members and Cloud Class Members are deemed to agree that they will not make any claim or demand or take any actions or proceedings against any Releasee or any other person or persons in which any claim could arise against any Releasee for damages and/or contribution and/or indemnity and/or other relief over under the provisions of the *Negligence Act*, R.S.O. 1990, c. N-3, or its counterpart in other jurisdictions, the common law, Quebec civil law or any other statute of Ontario or any other jurisdiction in relation to an Indian Residential School or the operation of Indian Residential Schools;

c) Canada's, the Church Organizations' and the Other Released Church Organizations' obligations and liabilities under this Agreement constitute the consideration for the releases and other matters referred to in Section 11.01(a) and (b) inclusive and such consideration is in full and final settlement and satisfaction of any and all claims referred to therein and the Class Members or and Cloud Class Members are limited to the benefits provided and compensation payable pursuant to this Agreement, in whole or in part, as their only recourse on account of any and all such actions, causes of actions, liabilities, claims and demands.

(2) Notwithstanding Section 11.01(1), no action, except for Family Class claims as set out in the Class Actions and the Cloud Class Action, capable of being brought by a Class Member or Cloud Class Member will be released where such an action would be released only by virtue of being a member of a Family Class in the Class Actions or the Cloud Class Action.

11.02 Non-resident Claimant Releases

(1) The Approval Orders will order and declare that Non-resident Claimants on being accepted into the IAP, must execute a Release in the form set out in Schedule "P" of this Agreement.

(2) Nothing in Section 4.06 (c), (d) or (f) or Section 11.01(1)(a) will prevent a Non-resident Claimant from pursuing his or her claim in the IAP.

(3) For greater certainty nothing in this Section 11.02 will prevent the bringing of an action contemplated in Section 4.06(i) and (j) of this Agreement.

11.03 Claims by Opt Outs and Others

If any person not bound by this Agreement claims over or brings a third party claim, makes any claim or demand or takes any action or proceeding against any defendant named in the Class Actions or the Cloud Class Action arising in relation to an Indian Residential School or the operation of Indian Residential Schools, no amount payable by any defendant named in the Class Actions of the Cloud Class Action to that person will be paid out of the Designated Amount Fund.

11.04 Cessation of litigation

(1) Upon execution of this Agreement, the representative plaintiffs named in the Class Actions and the Cloud Class Action, and counsel from each of the groups set out in Section 4.09(4)(c), (d), (e), (f) and (g) will cooperate with the defendants named in the Class Actions and in the Cloud Class Action to obtain approval of this Agreement and general participation by Class Members and Cloud Class Members and Non-resident Claimants in all aspects of the Agreement.

(2)   Each counsel from each of the groups set out in section 4.09(4)(c), (d), (e), (f) and (g) will undertake, within five days after the Approval Date, not to commence or assist or advise on the commencement or continuation of any actions or proceedings calculated to or having the effect of undermining this Agreement against any of the Releasees, or against any person who may claim contribution or indemnity from any of the Releasees in any way relating to or arising from any claim which is subject to this Agreement, provided that nothing in the Agreement will prevent any counsel from advising any person whether to opt out of the Class Actions and to continue to act for that person.

ARTICLE TWELVE
ADDITIONAL INDIAN RESIDENTIAL SCHOOLS

12.01   Request to Add Institution

(1)   Any person or organization (the "Requestor") may request that an institution be added to Schedule "F", in accordance with the criteria set out in Section 12.01(2) of this Agreement, by submitting the name of the institution and any relevant information in the Requestor's possession to Canada;

(2)   The criteria for adding an institution to Schedule "F" are:

a)   The child was placed in a residence away from the family home by or under the authority of Canada for the purposes of education; and,

b)   Canada was jointly or solely responsible for the operation of the residence and care of the children resident there.

(3)   Indicators that Canada was jointly or solely responsible for the operation of the residence and care of children there include, but are not limited to, whether:

a)   The institution was federally owned;

b)   Canada stood as the parent to the child;

c)   Canada was at least partially responsible for the administration of the institution;

d)   Canada inspected or had a right to inspect the institution; or,

e)   Canada did or did not stipulate the institution as an IRS.

(4)   Within 60 days of receiving a request to add an institution to Schedule "F", Canada will research the proposed institution and determine whether it is an Indian Residential

School as defined in this Agreement and will provide both the Requestor and the NAC with:

a) Canada's decision on whether the institution is an Indian Residential School;

b) Written reasons for that decision; and

c) A list of materials upon which that decision was made;

provided that Canada may ask the Requestor for an extension of time to complete the research.

(5) Should either the Requestor or the NAC dispute Canada's decision to refuse to add a proposed institution, the Requestor may apply to the Appropriate Court, or the NAC may apply to the court of the province or territory where the Requestor resides for a determination.

(6) Where Canada adds an institution to Schedule "F" under Section 12.01(4), Canada may provide the Requestor with reasonable legal costs and disbursements.

ARTICLE THIRTEEN
LEGAL FEES

13.01 Legal Fees

Canada agrees to compensate legal counsel in respect of their legal fees as set out herein.

13.02 Negotiation Fees (July 2005 – November 20, 2005)

(1) Canada agrees to pay each lawyer, other than lawyers representing the Church Organizations, who attended the settlement negotiations beginning July 2005 leading to the Agreement in Principle for time spent up to the date of the Agreement in Principle in respect of the settlement negotiations at his or her normal hourly rate, plus reasonable disbursements, and GST and PST, if applicable except that no amount is payable under this Section 13.02(1) for fees previously paid directly by OIRSRC.

(2) All legal fees payable under Section 13.02(1) will be paid no later than 60 days after the Implementation Date.

13.03 Fees to Complete Settlement Agreement (November 20, 2005 – Execution of Settlement Agreement)

    (1)   Canada agrees to pay each lawyer, other than lawyers representing the Church Organizations, for time spent between November 20, 2005 and the date of execution of this Agreement in respect of finalizing this Agreement at each lawyer's normal hourly rate, plus reasonable disbursements and GST and PST, if applicable except that no amount is payable under this Section 13.03(1) for fees previously paid directly by OIRSRC.

    (2)   No fees will be payable under Section 13.03(1) for any work compensated under Section 13.04 of this Agreement.

    (3)   All legal fees payable under Section 13.03(1) will be paid no later than 60 days after the Implementation Date.

13.04 Fees Accrued after November 20, 2005 (NCC Fees)

    (1)   Legal fees payable to legal counsel from November 20, 2005 forward will be paid in accordance with the terms set out in Section 13.10(1)(2)(4) and (5) of this Agreement.

    (2)   Subject to 13.07, all legal fees payable under Section 13.06 and 13.08 will be paid no later than 60 days after the Implementation Date.

13.05 No Fees on CEP Payments

No lawyer or law firm that has signed this Settlement Agreement or who accepts a payment for legal fees from Canada, pursuant to Sections 13.06 or 13.08, will charge an Eligible CEP Recipient any fees or disbursements in respect of the Common Experience Payment.

13.06 Fees Where Retainer Agreements

Each lawyer who had a retainer agreement or a substantial solicitor-client relationship (a "Retainer Agreement") with an Eligible CEP Recipient as of May 30, 2005, will be paid an amount equal to the lesser of:

    a)   the amount of outstanding Work-in-Progress as of the date of the Agreement in Principle in respect of that Retainer Agreement and

    b) $4,000, plus reasonable disbursements, and GST and PST, if applicable, and will agree that no other or further fee will be charged with respect to the CEP.

13.07 Proof of Fees

In order to receive payment pursuant to Section 13.06 of this Agreement, each lawyer will provide to OIRSRC a statutory declaration that attests to the number of Retainer Agreements he or she had with Eligible CEP Recipients as of May 30, 2005 and the amount of outstanding Work-in-Progress in respect of each of those Retainer Agreements as docketed or determined by review. OIRSRC will review these statutory declarations within 60 days of the Implementation Date and will rely on these statutory declarations to verify the amounts being paid to lawyers and will engage in such further verification processes with individual lawyers as circumstances require with the consent of the lawyers involved, such consent not to be unreasonably withheld.

13.08 The National Consortium and the Merchant Law Group Fees

(1)   The National Consortium will be paid forty million dollars ($40,000,000.00) plus reasonable disbursements, and GST and PST, if applicable, in recognition of the substantial number of Eligible CEP Recipients each of them represents and the class action work they have done on behalf of Eligible CEP Recipients. Any lawyer who is a partner of, employed by or otherwise affiliated with a National Consortium member law firm is not entitled to the payments described in Section 13.02 and 13.06 of this Agreement.

(2)   The fees of the Merchant Law Group will be determined in accordance with the provisions of the Agreement in Principle executed November 20, 2005 and the Agreement between Canada and the Merchant Law Group respecting verification of legal fees dated November 20, 2005 attached hereto as Schedule "V", except that the determination described in paragraph 4 of the latter Agreement, will be made by Justice Ball, or, if he is not available, another Justice of the Court of Queen's Bench of Saskatchewan, rather than by an arbitrator.

(3)   The Federal Representative will engage in such further verification processes with respect to the amounts payable to the National Consortium as have been agreed to by those parties.

(4)   In the event that the Federal Representative and either the National Consortium or the Merchant Law Group cannot agree on the amount payable for reasonable disbursements incurred up to and including November 20, 2005, under Section 13.08(1) of this Agreement, the Federal Representative will refer the matter to:

(a)   the Ontario Superior Court of Justice, or an official designated by it, if the matter involves the National Consortium;

(b)   the Saskatchewan Court of Queen's Bench, or an official designated by it, if the matter involves the Merchant Law Group;

to fix such amount.

(5)   The National Consortium member law firms are as follows:

Thomson, Rogers	Troniak Law Office
Richard W. Courtis Law Office	Koskie Minsky LLP
Field LLP	Leslie R. Meiklejohn Law Office
David Paterson Law Corp.	Huck Birchard
Docken & Company	Ruston Marshall
Arnold, Pizzo, McKiggan	Rath & Company
Cohen Highley LLP	Levene Tadman Gutkin Golub

All legal fees payable under Section 13.08 will be paid no later than 60 days after the Implementation Date.

White, Ottenheimer & Baker	Coller Levine
Thompson Dorfman Sweatman	Adams Gareau
Ahlstrom Wright Oliver & Cooper	

13.09   Cloud Class Action Costs, Fees and Disbursements

(1)   Canada will pay all cost awards in the Cloud Class Action that remain outstanding as of November 20, 2005 to Counsel for the Plaintiffs in that action. Canada will not seek to recover any portion of any costs paid pursuant to this Section 13.09(1) from the Anglican entities named as Defendants in the Cloud Class Action.

(2)   Canada will pay the fees and disbursements of the Plaintiffs in the Cloud Class Action as set out in Article 13 of this Agreement.

13.10   NCC Fees

(1)   Canada will pay members of the NCC fees based upon reasonable hourly rates and reasonable disbursements, but such fees will not include any fee for the Government of Canada, or the Church Organizations.

(2)   Subject to Section 13.10(4), any fees referred to in Section 13.10(1) and accrued after April 1, 2006 will be subject to a maximum operating budget of sixty-thousand dollars ($60,000.00) per month.

(3)   Notwithstanding Section 13.10(2) and subject to Section 13.10(4), the NCC may apply to Canada for additional funding in exceptional circumstances up to a maximum monthly amount of fifteen thousand dollars ($15,000.00).

(4)   The maximum operating budget referred to in Section 13.10(1) and the maximum additional funding in exceptional circumstances referred to in Section 13.10(3) will be reviewed and reassessed by Canada on July 1, 2006 and the first day of each month thereafter. Canada, in its sole discretion, may reduce or increase the maximum operating budget or the maximum additional funding or both.

(5)   Counsel who is designated by the NCC as counsel having carriage in respect of drafting, consent certification and approval of the settlement will be paid their normal hourly rates and reasonable disbursements to be billed by Counsel and paid by Canada on an ongoing basis. Such fees and disbursements are not subject to the maximum operating budget referred to in paragraph 13.10(2).

(6)   Other counsel who appear in court, if designated by the NCC and approved by Canada, will be paid an appearance fee of two thousand dollars ($2000.00) per diem. Such fees are not subject to the maximum operating budget referred to in paragraph 13.10(2).

(7)   The NCC, and counsel appointed on behalf of the NCC, will submit their accounts to the OIRSRC for payment, and will be paid within 60 days of such submission.

(8)   The NCC will submit its accounts to the OIRSRC for payment. The submitted accounts will be verified by OIRSRC to ensure compliance with the Treasury Board Travel Directive, attached as Schedule "Q", prior to payment.

13.11 NAC Fees

(1)   Members of the NAC will be compensated at reasonable hourly rates subject to the maximum monthly operating budget set out at Section 13.11(2) of this Agreement except the representatives for Canada or the Church Organizations, who will not be compensated under this Agreement.

(2)   Subject to Section 13.11(4), any fees referred to in Section 13.10(1) will be subject to a maximum operating budget of sixty-thousand dollars ($60,000.00) per month.

(3)   Notwithstanding Section 13.11(2) and subject to Section 13.11(4), the NAC may apply to Canada for additional funding in exceptional circumstances up to a maximum monthly amount of fifteen thousand dollars ($15,000.00).

(4)   The maximum operating budget referred to in Section 13.11(2) and the maximum additional funding in exceptional circumstances referred to in Section 13.11(3) will be reviewed and reassessed by Canada on the first day of the first month after the Implementation Date and on the first day of each month thereafter. Canada, in its sole discretion, may reduce or increase the maximum operating budget or the maximum additional funding or both.

(5) The NAC will submit its accounts to the OIRSRC for payment. The submitted accounts will be verified by OIRSRC to ensure compliance with the Treasury Board Travel Directive, attached as Schedule "Q", prior to payment.

13.12 RAC Fees

(1) Members of the RACs, will be compensated at reasonable hourly rates subject to the maximum monthly operating budget set out at Section 13.12(2).

(2) Canada will provide each RAC with an operating budget that will not exceed seven thousand dollars ($7,000.00) per month for each RAC except that each RAC may apply for additional funding in exceptional circumstances.

(3) The RACs will submit their accounts to the OIRSRC for payment. The submitted accounts will be verified by OIRSRC to ensure compliance with the Treasury Board Travel Directive, attached as Schedule "Q", prior to payment.

13.13 IAP Working Group Fees

(1) Canada agrees to pay each member of the IAP Working Group, other than lawyers representing Canada or the Church Organizations, who attended the IAP Working Group meetings beginning November 20, 2005 for time spent up to the Implementation Date, as requested in writing by Canada, at his or her normal hourly rate, plus reasonable disbursements, and GST and PST, if applicable except that no amount is payable under this Section 13.13(1) for fees previously paid directly by OIRSRC.

(2) No fees are payable under Section 13.13(1) for time billed under Section 13.02 or 13.03.

(3) The IAP Working Group, will submit their accounts to the OIRSRC for payment, and will be paid within 60 days of such submission.

13.14 Oversight Committee Fees

(1) Canada agrees to pay an honorarium to each member of the Oversight Committee, other than members representing Canada or the Church Organizations, at the same rate and on the same conditions as apply from time to time for adjudicators appointed for the IAP.

(2) Notwithstanding 13.14(1), Oversight Committee members will be paid the honorarium set out in 13.14(1) for a period not exceeding 3 days per month in those months where they attend in-person meetings or 1 day per month in those months where the meeting is held by teleconference or other means.

(2)   The Oversight Committee members will submit their accounts to the OIRSRC for payment. The accounts will be paid within 60 days of their submission. The accounts will be verified by OIRSRC to ensure compliance with the Treasury Board Travel Directive, attached as Schedule "Q", prior to payment.

ARTICLE FOURTEEN
FIRST NATIONS, INUIT, INUVIALUIT AND MÉTIS

14.01   Inclusion

For greater certainty, every Eligible CEP Recipient who resided at an Indian Residential School is eligible for the CEP and will have access to the IAP in accordance with the terms of this Agreement including all First Nations, Inuit, Inuvialuit and Métis students.

ARTICLE FIFTEEN
TRANSITION PROVISIONS

15.01   No Prejudice

The parties agree that the no prejudice commitment set out in the letter of the Deputy Minister of the OIRSRC dated July, 2005, and attached as Schedule "R" means that following the Implementation Date:

(1)   All Eligible CEP Recipients are entitled to apply to receive the CEP regardless of whether a release has been signed or a judgment received for their Indian Residential School claim prior to the Implementation Date.

(2)   Where a release of an Indian Residential School claim was signed after May 30, 2005 in order to receive the payment of an award under the DR Model:

a)   Canada will adjust the award to reflect the compensation scale set out at page 6 of the IAP attached as Schedule "D" of this Agreement;

b)   the Eligible IAP Claimant may apply to have their hearing re-opened to reconsider the assignment of points under the Consequential Loss of Opportunity category set out at page 6 of the IAP attached as Schedule "D" of this Agreement, and pursuant to the standards of the IAP, in any case where the adjudicator assessed their claim as falling within the highest level in the Consequential Loss of Opportunity category in the DR Model;

c)   an Eligible IAP Claimant who alleges sexual abuse by another student at the SL4 or SL5 category, where such abuse if proven would be the most serious proven abuse in their case, may have their hearing re-opened to consider such an allegation in accordance with the standards of the IAP.

(3) Following the coming into force of the Approval Orders, at the request of an Eligible IAP Claimant whose IRS abuse claim was settled by Canada without contribution from a Catholic Entity set out in Schedule "C" of this Agreement, such settlement having been for an amount representing a fixed reduction from the assessed Compensation, Canada will pay the balance of the assessed compensation to the Eligible IAP Claimant. Provided, however, that no amount will be paid to an Eligible IAP Claimant pursuant to this section until the Eligible IAP Claimant agrees to accept such amount in full and final satisfaction of his or her claim against a Catholic Entity set out in Schedule "C" of this Agreement, and to release them by executing a release substantially in the form of the release referred to in Section 11.02 of this Agreement.

(4) Until the Implementation Date, Canada will use its best efforts to resolve cases currently in litigation, including those that would not fit within the IAP.

15.02 Acceptance and Transfer of DR Model Claims

(1) No applications to the DR Model will be accepted after the Approval Date.

(2) DR applications received on or before the expiration of the Approval Date for which a hearing date had not been set as of the Implementation Date will be dealt with as follows:

   a) any application which alleges only physical abuse will be processed under the DR Model unless the claimant elects to transfer it to the IAP;

   b) any application which includes an allegation of sexual abuse will be transferred to the IAP unless the claimant, within 60 days of receiving notice of the proposed transfer, elects in writing to remain in the DR Model.

(3) An Individual whose claim is transferred under Section 15.02(2) of this Agreement is not required to complete an additional application to the IAP, but may modify their existing DR application to the extent necessary to claim the relief available under the IAP.

(4) Any Eligible IAP Claimant who received but did not accept a decision under the DR Model or a Pilot Project decision may apply to the IAP on the condition that all evidence used in the DR Model hearing or pilot project hearing will be transferred to the IAP proceeding.

ARTICLE SIXTEEN
CONDITIONS AND TERMINATION

16.01 Agreement is Conditional

This Agreement will not be effective unless and until it is approved by the Courts, and if such approvals are not granted by each of the Courts on substantially the same terms and conditions save and except for the variations in membership contemplated in Sections 4.04 and 4.07 of this Agreement, this Agreement will thereupon be terminated and none of the Parties will be liable to any of the other Parties hereunder, except that the fees and disbursements of the members of the NCC will be paid in any event.

16.02 Termination of Agreement

This Agreement will continue in full force and effect until all obligations under this Agreement are fulfilled.

ARTICLE SEVENTEEN CEP PAYMENTS TO APPROVED PERSONAL REPRESENTATIVES

17.01 Compensation if Deceased on or after May 30, 2005

If an Eligible CEP Recipient, dies or died on or after May 30, 2005 and the CEP Application required under Article Five (5) has been submitted to the Trustee by him or her prior to his or her death or by his or her Personal Representative after his or her death and within the period set out in Section 5.04(2), the Personal Representative will be paid the amount payable under Article Five (5) to which the deceased Eligible CEP Recipient would have been entitled if he or she had not died.

17.02 Deceased Cloud Class Members

Notwithstanding Section 17.01, if an Eligible CEP Recipient who is a member of a certified class in the Cloud Class Action died on or after October 5, 1996, and the CEP Application required under Article Five (5) has been submitted to the Trustee by his or her Personal Representative within the period set out in Section 5.04(2), the Personal Representative will be paid the amount payable under Article Five (5) to which the deceased Eligible CEP Recipient would have been entitled if he or she had not died.

17.03 Person Under Disability

If an Eligible CEP Recipient is or becomes a Person Under Disability prior to receipt of a Common Experience Payment and the CEP Application required under Article Five (5) has been submitted to the Trustee by him or her prior to becoming a Person Under Disability or by his or her Personal Representative after he or she becomes a Person Under Disability within the period set out in Section 5.04(2), the Personal Representative will be paid the amount payable under Article Five (5) to which the

Eligible CEP Recipient who has become a Person Under Disability would have been entitled if he or she had not become a Person Under Disability.

ARTICLE EIGHTEEN
GENERAL

18.01 No Assignment

No amount payable under this Agreement can be assigned and such assignment is null and void except as expressly provided for in this Agreement.

18.02 Compensation Inclusive

For greater certainty, the amounts payable to Eligible IAP Claimants under this Agreement are inclusive of any prejudgment interest or other amounts that may be claimed by Eligible IAP Claimants.

18.03 Applicable Law

This Agreement will be governed by the law of Ontario.

18.04 Dispute Resolution

The parties agree that they will fully exhaust the dispute resolution mechanisms contemplated in this Agreement before making any application to the Courts for directions in respect of the implementation, administration or amendment of this Agreement or the implementation of the Approval Orders. Application to the Courts will be made with leave of the Courts, on notice to all affected parties, or otherwise in conformity with the terms of the Agreement.

18.05 Notices

Any notice or other communication to be given in connection with this Agreement will be given in writing and will be given by personal delivery or by electronic communication addressed to each member of the NCC or NAC as the case may be or to such other address, individual or electronic communication number as a Party may from time to time advise by notice given pursuant to this Section. Any notice or other communication will be exclusively deemed to have been given, if given by personal delivery, on the day of actual delivery thereof and, if given by electronic communication, on the day of transmittal thereof if transmitted during normal business hours of the recipient and on the Business Day during which such normal business hours next occur if not so transmitted. The names and business addresses of the members of the NCC are attached as Schedule "S".

18.06 Entire Agreement

This Agreement constitutes the entire agreement between the Parties with respect to the subject matter hereof and cancels and supersedes any prior or other understandings and agreements between the Parties with respect thereto. There are no representations, warranties, terms, conditions, undertakings, covenants or collateral agreements, express, implied or statutory between the Parties with respect to the subject matter hereof other than as expressly set forth or referred to in this Agreement.

18.07 Benefit of the Agreement

This Agreement will enure to the benefit of and be binding upon the respective heirs, assigns, executors, administrators and successors of the Parties.

18.08 Counterparts

This Agreement may be executed in any number of counterparts, each of which will be deemed to be an original and all of which taken together will be deemed to constitute one and the same Agreement.

18.09 Official Languages

Canada will prepare a French translation of this Agreement for use at the Approval Hearings. Prior to Implementation Date, Canada will pay the costs of the preparation of an authoritative French version of this Agreement and

such cost shall include costs of review by a designate of the Parties. The authoritative French version shall be executed by the same Parties who executed this Agreement and, once executed, shall be of equal weight and force at law.

IN WITNESS WHEREOF the Parties have executed this Agreement.

SIGNED, SEALED AND) THE ATTORNEY GENERAL OF
DELIVERED CANADA

in the presence of:

Lump Sum Compensation Payment Project
Aboriginal Healing Foundation (AHF)
November 2006
KEY INFORMANT SURVEY GUIDE (recipients)

Introduction

The purpose of this survey is to gather information for the Lump Sum Compensation Payment Project being conducted by the Aboriginal Healing Foundation (AHF). Interviews will be held with key informants who have received large sum payments for the wrongs committed against them in residential schools. The results of the survey will be used in a report to be submitted to the AHF by January 30, 2007.

Identify and mention community counsellors who can help them if necessary.

On behalf of the AHF, we thank you for participating in this survey. Your input is important to us. The information you provide will be confidential. It will be combined with answers from other individuals who will be interviewed. Your name will not be included in the project report.

Questions

1. How have you been involved with residential schools? Did you attend one? Were you involved in a court case?

2. Have you received payment as a result of a court case or any other settlement process?

3. What was your experience with the payment process like? What was difficult for you? What was the most helpful part of the process?

4. In your opinion, what positive impacts has your payment had on you, your family and community?

5. In your opinion, what negative impacts has your payment had on you, your family and community?

6. Based on your experience, what kind of supports do individuals, families and communities need when large sum payments are made?

7. Looking at the payments that are about to be made to other residential school Survivors, what suggestions would you make to get the best possible results?

8. In your opinion, what are the barriers to your suggestions and how should these be addressed?

9. From your perspective, what role should Aboriginal organizations like the AHF play when large sum compensation payments are made? What about individuals, families, communities, governments, financial institutions, etc?

10. Is there anything we have not discussed that you would like to add?

Lump Sum Compensation Payment Project
Aboriginal Healing Foundation (AHF)
November 2006
KEY INFORMANT SURVEY GUIDE (non-recipients)

Introduction

The purpose of this survey is to gather information for the Lump Sum Compensation Payment Project being conducted by the Aboriginal Healing Foundation (AHF). Interviews will be held with key informants who know of individuals who have received large sum payments for the wrongs committed against them in residential schools. The results of the survey will be used in a report to be submitted to the AHF by January 30, 2007.

Identify and mention community counsellors who can help them if necessary.

On behalf of the AHF, we thank you for participating in this survey. Your input is important to us. The information you provide will be confidential. It will be combined with answers from other individuals who will be interviewed.

Questions

1. What involvement have you and your organization had with residential schools and Survivors?

2. How have you or your organization worked with community members who have received large sum compensation payments?

3. From your perspective, how well did the payment process work?

4. In your opinion, were individuals, families and the community satisfied with their experiences in applying for and receiving large sum payments?

5. From your perspective, what impact did the payments have on individuals, families and the community?

6. In your opinion, how did these payments add to or take away from healing opportunities?

7. In your opinion, how can the problems you've identified be effectively tackled?

8. Based on your past experiences, what supports have worked or not worked for the recipients of large sum payments, their families and the community?

9. In your opinion what are the barriers to your suggestions and how should these be addressed?

10. From your perspective, what role should Aboriginal organizations like the AHF play when large sum compensation payments are made? What about individuals, families, communities, governments, financial institutions, etc?

11. Is there anything we have not discussed that you would like to add?

Community Profiles

The following profiles draw upon a variety of government statistics, including data provided by Indian and Northern Affairs Canada (INAC) and information produced by Statistics Canada, among others. As a result, the different data sets may not correspond in all instances. Further, the following tables include totals that may not reflect total male and female counts as Statistics Canada has taken measures to protect the privacy of all individuals and, therefore, some population counts have been adjusted to ensure confidentiality. Readers should then refer to the cited source and date.

Gordon First Nation

P.O. Box 248
Punnichy, SK S0A 3C0
Phone: 306-835–2232
Fax: 306-835–2036
INAC Band No. 391

The Gordon First Nation is located 90 minutes north of Regina, Saskatchewan, five miles south of the village of Punnichy. Affiliated with the Touchwood Agency Tribal Council in Treaty Four Territory, Gordon includes members of Cree and Saulteaux heritage.

As of April 2007, Indian and Northern Affairs Canada's website lists Gordon's total registered status Indian population as 2,997, including 1,514 men and 1,483 women. There are 1,005 people living in Gordon First Nation (555 men; 450 women), and 1,992 people reside off-reserve or on other reserves (959 men; 1,033 women) (Indian and Northern Affairs Canada [INAC], n.d.).

Turning to population statistics, Gordon First Nation has a median age of 20.8 years, and close to 61 per cent of the population is 15 years and older, which means young people make up a sizeable proportion of the community. There are 70 people over 55 years of age (almost 10% of the total population), 25 of them aged 65–74, with no one over the age of 85. This table shows a more detailed breakdown (Statistics Canada, 2002).

Age, Gordon First Nation	Total	Male	Female
Total - All persons	740	375	360
Age 0–4	90	50	40
Age 5–14	200	100	95
Age 15–19	75	35	35
Age 20–24	50	25	30
Age 25–44	185	95	95
Age 45–54	65	35	35
Age 55–64	35	20	15
Age 65–74	25	10	15
Age 75–84	10	10	5
Age 85 and over	0	0	0

In terms of schooling, half of the 145 people aged 20–34 do not have high school certificates. Twenty-eight per cent did graduate high school and/or take some post-secondary education, with a small group of trades graduates (6.9%) and college graduates (10.3%). One age group up, and among the 90 people included here, about 44 per cent do not have a high school diploma, leaving nearly 17 per cent who did (and/or did some post-secondary education). As for trades graduates, 22 per cent succeeded, while nearly 17 per cent received a college education and no one completed a university degreee. This is not dissimilar to the population aged 45–64, wherein 40 per cent did not finish high school, and no one had graduated at the university level.

Community income statistics, meanwhile, were composed of 57.3 per cent earnings, and 39.3 per cent government transfers such as welfare. Gordon's 2001 labour force indicators shows a participation rate of 47.2 per cent, with an employment rate of 29.2 per cent and an unemployment rate of 40.5 per cent. Among the 175 Gordon first Nation members with labour force experience, 65 people were included in the "other services" sector. Next highest was health and education with 50 people. Manufacturing and construction had 30. Here is Statistics Canada community breakdown by occupation for 2001 (Statistics Canada, 2002):

Occupation, Gordon First Nation	Total	Male	Female
Total - Experienced labour force	175	90	85
Management	10	10	0
Business, finance, and administration	20	10	15
Natural/applied sciences and related occupations	0	0	0
Health	0	0	0
Social science, education, government service, and religion	30	0	30
Art, culture, recreation, and sport	10	10	0
Sales and service	45	15	30
Trades, transport and equipment operators, and related occupations	45	45	0
Occupations unique to primary industry	10	10	0
Occupations unique to processing, manufacturing, and utilities	0	0	0

Gordon was assigned a rating of "63" on INAC's Community Well-Being Index (INAC, n.d.), which puts it four points above the average Saskatchewan First Nation score, but 19 points below the non-First Nation provincial average. Covering 56 square miles, or 138 square kilometres, the community includes 207 private dwellings split among 738 people, according to a 2001 Statistics Canada report (Statistics Canada, 2002).

A seven-person council and one chief govern the community. Their two-year terms all end on March 31, 2008.

Chief Bryan McNabb
Councillor Dennis Bird

Councillor Dennis Hunter
Councillor Dale Grey
Councillor Arlene Morris
Councillor Kenneth Sinclair
Councillor Hugh Pratt
Councillor John McNab

The Aboriginal Healing Foundation funded Gordon First Nation – Residential School Recovery & Wellness Centre in 2001–2002 (Aboriginal Healing Foundation, n.d.). Its stated purpose was to "establish trust relationships with the survivors of the residential schools … through one on one contacts. The project will offer crisis intervention, family therapy and community outreach." It would also "record the legacy of the residential school abuses and the resulting traumas that occurred so that our history may be recovered in order to help us understand the root causes of our current social issues." Expected outcomes included the training of front-line workers on residential school effects, and the establishment of a resource centre to record residential school Survivor stories.

In a September 20, 2006 article in the *Regina Leader-Post* (Kyle, 2006), a Survivor from Gordon First Nation commented on the proposed Indian residential school settlement negotiated by the AFN:

> Ed Bitternose calculates he will receive about $1.38 an hour for the first year he attended a government-run residential school and 42 cents per hour for every hour – 24/7 – he attended school thereafter.

> Lawyers, however, will earn the equivalent of about $375 an hour under this deal, Bitternose said Wednesday.

Nonetheless, Bitternose said he thought the "agreement seems fair and reasonable and will help to put closure to my experience." He urged a Saskatchewan court to certify the settlement agreement. He reportedly felt, however, that the May 30, 2005 cut-off date was arbitrary and took issue with the fact that "families of former students who died prior to that date are not eligible for compensation."

Esketemc First Nation

P.O. Box 4479
Williams Lake, BC V2G 2V5
Phone: 250-440-5611
Fax: 250-440-5721
Email: esketemc@midbc.com
alib5@wlake.com
INAC Band No. 711

Esketemc First Nation (a.k.a. Alkali Lake) is a rural Aboriginal community situated in the British Columbia central interior, about 30 miles (or 48 km) southwest of Williams Lake. Its traditional territory spans the Alkali Lake area. Esketemc is one of 17 bands that make up the Secwepemc People, also known as the Shuswap Nation. They share a common language—Secwepemctsin—and a similar culture and belief system. Secwepemc member communities are also affiliated with the Shuswap Nation Tribal Council, the Cariboo Tribal Council, and the Secwepemc Cultural Education Society.

As of April 2007, INAC's website lists a total population of 745 registered status Indians; 411 on-reserve, 334 off-reserve. Of the 411 people on the Esketemc reserve, 214 are male and 197 are female, leaving 150 males and 164 females living off-reserve or on other reserves. This makes for a total of 384 men and 361 women altogether (INAC, n.d.). According to a 2001 Statistics Canada report, Esketemc's main reserve is 2.5 square kilometers, including 114 dwellings spread among 396 people, or one dwelling for every 3.47 people. Most were constructed before 1991 (Statistics Canada, 2002).

In terms of age demographics, the First Nation's Statistics Canada 2001 Community Profile indicates a median age of 25.8 (male: 28.3; female 24.6) across 395 people (220 male; 175 female). Just over two-thirds (70%) of the community are 15 years of age or older (74.4% male; 66.7 female). The age groups break down as follows (Statistics Canada, 2002):

Age, Esketemc First Nation	Total	Male	Female
Total - All persons	395	220	175
Age 0–4	35	15	20
Age 5–14	75	45	35
Age 15–19	45	30	15
Age 20–24	25	10	15
Age 25–44	115	65	50
Age 45–54	45	25	20
Age 55–64	30	20	10
Age 65–74	15	5	5
Age 75–84	10	5	5
Age 85 and over	0	0	0

Residents 55 years of age and up are in the minority on-reserve, totaling 55 people, or just 14 per cent of the 395 people in Esketemc, with no one above the age of 85 in 2001 (Statistics Canada, 2002).

Education statistics from the same year indicate that roughly half (52.9%) of the 85 people aged 20–34 years had graduated from high school and/or completed some post-secondary education. Virtually no one in this cohort has achieved a higher standing in their schooling. In the 35–44 age category, most of this group's 60 people (41.7%) have not completed high school, but nearly 17 per cent have a trade certificate/diploma, and nearly 17 per cent have a college certificate or diploma. For the 65 people aged 45–64, 38.5 per cent did not finish high school. The post-secondary performance is, relatively speaking, the best overall with 15.4 per cent graduating from a university program, 15.4 per cent from college, and just over 30 per cent obtaining a trades certificate/diploma (Statistics Canada, 2002).

In 2000, the median total income of persons 15 years of age and over in Esketemc was $11,680, of which roughly 68 per cent came from earnings and 32 per cent from government transfers such as welfare. Labour force indicators include a 60.7 per cent participation rate, a 37.5 per cent employment rate, and a 38.2

per cent unemployment rate. Of the 145 people in Esketemc's labour force with experience, 60 fell under "other services," but 30 people have worked in agriculture or other resource-based industries, 20 in health and education, and 15 in manufacturing and construction. Statistics Canada's community breakdown by occupation for 2001 is as follows (Statistics Canada, 2002):

Occupation, Esketemc First Nation	Total	Male	Female
Total - Experienced labour force	140	85	55
Management	15	0	10
Business, finance, and administration	20	10	15
Natural/applied sciences and related occupations	0	0	0
Health	0	0	0
Social science, education, government service, and religion	20	0	15
Art, culture, recreation, and sport	0	0	0
Sales and service occupations	30	10	15
Trades, transport and equipment operators, and related occupations	10	15	0
Occupations unique to primary industry	35	35	0
Occupations unique to processing, manufacturing, and utilities	10	10	0

Esketemc rated a "68" on INAC's Community Well-Being Index, which puts it two points below the average British Columbia First Nation score, and 17 points below the non-First Nation provincial average.

Seven councillors and one chief govern the community under the *Indian Act*. Their two-year terms expire in mid-February 2008 (INAC, n.d.).

Chief Fred Robbins
Councillor Alec Chelsea
Councillor Lucy Dick
Councillor Irene Johnson
Councillor James Paul
Councillor Wilfred Robbins
Councillor Phillip Robbins
Councillor Thomas Sampson

The Esketemc First Nation aspires to achieve self-government and a comprehensive treaty settlement within the treaty process of the BC Treaty Commission (n.d.). It entered the six-stage treaty process in December 1993, and has completed Stage 3.

In terms of its history, which some have called "nearly-legendary," Esketemc is well-known for its dramatic transformation from a reserve ravaged by two decades of severe, widespread alcoholism to a model community that has taken charge of much of its affairs. In its case study of Alkali Lake, the Four Worlds International Institute discusses this remarkable series of changes. Beginning with the shutting down of a bootlegging 'shuttle' run by liquor stores and taxi companies in nearby Williams Lake, to renegotiating the provision of social assistance as food vouchers instead of cash to curb the purchase of alcohol, the study describes how Esketemc gradually regained control of its community's situation. It discusses how links were made between healing and tangible progress on social and economic conditions. A traditional and spiritual revival sparked the return of various ceremonies to Esketemc, with concurrent efforts to create meaningful work that led to many new jobs. From all accounts, these initiatives were genuinely community-based and community-driven. The community has trained a number of its members to go out as 'teams' to carry out similar work in other tribal communities (Four Worlds International Institute, 1998).

As the Four Worlds case study notes, alcoholism was not the only problem Esketemc faced. The children of former alcoholics have had their own struggles to work out, not least the sexual and physical abuse many suffered during those dark years. One estimate puts the rate of sexual abuse at upwards of 90 per cent among young people. Many ultimately trace it back to what took place in the residential schools. The community saw that abusers were very often the people who had been victimized themselves. This led to the restorative justice approach, where the priority is to interrupt the cycle of abuse and restore healthy relationships between people (Four Worlds International Institute, 1998).

Roughly two decades after British Columbia became a province in 1871, two large 'industrial' schools were established in Secwepemc territory at Kamloops and near Williams Lake. They closed in the 1970s (Secwepemc Cultural Education Society, n.d.). The community held its own week-long Alkali Residential School Inquiry in May 1997 (Assembly of First Nations [AFN], n.d.). Its purpose was "to investigate the Esketemc Residential School experience that will assist to form the basis of healing of historical abuses in preparation for healthy families and community for self-government." Among its primary objectives were the documentation and validation of survivors' experiences, and an acknowledgement of the intergenerational trauma of residential schools. The three Inquiry Commissioners were British Columbia Judge Cunliffe Barnett, First Nations lawyer Ed John, as well as Elder and psychologist Joe Couture. With the exception of travel expenses, all services related to the Inquiry were performed on a voluntary basis by all involved (AFN, n.d.). The entire process was recorded on video, and featured real-time translation into Shuswap.

Esketemc's website describes the history of Canadian government policy as having a profoundly "negative impact on the life and development of our community," including the "violence and abuse in residential schools." Today, Esketemc works in partnership with the RCMP, Fisheries and Oceans Canada, BC Conservation officers, the Attorney General, and Justice Canada to coordinate community-driven interventions toward local crime (Justice Canada, n.d.). Esketemc Alternative Measures Program aims to "facilitate resolution of crimes, healing, recovery and prevention." Incidents are often resolved through traditional healing circles.

Overall, Esketemc is an active community that has pursued many opportunities within its territory. Examples on the economic front include a five-year, $1.7 million forestry agreement in 2004 with the British Columbia government (Government of British Columbia, 2004). In 2003, the Province gave the First Nation $339,400 for a three-year land use and economic development planning project, thereby enhancing Esketemc's forest management expertise (Government of British Columbia, 2003). In 2001, Esketemc helped make history as one of the first four British Columbia "community forest pilot sites," where almost 18,000 hectares of Crown and reserve lands would be used to create value-added products like log homes. On a much smaller (but just as important) scale, Esketemc received about $8,000 from the First Peoples' Heritage, Language and Culture Council (n.d.) in 2001–2002 for its Shuswap language revitalization project. In the area of health, Esketemc has signed an individual Health Transfer Agreement with the First Nations and Inuit Health Branch of Health Canada. The community directly delivers a variety of locally based health education, prevention, and awareness programs, including pre-natal nutrition, alcohol and drug programs, community health nursing, plus home and community care (Interior Health Authority, 2003).

Inuvik, NT

PO Box 1160
Inuvik, NT X0E 0T0
Phone: 867-777-8600
Fax: 867-777-8601

The town of Inuvik, referred as the "Place of Man" in the Inuvialuktun language, is considered the administrative and commercial hub of the Northwest Territory's Beaufort-Delta region. At 97 kilometre south of the Beaufort Sea, it is Canada's largest community north of the Arctic Circle (PR Services Ltd., n.d.). Unlike the other communities profiled here, Inuvik is not a reserve, but Aboriginal people from various groups make up a large proportion of the town.

In 2001, Statistics Canada reported Inuvik's population at 2,894 (Statistics Canada, 2002). In 2005, the NWT government reported a population of 3,521 (NWT Bureau of Statistics, n.d.). (Both figures are inclusive of Aboriginal and non-Aboriginal residents.) Inuvik's population hit its reportedly highest peak ever in 1990 at 4,200 people, which roughly corresponded to the end of a boom period in oil and gas exploration in the Mackenzie Valley and Beaufort Sea. However, since 1999, natural gas exploration has been once again undertaken in earnest (PR Services Ltd., n.d.), and territorial statistics report that the population has been steady at around 3,400 or so since 1996 (Statistics Canada, 2002).

About 50 square kilometres in area, Inuvik is home to 1,238 private dwellings. However, NWT 2004 statistics indicate that only 6 per cent of them house more than six residents, a figure that's been steadily declining since the early 1980s (Statistics Canada, 2002).

In terms of age, Inuvik's median age in 2001 for the overall population (Aboriginal and non-Aboriginal combined) was almost 30 years, and just over 73 per cent of its population was aged 15 and up. Here is a more detailed breakdown by age:

Age, Inuvik	Total	Male	Female
Total - all persons	2,890	1,465	1,430
Age 0–4	270	135	135
Age 5–14	510	265	245
Age 15–19	205	95	115
Age 20–24	225	115	105
Age 25–44	1,030	515	510
Age 45–54	370	180	185
Age 55–64	185	100	85
Age 65–74	70	45	30
Age 75–84	25	10	15
Age 85 and over	5	0	5

In 2001, 100 people in Inuvik were 65 years or older, with 25 of them falling within the 75–84 age range, and only five people in the 85 and older category. More recent NWT government statistics place the 60 years and older population at 272 people in 2005.

Educationally, just over 20 per cent of the people aged 20–34 (715 in total) had not completed high school, whereas almost 36 per cent had graduated and/or completed some post-secondary. A portion received a trades certificate/diploma (13.3%), some a college degree (16.1%), and others a university program (15.4%). The 510 people in the next age group up, aged 35–44, had a 17.6 per cent non-completion rate for high school versus a 25.5 per cent completion rate (and/or some post-secondary). Post-secondary statistics in this cohort saw 20.6 per cent finish a trades program, 18.6 per cent college, and 16.7 per cent university. Inuvik residents aged 45–64 saw a more or less even distribution across all five categories: 22.2 per cent less than high school; 22.2 per cent high school and/or some post-secondary; 20.4 per cent trades; 15.7 per cent college; and 19.4 per cent university (Statistics Canada, 2002).

The 2000 median income of people 15 years and older in Inuvik was $30,752 (this figure does not include the higher living costs often associated with the high North). Only 6.1 per cent of that income came from direct government transfers, the remainder came from earnings. Looking at labour force indicators in 2001, Inuvik's participation rate was 79.4 per cent, its employment rate at 74.6 per cent, and its unemployment rate at 6.7 per cent. As far as Inuvik residents' realm of experience, of the 1,630 people considered, 490 had been based in "other services," 380 in health and education, 275 in business services, 165 in wholesale and retail trade, and 150 in manufacturing and construction industries (Statistics Canada, 2002). In terms of occupation, Statistics Canada's 2001 breakdown is as follows:

Occupation, Inuvik	Total	Male	Female
Total - experienced labour force	1,630	865	760
Management	260	160	105
Business, finance, and administration	290	60	225
Natural and applied sciences and related occupations	105	80	25
Health	90	15	75
Social science, education, government service, and religion	190	70	125
Art, culture, recreation, and sport	35	10	25
Sales and service	330	145	185
Trades, transport and equipment operators, and related occupations	285	285	10
Occupations unique to primary industry	35	35	0
Occupations unique to processing, manufacturing, and utilities	10	10	0

The NWT Bureau of Statistics (n.d.) reported in 2004 that the employment rate among Aboriginal residents was just under 61 per cent, whereas the non-Aboriginal rate was close to 90 per cent.

A Statistics Canada report for 2001 indicated that 1,690 residents (790 male; 900 female) identified with at least one Aboriginal group, leaving 1,165 non-Aboriginal residents (Statistics Canada, 2002). The 2005 statistics from NWT show a split of 1,978 Aboriginal residents, 1,543 non-Aboriginal (NWT Bureau of Statistics, n.d.). Politically speaking, Inuvik's town council includes designated representation from the region's two main Aboriginal groups, the Gwich'in and the Inuvialuit (Town of Inuvik, n.d.). The Inuvialuit people settled their land claim in 1984; the Gwich'in in 1992. Inuvik is home to members and organizations of both groups (PR Services Ltd., n.d.).

New infrastructure includes a regional hospital built in 2003 as well as the Inuvik Family Centre, a meeting and recreation facility. Protection services for the town include RCMP officers and a volunteer fire department equipped with one truck. Inuvik receives medical services from three nurses and monthly doctor visits, plus two social services workers (INAC, n.d.). There is road access for the majority of the year, except for periods of freeze-up (late-October to mid-December) and thaw (roughly mid-May to mid-June), when there is air access only.

In terms of recent residential school initiatives, the federal and NWT governments and the Roman Catholic Diocese of MacKenzie settled in May 2002 with 28 victims that were abused at the Grollier Hall residential school in Inuvik. Part of the then-new ADR process, the Grollier Hall pilot project took three-and-half years from start to finish (Indian Residential Schools Resolution Canada [IRSRC], 2002).

Grollier Hall is infamous for the convictions of at least four former employees on abuse-related charges stemming from the 1960s and 1970s. It opened in 1959 and was run by the Catholic Church until 1985. When it closed in 1997 it was one of Canada's last residential schools (The Lethbridge Herald, 1998). Stringer Hall, meanwhile, was Inuvik's Anglican residential school, built side by side with Grollier Hall (Tindal, 2000).

Siksika Nation

P.O. BOX 1100
Siksika, AB T0J 3W0
Phone: 403-264-7250
Fax: 403-734-5110
INAC Band No. 430

The Siksika Nation in southern Alberta is located about 90 kilometres east of Calgary, and covers just under 71,000 hectares, or 696 square kilometres. Siksika, which literally means 'Blackfoot,' is immediately adjacent to the town of Gleichen, Alberta.

As of April 2007, INAC's website lists 6,192 registered status Indians in the Nation, including 3,150 men and 3,048 women. In terms of location, 3,442 people reside on-reserve (1,792 men; 1,650 women) and 2,605 people live off-reserve or on another reserve (1,358 men; 1,390 women) (INAC, n.d.).

Siksika rated a "64" on INAC's Community Well-Being Index or four points above the average Alberta First Nation score, but 20 points below the non-First Nation provincial average (INAC, n.d.). According to a Statistics Canada report for 2001, the community's 794 dwellings are divided among 2,767 people, a ratio of about one dwelling for every 3.5 people (Statistics Canada, 2002).

Age demographics for 2001 reveal a median age of 22.6 (male: 22.0; female 23.2) for 2,770 people (1,405 male; 1,365 female). Just over 64 per cent of the community is 15 years of age or older (62.6% male; 65.9 % female). The age group breakdown is as follows (Statistics Canada, 2002):

Age, Siksika Nation	Total	Male	Female
Total - All persons	2,770	1,405	1,365
Age 0–4	255	125	130
Age 5–14	735	395	335
Age 15–19	280	125	150
Age 20–24	185	95	95
Age 25–44	760	365	390
Age 45–54	270	130	135
Age 55–64	165	85	80
Age 65–74	75	50	30
Age 75–84	35	15	20
Age 85 and over	5	5	5

As seen here, just over 10 per cent (or 280 people) of Siksika's total on-reserve population was aged 55 years or older. Of those, 115 were 65 years and up.

Education statistics from 2001 show that while 30 per cent of the 565 people aged 20–34 years had finished high school, almost half had not. No one in this age cohort had completed university, though some received a trades certificate/diploma (13%) and an even smaller number a college certificate/diploma (7%). In the 35–44 age category, close to 43 per cent of this group's 375 people had not completed high school. Just over 21 per cent have a trade certificate/diploma, almost 11 per cent a college certificate/diploma, and close to 7 per cent had finished university studies. It is roughly the same breakdown for the 440 people in the 45–64 age group, with nearly 48 per cent not finishing high school, just over 18 per cent getting a trades certificate, close to 7 per cent completing college, and close to 7 per cent completing university studies (Statistics Canada, 2002).

In 2000, the median total income of persons 15 years of age and over in Siksika was $7,384, of which 61.6 per cent came from earnings and 29 per cent from government transfers such as social assistance. Labour force indicators include a 46.2 per cent participation rate, 35.6 per cent employment rate, and 23.5 per cent unemployment rate (Statistics Canada, 2002).

Among the 725 Siksika members with labour force experience, 240 fell under "other services," 220 people worked in health and education, 90 people worked in manufacturing and construction, and 85 people worked in business services. The Statistics Canada community breakdown by occupation for 2001 is as follows (Statistics Canada, 2002):

Occupation, Siksika Nation	Total	Male	Female
Total - Experienced labour force	720	395	330
Management	60	35	25
Business, finance, and administration	110	10	95
Natural/applied sciences and related occupations	15	10	10
Health	30	0	25
Social science, education, government service, and religion	90	30	55
Art, culture, recreation, and sport	15	10	0
Sales and service occupations	165	90	75
Trades, transport and equipment operators, and related occupations	155	130	25
Occupations unique to primary industry	65	60	0
Occupations unique to processing, manufacturing, and utilities	10	10	0

The Siksika Nation is governed under the *Indian Act* by a 12-member band council and its chief; their two-year terms will all expire at the end of November 2007. They use a custom electoral system.

Chief Adrian Stimson
Councillor Adolpho Bear Chief
Councillor Horace Bull Bear
Councillor Janice Doore
Councillor Jason Doore
Councillor Scotty Many Guns
Councillor Emery Medicine Shield
Councillor Kendall Panther Bone

Councillor Ruth Scalplock
Councillor Gerald Sitting Eagle
Councillor Eldon Weasel Child
Councillor Hector Winnipeg
Councillor Ernest Yellowfly

A signatory to Treaty #7 in 1877, the Siksika Nation aspires to greater self-government outside of the *Indian Act*. The Nation includes seven societies: Horn, Crow, Black Soldier, Motoki, Prairie Chicken, Brave Dog, and Ma'tsiyiiks. As a member of the Blackfoot Confederacy, Siksika has connections to the Piikani and Kainaiwa in southern Alberta and the Blackfeet in the U.S. state of Montana.

J.W. Tims was the first Anglican missionary to arrive on the Siksika reserve, and it was his church that operated the Old Sun's Indian Residental School on Siksika in 1929. An infamous reference to Old Sun in the Royal Commission on Aboriginal Peoples report extends from the 1907 Bryce Report, submitted by INAC's then-chief medical officer, Dr. P.H. Bryce. His statistical profile of tuberculosis among children in western residential schools revealed an infection rate of 47 per cent at Old Sun, the highest recorded at any school (Royal Commission on Aboriginal Peoples, 1996). The site has since given rise to the band-owned Old Sun Community College.

Today, Siksika is an active site with regard to residential school Survivor work. This includes the Indian Residential School Survivors Society of Alberta, which received $52,425 ($34,267 for 2005–2006 and $18,157 for 2006–2007) from the Indian Residential Schools Resolution Canada to help fund its assistance to Survivors proceeding as a group through the alternative dispute resolution process. The Eagle Shield Indian Residential School Society, also located in Siksika, received $43,000 for a similar initiative ($38,340 for 2005–2006 and $4,659 for 2006–2007) (IRSRC, 2006).

References

Aboriginal Healing Foundation (2006). A Healing Journey: Final Report Summary Points. Ottawa ON: Aboriginal Healing Foundation.

———(1999). Aboriginal Healing Foundation Program Handbook, 2nd Edition. Ottawa, ON: Aboriginal Healing Foundation.

———(no date). Funded Projects: Gordon First Nation - Residential School Recovery & Wellness Centre. Retrieved on 29 June 2007 from: http://www.ahf.ca/funded-projects/saskatchewan/gordon-first-nation-residential-school-recovery-wellness-centre

Assembly of First Nations (no date). Alkali Lake (Esketemc First Nation) Residential School Inquiry May 18–25, 1997. Retrieved 6 October 2006 from http://www.afn.ca/residentialschools/conference/Vancouver_pp/Day2_CBelleau_Alkali.pdf

Barber, Benjamin (1998). A Place for Us: How to Make Society Civil and Democracy Strong. New York, NY: Hill and Wang Publishers.

BC Treaty Commission (no date). Negotiation Update. Retrieved 12 October 2006 from http://www.bctreaty.net/nations_3/esketemc.html

Boyer, Y. (2006). First Nations, Métis and Inuit Women's Health. Discussion Paper Series in Aboriginal Health: Legal Issues. Ottawa, ON: National Aboriginal Health Organization.

Brant Castellano, Marlene (2004). Ethics of Aboriginal Research. Journal of Aboriginal Health (January):98–114. Retrieved 5 March 2007 from: http://www.naho.ca/english/pdf/journal_p98-114.pdf

Brown A. (1999). Patterns of abuse among Native American elderly. In T. Tatara (ed.), Understanding elder abuse in Minority Populations. Philadelphia, PA: Brunner/Mazel: 143–159.

Canadian Institute for Health Information (2004). Aboriginal People's Health in Improving the Health of Canadians. Ottawa, ON: Canadian Population Health Initiative.

Canadian Intergovernmental Conference Secretariat (2003). 2003 First Ministers' Accord on Health Care Renewal. Retrieved on 27 June 2007 from: http://www.scics.gc.ca/pdf/800039004_e.pdf

Carson, D.K. and C. Hand (1999). Dilemmas surrounding elder abuse and neglect in Native American communities. In T. Tatara (ed.), Understanding elder abuse in Minority Populations. Philadelphia, PA: Brunner/Mazel: 161–184.

Corrado, Raymond R. and Irwin M. Cohen (2003). Mental Health Profiles for a Sample of British Columbia's Aboriginal Survivors of the Canadian Residential School System. Ottawa, ON: Aboriginal Healing Foundation.

Crossing Boundaries National Council and KTA Center for Collaborative Government (2006). Volume Four { Aboriginal Voice National Recommendations: From Digital Divide to Digital Opportunity. Ottawa, ON: The Crossing Boundaries National Council. Retrieved 15 May 2007 from: http://www. crossingboundaries.ca/files.av/digital_opportunieis_(vol_4).pdf

De Bruth, Lemyra, Karen Hymbrough, Daniel Simpson, Beverly Wilkins, and Scott Nelson (1994). When Communities are in Crisis – Planning for Response to Suicides and Suicide Attempts Among American Indian Tribes. American Indian and Alaska Native Mental Health Research 4(4):223–231.

Dion Stout, Madeleine and Gregory Kipling (2003). Aboriginal People, Resilience and the Residential School Legacy. Ottawa, ON: Aboriginal Healing Foundation.

Dion Stout, Madeleine and Nadine Jodoin (2006). Lump Sum Payment Project: Literature Review (Phase One). Aboriginal Healing Foundation [unpublished].

Dion Stout, Madeleine, Gregory D. Kipling, and Roberta Stout (2001). Aboriginal Women's Health Research Synthesis Project: Final Report, Centres of Excellence for Women's Health. Retrieved 5 March 2007 from: http://www.cewh-cesf.ca/PDF/cross_cex/synthesisEN.pdf

Donna Cona (2002). Report: Department of Indian Affairs and Northern Development, National Connecting Aboriginal Canadians Forum: Overview of Events, May 9, 2002. Retrieved on 3 July 2007 from: http://www. aboriginalcanada.gc.ca/abdt/lookups/cacwebsitegraphics.nsf/vDownload/DonaConna_final_finalreport. pdf/$file/DonaConna_final_finalreport.pdf

Durie, Mason (2006), Indigenous Resilience: from disease to disadvantage to the realization of potential. Rapou Oranga. Pacific Region Indigenous Doctors Congress, December 7, 2006 [unpublished report].

First Peoples' Heritage, Language, and Culture Council (n.d.). 2001/2002 Aboriginal Language Initiative Grants. Retrieved 12 October 2006 from: http://www.fphlcc.ca/assets/toolkit/grantsummaries/ALI-01-02.pdf

Four Worlds International Institute (1998). Part IV: A. The Alkali Lake Community Story. Community Healing and Aboriginal Social Security Reform: A study prepared for the Assembly of First Nations - Aboriginal Social Security Reform Strategic Initiative. Retrieved 12 October 2006 from: http://www.4worlds.org/4w/ssr/Partiv.htm

Geller, Jeffry L., William H. Fisher, and Melissa McDermitt (1995). A National Survey of Mobile Crisis Services and their Evaluation. Psychiatric Services 46(9): 893.

Government of British Columbia (2004). First Nations Agreement to Help Battle Dive Beetle. Retrieved 12 October 2006 from: http://www.for.gov.bc.ca/pscripts/pab/newsrel/mofnews.asp?refnum=2004FOR0019-000

———(2003). Funds to Enhance First Nations Forestry Opportunities. Retrieved 12 October 2006 from: http://www2.news.gov.bc.ca/nrm_news_releases/2003TNO0020-000511.htm

Hodgson, Maggie (no date). Moving Forward Together by Building Bridges [unpublished paper].

Indian and Northern Affairs Canada (no date). Welcome to First Nation Profiles [search by First Nation]. Retrieved 4 October 2006 from: http://sdiprod2.inac.gc.ca/FNProfiles/

Indian Residential Schools Adjudication Secretariat (no date). Adjudication. Retrieved 12 February 2007 from: http://www.irsad-sapi.gc.ca/english/adjudication.html

Indian Residential Schools Resolution Canada (2006). Settlement Agreement. Schedule "D." Independent Assessment Process (IAP) for Continuing Indian Residential School Abuse Claims. Retrieved 12 June 2007 from http://www.residentialschoolsettlement.ca/Schedule_D-IAP.PDF

———— (2003). Guide for the Alternative Dispute Resolution Process: A process to resolve claims of physical abuse, sexual abuse and wrongful confinement, suffered at Indian residential schools. Ottawa, ON: Her Majesty the Queen in Right of Canada.

———— (2002). News Releases: Government of Canada, NWT, and the Catholic Church Settle With Abuse Victims. Retrieved 8 October 2006 from: www.irsr-rqpi.gc.ca/english/news_06_05_02.html

———— (no date a). Advance Payment Program: Statistics – as of April 2, 2007. Retrieved 12 June 2007 from: http://www.irsr-rqpi.gc.ca/english/advance_payment_program.html

———— (no date b). Alternative Dispute Resolution. Retrieved 12 February 2007 from: http://www.irsr-rqpi.gc.ca/english/dispute_resolution.html

———— (no date c). Indian Residential School Statistics: Claims in ADR Process as of May 14, 2007. Retrieved 20 May 2007 from: http://www.irsr-rqpi.gc.ca/english/dispute_resolution_adr_decisions.html

Interior Health Authority (2003). Aboriginal Health and Wellness Plan: 2002/03–2005/06. Retrieved 12 October 2006 from: http://www.interiorhealth.ca/NR/rdonlyres/B8D2BD87-FDFE-437A-ACB2-D1C3CA255A38/1132/IHAboriginalHealthPlanRevisedFeb03.pdf

Justice Canada (no date). Community-Based Justice Programs - British Columbia. Retrieved 12 October 2006 from: http://www.justice.gc.ca/en/ps/ajs/programs/bc.html

Kyle, Anne (2006). Residential settlement hearing continues. Regina Leader-Post 20 September 2006. Retrieved 10 October 2006 from: http://www.canada.com/reginaleaderpost/news/story.html?id=3501675b-5e8b-49a6-90cb-fa1eed33f0a8

Lane, Phil, Jr., Michael Bopp, Judie Bopp, and Julian Norris (2002). Mapping the Healing Journey: the Final Report of a First Nation Research Project on Healing in Canadian Aboriginal Communities. Ottawa, ON: Solicitor General Canada and the Aboriginal Healing Foundation.

Llewellyn, Jennifer J. (2002). Dealing with the Legacy of Native Residential School Abuse in Canada: Litigation, ADR, and Restorative Justice. University of Toronto Law Journal 52(3):253–300. Retrieved 3 March 2007 from: http://www.utpjournals.com/product/utlj/523/523_llewellyn.html

Mahoney, Kathleen (2006). Resolving the IRS Legacy: The Indian Residential Schools Settlement. Assembly of First Nations IRS Unit. PowerPoint presentation at the Residential Schools Settlement Agreement Conference for Frontline Workers, September 11, 2006.

Mussell, W.J. (2005). Warrior-Caregivers: Understanding the Challenges and Healing of First Nations Men, A Resource Guide. Ottawa, ON: Aboriginal Healing Foundation.

Mutha S., C. Allen, and M. Welch (2002). Toward Culturally Competent Care: A Toolbox for Teaching Communication Strategies. San Francisco, CA: University of California.

National Aboriginal Health Organization (2004). Briefing Note #FNC04-040: Indian Residential School Alternative Dispute Resolution Process. Retrieved on 3 July 2007 from: http://www.naho.ca/firstnations/english/pdf/FNC04-040_indian_residential_schools.pdf

———— (2002). Urban Aboriginal Health Centres Meeting, March 19-21, 2002, Winnipeg, Manitoba, Final Meeting Report. Retrieved on 29 June 2007 from: http://www.naho.ca/english/pdf/UAHCM.pdf

NWT Bureau of Statistics (no date). Inuvik - Statistical Profile. Retrieved 8 October 2006 from: http://www.stats.gov.nt.ca/Profile/Profile%20PDF/Inuvik.pdf

O'Connor, Pauline (1998). Mapping Social Cohesion. CPRN Discussion Paper No. F|01. Ottawa, ON: Canadian Policy Research Networks. Retrieved on 4 July 2007 from: http://epe.lac-bac.gc.ca/100/200/300/cprn/english/msc_e.pdf

Ontario Court of Appeal (2004). Cloud vs. Canada (Attorney General), [2004] O.J. No. 4924. Retrieved 19 February 2007 from: http://www.ontariocourts.on.ca/decisions/2004/december/C40771.htm

PR Services Ltd. (no date). Travel Yukon: Inuvik History. Retrieved 8 October 2006 from: http://www.yukoninfo.com/inuvik/info/inuvikhistory.htm

Public Health Agency of Canada (2004). Reducing Health Disparities – Roles of the Health Sector: Discussion Paper. Health Disparities Task Group of the Federal/Provincial/Territorial Advisory Committee on Population Health and Health Security. Retrieved 2 March 2007 from: http://www.phac-aspc.gc.ca/ph-sp/disparities/ddp_e.html

Purnell, L.D. and B.J. Paulanka (1998). Transcultural Health Care: A Culturally Competent Approach, Volume 1. Philadelphia, PA: F.A. Davis Company.

Putnam, Robert D. (1996). The Decline of Civil Society: How Come? So What? Ottawa, ON: The Canadian Centre for Management and Development.

Royal Canadian Mounted Police (no date). Elder Abuse: What to Watch Out For. PowerPoint presentation created by Beauval R.C.M.P. Constables Evan Anderson, Rob Wilson, and Craig Reid and delivered by Sargeant Clayton Lerat, "F" Division, Aboriginal Policing Services, Regina, Saskatchewan.

Royal Commission on Aboriginal Peoples (1996). Volume 1: Looking Forward, Looking Back. Report of the Royal Commission on Aboriginal Peoples. Ottawa, ON: Minister of Supply and Services Canada.

Rutter, M. (2001). Psychosocial Adversity: Risk, Resilience and Recovery. In J. Richmond and M. Fraser (eds.), The context of youth violence: Resilience, risk, and protection. Westport, CT: Praeger Publishers: 13–43.

Secwepemc Cultural Education Society (no date). Our Story. Retrieved on 3 July 2007 from: http://www.secwepemc.org/about/ourstory

Statistics Canada (2006). Measuring Violence Against Women: Statistical Trends 2006. Ottawa, ON: Minister of Industry. Retrieved 5 March 2007 from: http://www.statcan.ca/english/research/85-570-XIE/85-570-XIE2006001.pdf

——— (2002). 2001 Community Profiles. Catalogue no. 93F0053XIE [search by community name and province]. Retrieved at: http://www12.statcan.ca/english/profil01/CP01/Index.cfm?Lang=E

Status of Women Canada (1998). Gender-based Analysis: A Guide for Policy-making (Revised edition). Retrieved 5 March 2007 from: http://www.swc-cfc.gc.ca/pubs/gbaguide/gbaguide.pdf.

Swift, Jamie (1999). Civil Society in Question. Toronto, ON: Between the Lines.

The Lethbridge Herald (1998). Former Residential School Supervisor Gets 10-year Jail Sentence for Abuse. August 16, 1998. Retrieved 8 October 2006 from: http://www.4worlds.org/4w/resschool/ newclips.html

Tindal, Doug (2000). The system was wrong. Ministry Matters (Winter 2000) [e-journal]. Retrieved 4 October 2006 from: http://generalsynod.anglican.ca/ ministries/departments/mm/2000/legacy/mm11.html

Torjman, Sherri (1997). Civil Society: Reclaiming Our Humanity, Caledon Institute. Ottawa, ON: Caledon Institute of Social Policy.

Town of Inuvik (no date). Inuvik - Town Hall. Retrieved 15 October 2006 from: http://www.inuvik.ca/townhall/ council.html

Vaillant, George (1993). The wisdom of the ego. Cambridge, MA: Harvard University Press.

Wesley-Esquimaux, C.C. and M. Smolewski (2004). Historic Trauma and Aboriginal Healing. Ottawa, ON: Aboriginal Healing Foundation.

Women's Health Victoria (no date). Gender And Health: Defining the terms. Retrieved 5 March 2007 from: http://www.whv.org.au/health_policy/gender.htm

World Health Organization (2000). General Guidelines for Methodologies on Research and Evaluation of Traditional Medicine. Geneva, SWI: World Health Organization.

Yellow Horse Brave Heart, Maria and Birgil Kills Straight (2003). Historical Trauma and Indigenous Knowledge and Healing - The Takini Network. Notes from a presentation at the National Aboriginal Health Organization's First Annual Conference and Health Information Fair, January 21–23, 2003 [unpublished].